The Sixth Patriarch's Dharma Jewel Platform Sutra

The Sixth Patriarch's Dharma Jewel Platform Sutra

With the Commentary of
Tripitaka Master Hua

English translation by the
Buddhist Text Translation Society

Buddhist Text Translation Society
Dharma Realm Buddhist University
Dharma Realm Buddhist Association
Burlingame, California U.S.A.

The Sixth Patriarch's Dharma Jewel Platform Sutra

Published and translated by:

Buddhist Text Translation Society
1777 Murchison Drive, Burlingame, CA 94010-4504
http://www.bttsonline.org
http://www.drba.org

First edition (Hong Kong) 1971
Second edition (USA) 1977
Third edition (USA) 2002

11 10 09 08 07 06 05 04 03 02   10 9 8 7 6 5 4 3 2 1

ISBN 0-88139-316-9

Printed in Malaysia. Printed on non-acid paper.

Addresses of DRBA branches are listed at the back of this book.

Library of Congress Cataloging-in-Publication Data

Huineng, 638-713.
[Liuzudashi fa bao tan jing. English]
The Sixth Patriarch's Dharma jewel platform sutra : with the commentary of Venerable Master Hsuan Hua, English translation by the Buddhist Text Translation Society.
p. cm
Includes index.
Originally published: San Francisco : Sino-American Buddhist Association, 1977.
ISBN 0-88139-316-9
1. Zen Buddhism-Early works to 1800. I. Hsüan Hua, 1908- II. Hsüan Hua, 1908- Liuzu fa bao tan jing qian shi. English. III. Buddhist Text Translation Society. IV. Title.

BQ9299.H854 L613 2002
294.3'85--dc21   2001037450

Contents

The Eight Guidelines of The Buddhist Text Translation Society

1. A volunteer must free him/herself from the motives of personal fame and profit.
2. A volunteer must cultivate a respectful and sincere attitude free from arrogance and conceit.
3. A volunteer must refrain from aggrandizing his/her work and denigrating that of others.
4. A volunteer must not establish him/herself as the standard of correctness and suppress the work of others with his or her fault-finding.
5. A volunteer must take the Buddha-mind as his/her own mind.
6. A volunteer must use the wisdom of Dharma-Selecting Vision to determine true principles.
7. A volunteer must request Virtuous Elders in the ten directions to certify his/her translations.
8. A volunteer must endeavour to propagate the teachings by printing Sutras, Shastra texts, and Vinaya texts when the translations are certified as being correct.

Dharma is neither sudden nor gradual,
Delusion and awakening are slow and quick.
But deluded people cannot comprehend
This Dharma-door of seeing-the-nature.

Although it is said in ten thousand ways,
United, the principles return to one;
In the dark dwelling of defilements,
Always produce the sunlight of wisdom.

from Sixth Patriarch's Verse of No Mark

Editor's Introduction

The Sixth Patriarch's Dharma Jewel Platform Sutra is the fundamental text of Ch'an Buddhism. It relates the life and teachings of Master Hui Neng, the Great Master the Sixth Patriarch, as set down by one of his disciples. During the seventh and eighth centuries under the T'ang Dynasty, Master Hui Neng taught the doctrines of no-thought and of sudden enlightenment, which, as expounded in this text, continue to be the heart of Ch'an wherever it is practiced. As such, these are the only teachings of a Chinese high monk which are regarded by Buddhists as a Sutra, that is, as a sacred text equal to those compiled by the earlier South Asian masters.

Interest in Buddhism in general and in Ch'an in particular is now swiftly growing in the West, especially in America. Translations and re-translations of many of the central Buddhist texts have been appearing in consequence. A good deal of confusion has been an unfortunate by-product. Because Ch'an is so foreign to traditional Western thought, the rendering of Ch'an teachings into a Western language requires, even in the most literal translation, the virtual invention of a new vocabulary of concepts; and each new translation has tended to present a distinctly different rendition of the central Buddhist ideas. To elucidate them, commentaries are often added by the translators.

But all of these translations and commentaries have been written by scholars who are not Buddhists. While that kind of non-membership is hardly important to a translator of ordinary philosophical writings, it becomes a severe stumbling-block for the translator of Ch'an teachings. For Ch'an is not a system of thought at all, but a special kind of moral and psychological work, aimed at a particular personal transformation which the Buddhists call enlightenment. Only one who through difficult practice has undergone that transformation can hope to teach Ch'an authoritatively and translate and comment on the sayings of other masters without having to resort to guesswork about what the sayings mean.

Fortunately for students of the Way, an effort to establish an authoritative Buddhist canon in English has now been undertaken by Tripitaka Master Hsüan Hua and his American disciples.

Master Hua stands in the direct line of orthodox Buddhist leadership as it has been handed down from the time of Shakyamuni Buddha.

The present translation of *The Sixth Patriarch's Sutra*, here presented in its third edition, was the first work of Master Hua to appear in America (the first edition appeared in 1971). The translation itself was carried out under the Master's supervision by the Buddhist Text Translation Society, composed of the Master's disciples who are scholars both of the Chinese language and of Buddhism. With his Western readers in mind, the Master has provided a running commentary to the Sutra text. The commentary was first spoken in a series of lectures in 1969. The Master's sure and witty manner of making the most difficult concepts plain, already well known to Buddhists on both sides of the Pacific, has been rendered in English by his disciples with an eye to retaining the lively spoken style of the original.

In his commentary, Master Hua's method is to read a few lines from the Sutra text and then expound upon their meaning or expand on the doctrines in question, often by reference to contemporary American problems. This style of exposition follows the tradition of lecturing Sutras that has existed in China for many centuries. Until the appearance of this volume in its first edition, there had been in the West little or no record or even description of the verbal teachings of Buddhism. The present volume serves as a rare example of Buddhism in action, as it has survived intact through the centuries.

Upasaka Kuo Chou Rounds

Buddhist Text Translation Society, San Francisco, 1977.

Biography of the Venerable Master

Discovering and perfecting the method to extricate living beings from the most fundamental problem of human existence–that of birth and death–has been the primary focus of the Venerable Master Hsüan Hua's life.

On the sixteenth day of the third lunar month in 1908, his mother saw Amitabha Buddha emitting a light which illumined the entire world, and when she awoke from this dream she gave birth to the Venerable Master. A rare fragrance lingered in the room following her dream and throughout the birth.

The Master's initial awareness of death came at eleven years old when he saw a lifeless infant. The realization that death and birth follow upon one another without cease and that both bring suffering, pain and sorrow, awakened a profound sense of compassion in the Master and prompted his immediate resolution to leave the home life and learn to bring an end to the cycle of birth and death. He honored his mother's wishes that he remains at home to serve his parents until their deaths, however.

The following year on Gwan Yin Bodhisattva's birthday, he dreamed that an old woman wearing a patchwork robe and a string of beads appeared to guide him through a wilderness in which he was lost. She radiated compassion as she led him over the road which was gutted with deep and dangerous holes. He knew that if he had tried to traverse this road alone it would have been difficult if not impossible to reach safety, but as she guided him, the road became smooth and safe and he could see clearly in all directions. Ahead was his home. Glancing back on the dangerous road, he saw many people following him–old and young, men and women, sangha and scholars. "Who are those people?" he asked, "Where did they come from and where are they going?"

"They have affinities with you," she said, "and they also want to go home. You must guide them well and show them the Way so that you may all arrive at nirvana. I have important work to do elsewhere, and so I shall leave you now, but soon we shall meet again."

The Master asked her name and where she lived. "You will find out when you arrive home," she said. "There's no need to ask so many questions." Suddenly she whirled around and disappeared. The Master led the people safely home and woke from his dream feeling extremely happy.

During that same year he began bowing to his parents three times each, in the morning and evening–twelve bows a day. Then he thought "The world is bigger than just my father and mother," and he began to bow to the heavens, to the earth, to the Emperor, and to his teachers as well. He also bowed to his master, even though he had not yet met him. The Master knew that without the aid of a good knowing advisor, it is impossible to cultivate, and he felt that he would meet his master soon. He also bowed to the Buddhas, Bodhisattvas, Pratyeka Buddhas, and Arhats, and to all the good people in the world to thank them for all the good deeds they had done; he bowed on behalf of the people they had helped.

"Evil people are to be pitied," he thought, and he bowed for them, asking that their karmic offences might be lessened and that they might learn to repent and reform. When doing this, he thought of himself as the very worst offender. Each day he thought of new people to bow for and soon he was bowing 837 times in the morning and 837 times in the evening, which took about three hours a day in all.

The Master didn't let others see him bow. He rose at four in the morning, washed his face, went outside, lit a stick of incense, and bowed, regardless of the weather. If there was snow on the ground, he would just bow in the snow. In the evening, long after everyone was asleep, he went outside and bowed again. He practiced this way every day for six years.

During these years his filial devotion became known far and wide and he was referred to as "Filial Son Pai." Nor did his filial devotion end at the death of his parents. On the day his mother was buried, he remained behind after the ceremonies were completed to begin a three-year vigil beside her grave. Shortly after, he left his mother's grave long enough to go to Three Conditions Temple at P'ing Fang Station south of Harbin to receive the shramanera precepts from Great Master Ch'ang Chih. He then returned to his mother's grave and built a five by eight hut out of five inch sorghum stalks which kept out the wind and rain but actually set up little distinction between inside and outside. He commenced to observe the custom of filial piety by watching over his mother's grave for a period of three years. Clothed only in a rag robe, he endured the bitter Manchurian snow and blazing summer sun. He ate only one meal a day, when there was food, and he simply did not eat if no food was offered to him. He never lay down to sleep.

At the side of the grave, the Master read many sutras. When he first read the *Lotus Sutra*, he jumped for joy. He knelt and recited it for seven days and seven nights, forgetting to sleep, forgetting to eat, until eventually blood flowed from his eyes and his vision dimmed. Then he read the *Shurangama Sutra*, thoroughly investigating the Great Samadhi and quietly cultivating it: the three stoppings, the three contemplations, neither moving nor still. The Master relates of this experience:

"I began to obtain a single-minded profound stillness, and penetrate the noumenal state. When I read the *Avatamsaka*, the enlightenment became boundless in its scope, indescribable in its magnificence, unsurpassed in its loftiness, and ineffable in its clarity. National Master Ch'ing Liang said,

> *Opening and disclosing the mysterious and subtle,*
> *Understanding and expanding the mind and its states,*
> *Exhausting the principle while fathoming the nature,*
> *Penetrating the result which includes the cause,*
> *Deep and wide, and interfused,*
> *Vast and great and totally complete.*

> *"It is certainly so! It is certainly so! At that time I could not put down the text, and bowed to and recited the Great Sutra as if it were clothing from which one must not part or food which one could not do without for even a day. And I vowed to myself to see to its vast circulation."*

When his filial duties were completed, the Master went into seclusion in Amitabha Cave in the mountains east of his home town. There he delved deeply into dhyana meditation and practiced rigorous asceticism, eating only pine nuts and drinking spring water. The area abounded with wild beasts, but they never disturbed the Master. In fact, wolves and bears behaved like house pets, tigers stopped to listen to his teaching, and wild birds gathered to hear the wonderful Dharma.

After his stay in the mountains, the Master returned to Three Conditions Monastery where he helped the Venerable Master

Ch'ang-chih and the Venerable Master Ch'ang-jen to greatly expand the monastery, while simultaneously devoting his time to the propagation of the Dharma.

For more than three decades in Manchuria, the Master adhered strictly to ascetic cultivation, diligently practiced dhyana meditation, and worked tirelessly for the expansion and propagation of the Dharma. During those years, he visited many of the local Buddhist monasteries, attended intensive meditation and recitation sessions, and walked many miles to listen to lectures on the Sutras, in addition to lecturing on the Sutras himself. He also visited various non-Buddhist religious establishments and obtained a thorough grounding in the range of their specific beliefs.

In 1946 the Master made a major pilgrimage which took him to P'u T'o Mountain to receive the complete precepts in 1947. Then in 1948, after three thousand miles of travel, the Master went to Nan-hua Monastery and bowed before the Venerable Master Hsü Yün, the 44th Patriarch from Shakyamuni Buddha. At that first meeting the Venerable Master Yün, who was then 109 years old, recognized the Master to be a vessel worthy of the Dharma and capable of its propagation. He sealed and certified the Master's spiritual skill and transmitted to him the wonderful mind-to-mind seal of all Buddhas. Thus the Master became the 45th generation in a line descending from Shakyamuni Buddha, the nineteenth generation in China from Bodhidharma, and the ninth generation of the Wei-yang lineage. Of their meeting the Master has written:

The Noble Yün saw me and said, "Thus it is."
I saw the Noble Yün and verified, "Thus it is."
The Noble Yün and I, both Thus,
Universally vow that all beings will also be Thus.

The mind-to-mind transmission is performed apart from the appearance of the spoken word, apart from the mark of the written word, apart from the characteristic of the conditioned mind–apart from all such appearances. Only sages who have genuine realization understand it; ordinary people have no idea what is happening. It is a mutual recognition of the embodiment of the principle of true suchness.

Nearly eight years later, in May of 1956, the Venerable Yün sent to the Master a document entitled "The Treasury of the Orthodox Dharma Eye: the Source of Buddhas and Patriarchs." The document bears the seals of Yün-chu Monastery and of the Venerable Yün. It serves as tangible and public certification of the transmission of the mind-to-mind seal from the Venerable Yün to the Master, which took place during their initial meeting in 1948.

In 1950 the Master resigned his post at Nan Hua Monastery as the Director of the Nan Hua Institute for the Study of the Vinaya, and journeyed to Hong Kong where he lived in a mountainside cave in the New Territories. He stayed in the cave until the large influx of Sangha members fleeing the mainland required his help in establishing new monasteries and temples throughout Hong Kong. He personally established two temples and a lecture hall and helped to bring about the construction of many others. He dwelt in Hong Kong for twelve years, during which many people were influenced by his arduous cultivation and awesome manner to take refuge with the Triple Jewel, cultivating the Dharma-door of recitation of the Buddha's name, and to support the propagation of the Buddhadharma.

In 1962 the Master carried the Buddha's Dharma banner farther west to the shores of America where he took up residence in San Francisco, sat in meditation, and waited for past causes to ripen and bear their fruit. In the beginning of the year 1968 the

Master declared that the flower of Buddhism would bloom that year in America with five petals; in the summer of that year the Master conducted the *Shurangama Sutra* dharma assembly which lasted 96 days–five of the people who attended that session left the home-life and became bhikshus and bhikshunis under the Master's guidance. Since that time more than twenty people have left the home life under his guidance.

Since 1968 the Master has delivered complete commentaries on *The Heart Sutra*, *The Diamond Sutra*, *The Sixth Patriarch's Sutra*, *The Amitabha Sutra*, *The Sutra of the Past Vows of Earth Store Bodhisattva*, *The Great Compassion Heart Dharani Sutra*, *The Dharma Flower Sutra*, *The Sutra in Forty-two Sections*, *The Shramanera Vinaya* and others. In June of 1971, the Master commenced a Dharma Assembly on the king of sutras, the *Avatamsaka*. With such tireless vigor the Master has firmly planted the roots of Dharma in western soil so that it can become self-perpetuating. He has spent many hours every day explaining the teachings and their application to cultivation, steeping his disciples in the nectar of Dharma that they might carry on the Buddha's teachings.

The miraculous events that have taken place in the Master's life are far too numerous to relate in this brief sketch. This is but a brief outline of how the Master has worked with selfless devotion to lay the foundation of the Buddha's teaching on western soil.

Tripitaka Master Hua's Introduction

All of the Sutras are guides to use in cultivating the Way. They may be spoken by the Buddhas, the Bodhisattvas, the Patriarchs, and also by Arhats, transformation beings, and gods. Although they all serve the same purpose, the doctrines within them differ.

The Sutras spoken by the Buddha were translated from the Indian languages into Chinese, and thus worked their way into Chinese society. In China, then, all the Sutras are translations, with the sole exception of this present work *The Sixth Patriarch's Sutra*, which was spoken by the great Chinese master the Sixth Patriarch. The Great Master was originally an illiterate peasant. When he heard the sentence of *The Vajra (Diamond) Sutra* which said, "One should produce that thought which is nowhere supported," he experienced an awakening and went to Huang Mei to draw near to the Fifth Patriarch, the Great Master Hung Jen. The Fifth Patriarch transmitted to him the wonderful Dharma, "using the mind to seal the mind," which has been handed down in unbroken Patriarchal succession. The Sixth Patriarch inherited this mind-seal Dharma-door and proceeded to carry out the wisdom-life of the Buddha in his speaking of *The Sixth Patriarch's Sutra*.

Now, it has been translated into English and the mind-seal Dharma-door of the Buddha has thereby been transmitted in perpetuity to the West. It is hoped that Westerners will now read, recite, and study it, and all become Buddhas, Bodhisattvas, and/

or Patriarchs. This is the main objective of this translation. May all who see and hear it quickly accomplish the Buddha Way.

Wherever this Sutra is transmitted, the Orthodox Dharma may be found right in that place, causing living beings quickly to accomplish Buddhahood; such is the importance of this new translation. The Sutra is indeed a treasure trove; it is the true body of the Buddha, the compassionate father and mother of all living beings. It can give rise to limitless Buddhas, Bodhisattvas, and Patriarchs! May all in the West who now read this Sutra realize Bodhi and accomplish the Buddha Way!

The Sutras contain the precious wisdom of the Buddha. There are some, let us call them "garbage-eating" scholars who claim that *The Shurangama Sutra* was not spoken by the Buddha. This is most certainly not the case, and I have made the following vow: If *The Shurangama Sutra* is false, I will fall into the uninterrupted hells forever.

Ch'ang Pai-shan Seng

San Francisco, August 1977

Translator's Introduction

This is the third edition of the first commentary to *The Sixth Patriarch's Dharma Jewel Platform Sutra* ever to express the essence of the Sixth Patriarch's heart. Since the time the Great Master spoke this Sutra, no other commentary has revealed his basic principles, the Dharma of his heart. Tripitaka Master Hsüan Hua's commentary unfolds the heart Dharma, the mind-seal, before the reader.

If you wish to understand the wonderful meaning of this Sutra, you should study this commentary, for within it are set forth the limitless, inexhaustible, profound principles of the Buddhadharma. Among Western and Eastern peoples it is the flower of wisdom, the real fruit of Bodhi.

Furthermore, this translation has been prepared by the Buddhist Text Translation Society of the Sino-American Buddhist Association. Each of its members, Bhikshus, Bhikshunis, Upasakas, Upasikas, many of whom hold Master's and Doctor's degrees, have read the manuscript with care over a period of several years to insure its accuracy.

Essentially, the mind-seal cannot be spoken or expressed in writing, but in his commentary the Master has done just that, using numerous analogies and expedient devices to cause people to understand what they have never understood before.

Tripitaka Master Hua was born in northern China, and after his mother's death he practiced filial piety by sitting beside her grave for a period of three years. He built a small grass hut to keep out the wind and rain, and sat there in meditation. If food was brought to him, he ate; if no food was brought, he did not.

The Master later traveled south to Canton, where he was appointed by the Venerable Master Hsü Yün to serve as Head of the Vinaya Academy at Nan Hua Monastery, the temple of the Sixth Patriarch. He later received in transmission the Dharma of Master Hsü Yün and became his Dharma successor.

Since arriving in America, the Master has turned the Great Dharma Wheel, lecturing on such Sutras as *The Shurangama Sutra*, *The Lotus Sutra*, *The Earth Store Bodhisattva Sutra*, *The Vajra Sutra*, and *The Heart Sutra*, and others. He teaches an ever-growing number of American disciples, many of whom have left home to become Bhikshus and Bhikshunis.

In San Francisco, the Master has founded Gold Mountain Monastery where he is lecturing on *The Avatamsaka Sutra*. He has also founded the International Institute for the Translation of Buddhist Texts. He has made the solemn vow that wherever he goes the Orthodox Dharma will prevail and the Dharma-ending Age shall not set in. Most recently, the Master established the City of Ten Thousand Buddhas, near Talmage, California, a vast complex of 237 acres and 60 buildings, to serve as a center of World Buddhism. The City of Ten Thousand Buddhas now holds Dharma Realm Buddhist University, of which the Master is President, and soon to be established are many programs to benefit living beings in many ways.

The Master upholds firmly the Orthodox Dharma, for the Dharma he teaches proceeds from direct and authoritative transmission, and he works unceasingly for the Buddha, the Dharma, and the Sangha. This lively commentary constitutes the first authentic transmission to the West of the mind-seal of all Buddhas which has passed in unbroken Patriarchal succession from Shakyamuni Buddha to the present day. We present this volume as the foundation for the flourishing of the Buddhadharma in the West.

Bhikshuni Heng Yin

Buddhist Text Translation Society/Co-chairperson,
Primary Translation Committee,
International Institute for the Translation of Buddhist Texts.
San Francisco, August 1977

Reviewer's Preface

When the Fifth Patriarch transmitted the Dharma to the Sixth Patriarch he said to him, "Do not speak too soon, for the Buddhadharma arises from difficulty."

Centuries later in Northern China, Tripitaka Master Hsüan Hua, then known as Filial Son Pai, was practicing filial piety. He cultivated and meditated for three years beside his mother's grave. His only protection from the northern winds and rains was a five foot square hut made from stalks of sorghum bound together in an A-frame which left both ends exposed to the elements.

One time while cultivating there a miracle happened. Filial Son Pai saw the Great Master the Sixth Patriarch come to his hut. He entered through one of the openings and talked to the filial son just like an ordinary person. Filial Son Pai thought that he was real, forgetting at that time that the Great Master had entered Nirvana over a thousand years ago. The Sixth Patriarch said to the Filial Son:

"In the future you can go to America.
You will meet this person and that person...
Five schools will divide into ten,
to teach and transform living beings.
Ten will become a hundred,
a hundred will become a thousand,
and so forth to endless, endless numbers,

in abundance, abundance, abundance,
endless abundance–numbers incalculable
as grains of sand in the River Ganges.
This marks the true beginning of
the Proper Dharma in the West."

After they had talked, when the Great Master moved to leave, the filial son rose to escort him. They walked together a few steps and suddenly the Sixth Patriarch was gone. It was then that Filial Son Pai realized, "Oh! The Sixth Patriarch entered Nirvana hundreds of years ago, but nonetheless, I met him today!"

Several decades after this miracle, following years of difficulty and hard cultivation, in a cold and tiny temple in San Francisco's Chinatown, Tripitaka Master Hsüan Hua began transmitting the Dharma of the mind-seal of all Patriarchs. He continues to do so every day. Those who recognize him listen to it, consider it, and cultivate it.

In this commentary on *The Sixth Patriarch's Sutra* the Master says, "...you will succeed only if you do not fear suffering. The Buddhadharma arises from difficulty, the more difficult, the better. So now you must endure suffering. This is difficult, but you can do it, for it is the opening of your wisdom."

Bhikshuni Heng Ch'ih

Buddhist Text Translation Society/Co-chairperson,
Primary Translation Committee,
International Institute for the Translation of Buddhist Texts
San Francisco, August 1977

釋迦牟尼文佛

Na Mwo Original Teacher Sakyamuni Buddha

二十八祖菩提達摩大師

Twenty-eighth Patriarch Arya Bodhidharma
The First Patriarch in China

二十九祖慧可大師

Twenty-ninth Patriarch Great Master Hui-k'o
The Second Patriarch in China

Thirtieth Patriarch Great Master Seng-ts'an
The Third Patriarch in China

三十一祖道信大師

Thirty-first Patriarch Great Master Tao-hsin
The Fourth Patriarch in China

三十二祖弘忍大師

Thirty-second Patriarch Great Master Hung-jen
The Fifth Patriarch in China

三十三祖慧能大師

Thirty-third Patriarch Great Master Hui-neng
The Sixth Patriarch in China

Verse for Opening a Sutra

The unsurpassed, profound, and wonderful Dharma,
Is difficult to encounter in hundreds of millions of eons,
I now see and hear it, receive and uphold it,
And I vow to fathom the Tathagata's true meaning.

FOREWORD

The Sixth Patriarch's Dharma Jewel Platform Sutra has been explained in America before, but I do not know how well it has been done. Some lecturers simply read the text aloud, and, since each Sutra has its own special interpretation, merely reading it aloud does not reveal the meaning.

The Buddhadharma flourished in China, but only the teachings of the Sixth Patriarch, the illiterate Patriarch, were made into a Sutra. It was recorded by the Master's disciple Fa Hai[1]. Although his transcription may not mirror the Patriarch's exact words, the meanings expressed are correct.

I hope that everyone will study the Buddhadharma with his true mind, and not hold the opinion that it is very easy. It is only by regarding the Buddhadharma as extremely important that you will be able to comprehend the principles which I explain.

---

1. Dharma Master Fa Hai was a "room entering disciple" of the Sixth Patriarch. That means that the Sixth Patriarch had transmitted the wonderful mind-seal Dharma to him and he was therefore privileged to enter the Patriarch's room.

INTRODUCTION

The Sixth Patriarch's Dharma Jewel Platform is the specific title of this Sutra, and the word Sutra is a general term for all discourses given by the Buddha. In order to clarify their content, Sutra titles are classified into seven types, according to their reference to person, dharma, and analogy, as follows:

A. Three Single: Three of the seven types of titles refer to only one of the categories of person, dharma, or analogy, and so they are called the "three single." For example:

1. *The Buddha Speaks of Amitabha Sutra* is a title established solely by reference to person; both the Buddha and Amitabha are persons, for only a person can cultivate and realize Buddhahood. The Buddha is a person, and people are just Buddhas. In Chinese, when we write the word Buddha (佛), the symbol for "person" (人) stands on the left-hand side.
2. *The Mahaparinirvana Sutra* is a title established by reference to the dharma, "nirvana." Nirvana is a Sanskrit word which in Chinese is composed of two characters "(涅槃)–nieh p'an" which may be explained as "not produced and not destroyed."
3. *The Brahma Net Sutra* is a title established by reference to analogy. In this Sutra the Buddha explains the precepts. If you keep these precepts, you will give forth light, like the great net in the heaven of the Brahma King. But if you carelessly break the precepts, you

commit the grave offense of "knowing and yet deliberately violating dharma." Your light then flows into the three evil paths: the hell beings, animals, and hungry ghosts, where there is not the slightest trace of merciful treatment.

B. Three Double: Titles established by reference to person and dharma, person and analogy, or dharma and analogy are called the "three double." For example:

4. *The Wonderful Dharma Lotus Flower Sutra* is a title established by reference to dharma and analogy since the Wonderful Dharma is analogous to the Lotus Flower.
5. *The Lion Roar of the Thus Come One Sutra* is a title established by reference to person and analogy. Thus Come One is the first of ten honorific titles given to every Buddha and therefore represents a person. The Lion Roar is analogous to his speaking the Dharma.
6. *The Sutra of the Questions of Manjushri* is a title established by reference to a person, the Bodhisattva Manjushri of great wisdom, and the dharma he requested, Prajna.

C. Complete in One: The seventh classification contains references to person, dharma, and analogy.

7. *The Great Universal Buddha Flower Adornment Sutra (Avatamsaka Sutra)* refers to the Buddha as a person, Great and Universal as a dharma, and Flower Adornment as an analogy.

The Sixth Patriarch's Dharma Jewel Platform Sutra is a Chinese, not an Indian Sutra, and its title is not classified according to the seven topics mentioned above. This sutra is classified according to person, dharma, and a place. The Sixth

Patriarch is a person, the Dharma Jewel is a dharma, and the Platform is a place.

I will now explain the specific title of this Sutra.

The Sixth Patriarch. Master Hui Neng of Nan Hua Temple, who spoke the Sutra at the beginning of the eighth century A.D., was the Sixth Chinese Patriarch. He lived six generations after Bodhidharma, who brought the Mahayana teaching to China from India and who became the First Chinese Patriarch. Bodhidharma was also the twenty-eighth Indian Patriarch, and so from the time of Shakyamuni Buddha, the Great Master Hui Neng is counted as the Thirty-Third Generational Patriarch.

Dharma. Dharma is a method. It is like a rule, a model, or a pattern. If one cultivates according to this method, that is practicing "Dharma."

Jewel. The Dharma is like a precious jewel.

Platform. The platform is the place where this Sutra was spoken. This Dharma Seat may be raised above the ground by three, five or nine feet, but never more than ten feet. In front of it sits a small table which holds Sutras. Dharma Masters speak Dharma, administer the Three Refuges[2], and transmit precepts from the Dharma Seat, which Dharma protectors, good spirits, and numerous diamond-treasury Bodhisattvas[3] take turns protecting.

---

2. One formally becomes a Buddhist only when one has received the Three Refuges, transmitted in a traditional ceremony by a qualified member of the Sangha. They are: refuge in: 1) the Buddha, 2) the Dharma (the teachings), and 3) the Sangha (Buddhist monks and nuns of the past, present and future).

3. Bodhisattva is a Sanskrit word. Bodhi means "enlightenment" and sattva, "being". They do not enter Nirvana but choose instead to remain in the world and save living beings. Thus Bodhisattvas are enlightened beings who enlighten other beings. "Diamond-treasury" refers to a division of Dharma-protecting Bodhisattvas.

Sutra. The Sixth Patriarch's Dharma Jewel Platform is the specific name of the Sutra, and the word "Sutra" is its general name. "Sutra" is a Sanskrit word which means "a tally." Above, it tallies with the true principle of all Buddhas, and below, with the opportunities for teaching living beings. Above, it tallies with true suchness, the miraculous principle of all Buddhas, and below, it tallies with the living beings who need the teaching. Thus, a Sutra tallies with both the principle and the opportunity.

The word Sutra has four additional meanings:

1. *Stringing together.* The principles of the Buddhadharma are linked together by the Sutras just like beads are strung together on a string.
2. *Attracting.* Creating the opportunities for teaching living beings, a Sutra attracts living beings just like a magnet attracts iron filings. All living beings who wish to study the Buddhadharma will be drawn to the principles in the Sutras, like iron filings to a magnet.
3. *Permanent.* From antiquity to the present, a Sutra does not change. Not one word can be deleted; not one meaning can be added. Not increasing or decreasing, a Sutra is permanent, unchanging.
4. *Method.* A Sutra is a method respected by living beings in the three periods of time. In the past, living beings relied upon this method to cultivate and attain Buddhahood. In the present, living beings depend upon it to move from the position of foolish common people to that of Buddhahood. In the future, living beings will also cultivate according to this method. A Sutra is a method, then, venerated throughout the three periods of time.

The word Sutra has many more meanings. For example, a Sutra is like a bubbling spring; principles flow from it like water bubbling up out of the earth. It is also like a carpenter's chalk-line, which makes a perfectly clear, straight guide. But if you understand the first four meanings, you understand the basic meanings.

To explain a Sutra correctly, one must first outline it according to the Five Profound Meanings of the T'ien T'ai School:

1. *Explaining the Name.* According to the seven kinds of Sutra titles explained previously, this Sutra is established by reference to person, Dharma, analogy, and place.
2. *Discriminating the Substance.* This Sutra takes the Real Mark[4] as its substance. The Real Mark is without a mark, and yet there is nothing which is not marked by it.
3. *Clarifying the Principle.* The principle of this Sutra is the realization of Buddhahood. If you cultivate according to this Sutra, you can realize the Buddha position.
4. *Discussing the Function.* This Sutra's function is to lead you to understand the mind and see your own nature. If you understand the mind, you have no worries. If you see your own nature, you have no cares. No longer do you quit worrying about one problem only to begin worrying about another and, when that one is solved, find yet another one coming to take its place. If

4. The Real Mark denotes true reality, devoid of external appearances, attachments, and discriminations

you understand the mind and see your own nature, then everything is easy.

5. *Determining the Teaching Mark.* This Sutra is like sweet dew, the heavenly elixir of immortality. Drink it once and you will never die. The Sutra is also like ghee, a clarified butter with the most miraculous and subtle of tastes. Ghee is also used to describe the Sutras spoken by Shakyamuni Buddha during the Dharma Flower and Lotus-Nirvana periods of his teaching[5].

---

5. The T'ien T'ai School, systematized by the Great Master Chih-i (538-597), is one of the great teaching schools of Chinese Buddhism. It takes as its basic text the *Wonderful Dharma Lotus Flower Sutra*, and divides the Buddha's teaching into five periods; each period is represented by an analogy to a milk product.

Period	**Milk Product**
Avatamsaka (21 days)	whole milk
Agama (12 years)	coagulated milk
Vaipulya (8 years)	curdled milk
Prajna-paramita (22 years)	butter
Lotus Flower-Nirvana (8 years)	clarified butter (ghee)

The original dharma of the *Avatamsaka* is like fresh milk. With each new teaching, it becomes richer and purer, yet it is still the same basic substance–Dharma Food.

The Five Previous Chinese Patriarchs

It wasn't easy being the Sixth Patriarch. Many people wished to kill him and his disciples as well. For this reason, after the Great Master obtained the Dharma, he went into hiding, dwelling among hunters for sixteen years. Even after establishing his Dharma platform at Nan Hua Temple, followers of other religions tried to kill him, and so the Great Master hid inside a big rock. He sat there in meditation, and although they set the mountain on fire, he was untouched by the flames. The rock could still be seen when I was at Nan Hua Temple.

Who wanted to kill him? In general, it wasn't you and it wasn't me. On the other hand, if you consider the insane things we have done in past lives, it might well have been you or it could have been me. But in this life it wasn't you or me and so there is no need to worry about having broken precepts in this case.

As I told you, the Great Master is counted as the Sixth Patriarch from the First Patriarch, Bodhidharma, who was the Twenty-eighth Indian Patriarch. "Bodhi" means enlightenment and "Dharma" means law. When Bodhidharma set sail from India, fulfilling Shakyamuni Buddha's prediction that the Mahayana[6] teaching would be transmitted to China during the time of the Twenty-eighth Patriarch, the Buddhadharma already existed in China, yet it was as if it were not there at all. Although there were men who studied, there were few who lectured or recited the sutras and repentance ceremonies were seldom practiced. Cultivation was superficial. Scholars debated and argued, but none of them truly understood.

The principles in the Sutras must be cultivated, but at that time in China they were not cultivated because everyone feared suffering. Now, in America, it is just the same. People sit in meditation. However, as soon as their legs begin to ache, they wince and fidget and then gently unbend them. People are just people and nobody likes to have aching legs.

While still in India, Patriarch Bodhidharma sent two of his disciples, Fo T'o and Yeh She, to China to transmit the sudden enlightenment Dharma door. But no one, not even Chinese Bhikshus[7], would speak to them. So they went to Lu Mountain where they met the Great Master Yüan Kung, who lectured on mindfulness of the Buddha.

Master Yüan asked, "What Dharma do you transmit that causes people to pay you so little respect?"

Fo T'o and Yeh She could not speak Chinese, so they used sign language instead. Raising their arms in the air, they said, "Watch! The hand makes a fist and the fist makes a hand. Is this not quick?"

Master Yüan replied, "Quick indeed."

"Bodhi (enlightenment) and affliction," they said, "are just that quick."

At that moment, Dharma Master Yüan became enlightened, realizing that originally Bodhi and affliction are not different, for Bodhi is affliction and affliction is Bodhi. He made offerings to

6. The Mahayana or "great vehicle" teaching stresses the salvation of all beings, since all beings possess the Buddha nature and may realize Buddhahood. It is called "great" in comparison with the Hinayana or "lesser vehicle", whose followers pursue personal salvation.

7. A Bhikshu is a Buddhist Monk.

Fo T'o and Yeh She, and shortly thereafter, the two Indian Bhikshus died on the same day, in the same place. Their graves may still be seen at Lu Mountain.

Patriarch Bodhidharma saw that the roots of the Mahayana, the Great Vehicle Buddhadharma, were ripe in China. Fearing neither the distance nor the hardship of travel, he took the Dharma there. The Chinese called him "barbarian" because he talked in a way that no one understood. When children looked up at the bearded Bodhidharma, they ran away in terror. Adults feared that he was a kidnapper and so told their children to stay away from him.

Patriarch Bodhidharma went to Nan Ching where he listened to Dharma Master Shen Kuang explained the Sutras. When Shen Kuang spoke, the heavens rained fragrant blossoms and a golden-petalled lotus rose from the earth for him to sit upon. However, only those with good roots, who had opened the five eyes[8] and the six spiritual penetrations were able to see that. Now! Isn't this wonderful?

After listening to the Sutra, Bodhidharma asked, "Dharma Master, what are you doing?"

"I am explaining Sutras," Shen Kuang replied.

"Why are you explaining Sutras?"

"I am teaching people to end birth and death."

"Oh?" said Bodhidharma, "exactly how do you do that? In this Sutra which you explain, the words are black and the paper is white. How does this teach people to end birth and death?"

Dharma Master Shen Kuang had nothing to say. How *did* he teach people to end birth and death? He fumed in silence. Then, even though heavenly maidens rained down flowers and the

---

8. Opened through cultivation, the Five Eyes are: 1) the Buddha Eye, 2) the Dharma Eye, 3) the Flesh Eye, 4) the Heavenly Eye, and 5) the Wisdom Eye.

earth gave forth golden lotuses, Dharma Master Shen Kuang got angry. This is what I mean when I say that the Buddhadharma existed in China, but it was as if it were not there at all.

When angry, Dharma Master Shen Kuang used his heavy iron beads to level opposition. In response to Bodhidharma's question, he reddened with anger and raged like a tidal wave smashing a mountain. As he whipped out his beads, he snapped, "You are slandering the Dharma!" and cracked Bodhidharma across the mouth, knocking loose two teeth. Bodhidharma neither moved nor spoke. He hadn't expected such a vicious reply.

There is a legend about the teeth of holy men. You must not ask about the principle, however, because it is too inconceivable. The legend says that if a sage's teeth fall to the ground, it won't rain for three years. Patriarch Bodhidharma thought, "If it doesn't rain for three years, people will starve! I have come to China to save living beings, not to kill them!" So Bodhidharma did not let his teeth fall to the ground. Instead, he swallowed them and disappeared down the road. Although he had been beaten and reviled, Bodhidharma could not go to the government and file suit against Dharma Master Shen Kuang. Those who have left home have to be patient. How much more so must a patriarch forbear.

Bodhidharma then met a parrot imprisoned in a wicker cage. This bird was much more intelligent than Dharma Master Shen Kuang. Recognizing Bodhidharma as the First Patriarch, the bird said,

Mind from the West,
Mind from the West,
Teach me a way
To escape from this cage.

Although Bodhidharma had received no response from people, this parrot recognized him. Hearing the bird's plea for help, Bodhidharma whispered a secret expedient teaching to teach this bird how to end suffering. He said,

To escape from the cage;
To escape from the cage;
Put out both legs,
Close both eyes.
This is the way
To escape from the cage!

The parrot listened attentively and said, "All right! I understand," and stuck out his legs, closed his eyes, and waited.

When the bird's owner came home from work, he always played with his parrot. But this time when he looked in the cage he was shocked. The owner was on the verge of tears. He couldn't have been more upset if his own son had died. He pulled open the cage door and scooped up the bird, which lay still and quiet in his hand. The body had not yet chilled. The owner looked with disbelief at the little body. He peeked at it from the left and right...it didn't even quiver. Slowly, he opened his hand...PHLLRTTPHLRTTPHLRTT! The bird broke loose from his hand and flew away!

Now, like the parrot, we are in a cage. How do we escape? You may say, "I am really free. If I want to eat, I eat; if I want to drink, I drink. I do not have to follow rules. I can do anything."

Don't think you are quite so clever. This is not freedom, it is just confusion. To be free, you must be free of birth and death, and then, if you wish to fly into space you can fly into space, and if you wish to drop into the earth, you can drop into the earth. If you can do this, you are truly independent. Like the parrot, you are free.

As I explain *The Sixth Patriarch Dharma Jewel Platform Sutra*, I do not lecture well. This is not polite talk; it's true. Some lecture well, yet do not dare explain. After I have lectured, you of true eloquence may follow. When you have opened your wisdom, you will understand.

In his great anger, Dharma Master Shen Kuang knocked out two of Bodhidharma's teeth. He thought he had won a great victory because the Barbarian put forth no opposition. But not long after, the Ghost of Impermanence, wearing a high hat, paid a call on Master Shen Kuang:

"Your life ends today," said the ghost. "King Yama, the King of the Dead, has sent me to escort you."

Master Shen Kuang said, "What? Must *I* die? When I speak the Dharma, flowers fall from the heavens and the earth bubbles forth golden lotuses, yet I still have not ended birth and death? Tell me, is there a person in this world who has ended birth and death?"

"There is," came the reply.

"Who?" asked Shen Kuang. "Tell me, and I'll follow him to study the Way."

"He's that black-faced Bhikshu whose teeth you just knocked out. King Yama bows to him every day."

"Please, Old Ghost, speak to King Yama on my behalf. I want to follow that Bhikshu. I am determined to end birth and death. Can't you allow me some more time?"

"All right," said the ghost. "Since you are sincere, King Yama will wait."

Dharma Master Shen Kuang was delighted. He was so quick to rush after Bodhidharma, that he forgot to thank the Ghost of Impermanence; in fact, he even forgot to put on his shoes. He ran until he met the parrot whom Bodhidharma had freed, and suddenly he understood, "Originally it is just this way! I need only act dead. I need only be a living dead person!"

Bodhidharma walked on, ignoring the barefoot Dharma Master following behind. Arriving at Bear's Ear Mountain in Loyang, the Patriarch sat down to meditate facing a wall. Dharma Master Shen Kuang knelt close by. For nine years, Patriarch Bodhidharma sat meditating and Dharma Master Shen Kuang knelt beside him, seeking the Dharma.

Earlier, when I spoke this public record, an eleven year old child asked me, "During the nine years he knelt, did he eat or not?" I replied, "How could anyone kneel for nine years without eating and still live? When the Patriarch meditated, Shen Kuang knelt, and when the Patriarch ate, Shen Kuang ate." But this is not recorded in the books. While the Patriarch was sitting, many people came to bow to him and were received as his disciples.

One day a great snow fell, and it rose in drifts as high as Shen Kuang's waist, and yet he continued to kneel. Finally, Patriarch Bodhidharma asked him, "Why are you kneeling here in such deep snow?"

"I want to end birth and death," replied Shen Kuang. "When I was lecturing Sutras I was unsuccessful. Please, Patriarch, transmit this dharma to me."

"What do you see falling from the sky?" asked Bodhidharma.

"Snow," said Shen Kuang.

"What color is it?" asked Bodhidharma.

"It's white, of course."

"When red snow falls from the sky," said Bodhidharma, "I will transmit the Dharma to you. You knocked out two of my teeth, and I have been most compassionate in not taking revenge. Do you really expect me to give you the Dharma?" This was the test Patriarch Bodhidharma gave to Master Shen Kuang.

How did Shen Kuang complete the test? Cultivators of the Way carry a knife to protect the substance of their precepts. A true cultivator would rather cut off his head than break a precept.

Shen Kuang drew his precept knife, and with one slice, cut off his arm and thus passed his test. His blood flowed onto the new fallen snow. He scooped up a bucket full of crimson snow, dumped it before Bodhidharma, and said, "Patriarch, do you see? The snow is red!"

Bodhidharma said, "So it is, so it is." He had tested Shen Kuang's sincerity, and now the Patriarch was extremely happy. "My coming to China has not been in vain. I have met a person who dares to use a true mind to cultivate the Way, even forsaking his arm in search of the Dharma."

The Patriarch then spoke the Dharma door of "using the mind to seal the mind."[9] It points straight to the mind to see the nature and realize Buddhahood.

While hearing this dharma, Shen Kuang didn't think about the pain in his arm, and before that he had thought only of making the snow turn red. But now, he once again produced discursive thought: "My arm really hurts!" he said. "My mind is in pain. Please, Patriarch, quiet my mind."

"Find your mind," said Bodhidharma. "Show it to me and I will quiet it for you."

Dharma Master Shen Kuang searched for his mind. He looked in the ten directions: north, east, south, west, in the intermediate points, and up and down. He also looked in the same seven places that the Venerable Ananda looked when

9. 以心印心 – i hsin yin hsin, refers to the mind-to-mind transmission of Dharma passed through each generation from the time of Shakyamuni Buddha onwards.

Shakyamuni Buddha asked him the same question in *The Shurangama Sutra*[10]. That is,

1. He looked inside his body;
2. He looked outside his body;
3. He looked for it hidden somewhere in his sense organs.
4. He looked where there was light;
5. He looked at the place where conditions came together.
6. He looked in the middle, between the organs and their objects;
7. And, finally, he looked in the place of non-attachment, which is no-place.

At last Shen Kuang said to Bodhidharma, "I can't find my mind! Great Master, it is nowhere to be found."

"This is how well I have quieted your mind," said the Patriarch. At these words, Shen Kuang understood the meaning of the Dharma transmission, the wonderful, ineffable principle.

Ten thousand dharmas return to one;
Where does the one return?
Shen Kuang did not understand,
And ran after Bodhidharma;
Before him at Bear's Ear Mountain
Knelt nine years
Seeking Dharma to escape King Yama

With the transmission of the Dharma, Shen Kuang received the name "Hui K'o" which means "Able Wisdom."

---

10. *Shurangama Sutra*, 楞嚴經– leng yen ching, from Roll I. T. 945.

Master Hui K'o asked Bodhidharma, "In India, did you transmit the Dharma to your disciples? Did you also give the robe and bowl as certification?"

"I transmitted the Dharma in India," replied Bodhidharma, "but I did not use the robe and bowl. Indian people are straightforward. When they attain the fruit, they know they must be certified. If no one certifies them, they do not say, 'I have attained the way! I have given proof to Arhatship! I am a Bodhisattva!' They do not speak like this."

"Chinese people, however, are different. Many Chinese have the Great Vehicle Root Nature[11], but there are also many people who lie. Having cultivated without success, such people claim to have the Way. Though they have not certified to the fruit, they claim to be certified sages. Therefore I transmit the robe and bowl to prove that you have received the transmission. Guard them well and take care."

While the Patriarch Bodhidharma was in China, he was poisoned six times. Dharma Master Bodhiruci and Vinaya Master Kuang T'ung were jealous of him. They prepared a vegetarian meal which contained an invariably fatal drug, and offered it to the Patriarch. Although he knew it was poisoned, he ate it. Then he vomited the food on to a tray, and it was transformed into a pile of writhing snakes.

After this unsuccessful attempt, Bodhiruci tried again, using an even more potent poison. Again, Bodhidharma ate the food. Then he sat atop a huge boulder and spat out the poison. The

11. "Great Vehicle Root Nature" refers to the strong karmic affinity of those who in past lives have cultivated the Great Vehicle and who, by their meritorious actions, have sent down "deep roots," that is, have established a firm foundation in the Buddhadharma, which enables them to successfully understand and practice it in the present.

boulder crumbled into a heap of dust. In four more attempts, jealous people tried without success to poison the Patriarch.

One day, the Great Master Bodhidharma said to Hui K'o, "I came to China because I saw people here with the Great Vehicle Root Nature. Now I have transmitted the Dharma and am ready to complete the stillness." After his death, the Patriarch's body was buried. There was nothing unusual about his funeral.

In Northern Wei (386-532 A.D.), however, an official called Sung Yün, met Bodhidharma on the road to Chung Nan Mountain in Ts'ung Ling. When they met, Bodhidharma was carrying one shoe in his hand. He said to Sung Yün, "The king of your country died today. Return quickly! There is work to be done."

The official asked, "Great Master, where are you going?"

"Back to India," the Great Master replied.

"Venerable One, to whom did you transmit your Dharma?"

"In China, after forty years, it will be 'K'o.'"

Sung Yün returned to his country and reported the incident. "Recently, in Ts'ung Ling, I met the Patriarch Bodhidharma who told me that the king of our country had died and instructed me to return to the capital. When I arrived I found it exactly as he had said. How did he know?"

His countrymen scoffed, "Bodhidharma is already dead. How could you have met him on the road?" Then they rushed to the Patriarch's grave and found it empty, with nothing inside but one shoe.

Where did Bodhidharma go? No one knows. Perhaps he came to America. Wherever he wanders, no one can recognize him, because he can change and transform according to his convenience. When he came to China, he said he was one hundred and fifty years old, and when he left, he was still one hundred and fifty years old. No historical references can be found.

When Bodhidharma was about to enter Nirvana he said, "I came to China and transmitted my Dharma to three people. One received my marrow, one my bones, and one my flesh." After the transmission, the Patriarch himself no longer had a body. Great Master Hui K'o received the marrow and Ch'an Master Tao Yü received the bones.

Bhikshuni Tsung Ch'ih could recite *The Lotus Sutra* from memory. After she died, a green lotus flower grew from her mouth. She received Bodhidharma's flesh. In the end, the Patriarch had no body at all. So don't look for him in America; you won't find him.

The Second Patriarch, Hui K'o of the Northern Ch'i (550-577 A.D.) whose family name was Chi, was formerly Shen Kuang. When he was born, his parents saw Wei T'ou Bodhisattva, the golden armored spiritual being, come to offer protection; thereupon they named their son "Shen Kuang" which means "spiritual light." Not only was the Patriarch intelligent, but he had an excellent memory as well, and his skill and powers of discrimination were so remarkable that he could read ten lines in the time it took an ordinary person to read one. In a gathering of one hundred people, all talking at once, he could clearly distinguish each conversation.

The Great Master, however, had great anger; he disagreed with everyone and was always ready to fight. When Shen Kuang explained Sutras, as I have told you, he used his iron beads to win his arguments. Later, after he knelt for nine years in quest of the Dharma, it was his great anger which enabled him to cut off his arm and feel no pain. It was also because of this anger that he later felt pain. Unafflicted by anger, he would have felt no pain. Pain is just an affliction and affliction is the cause of pain.

The Second Patriarch was forty years old when he left Bodhidharma. Having obtained the Dharma, he went into hiding because Bodhiruci and Vinaya Master Kuang T'ung, who had made six attempts on the life of Bodhidharma, also wished to kill his disciples. So although Hui K'o had great anger, he nevertheless obeyed his teacher and went into hiding for forty years. When he was eighty, he began to propagate the Buddhadharma, teaching and transforming living beings.

Later, the disciples of Bodhiruci and Vinaya Master Kuang T'ung tried to kill Master Hui K'o, who feigned insanity to lessen the jealousy of his rivals. But he never ceased to save living beings who were ready to receive his teaching. Because so many people continued to trust the Second Patriarch, Bodhiruci's disciples were still jealous. They reported Hui K'o to the government, accusing him of being a weird inhuman creature. "He confuses the people who follow him," they charged; "he is not even human." The Emperor ordered the district magistrate to arrest him, and Hui K'o was locked up and questioned:

"Are you human or are you a freak?" asked the Magistrate.

"I'm a freak," replied Master Hui K'o.

The magistrate knew that the Patriarch said this to avoid causing jealousy, so he ordered him to tell the truth. "Speak clearly," he demanded, "what are you?"

The Great Master replied, "I'm a freak."

Governments can't allow strange freaks to roam the earth, and so Hui K'o was sentenced to die. Now, isn't this the way of the world?

The Patriarch wept when he told his disciples, "I must undergo this retribution." He was a courageous man, certainly not one to cry out of fear of death. He was sad because the Dharma had not become widely understood during his lifetime.

"The Buddhadharma will not flourish until the time of the Fourth Patriarch," he announced, and then he faced the executioner.

"Come and kill me!" he said. The executioner raised his axe and swung it towards the Master's neck. What do you think happened?

You are probably thinking, "He was a Patriarch with great spiritual power. Certainly the blade shattered and his head was not even scratched." No. The axe cut off his head, and it didn't grow back. However, instead of blood, a milky white liquid flowed onto the chopping block.

You think, "Now really, this is just too far out." If you believe it, that is fine. If you do not believe it, that is fine too; just forget it. However, I will give you a simple explanation of why blood did not flow from the Patriarch's neck: When a sage enters the white *yang* realm[12] his blood becomes white because his body has transformed completely into *yang*, leaving no trace of *yin*. "I don't believe it," you say. Of course you don't. If you did, you would be just like the Second Patriarch.

When the executioner saw that the Master did not bleed, he exclaimed, "Hey! He really is a freak! I chopped off his head, but what came out was not blood, but this milky white fluid. And his face looks exactly as it did when he was alive!" The Emperor knew that he had executed a saint, because he remembered that the Twenty-fourth Indian Patriarch, Aryasimha, had also been beheaded and had not bled, but a white milky liquid had poured forth, because he had been without outflows. When one has no ignorance, one may attain to a state without outflows and enter the white *yang* realm.

---

12. 白陽世界 – pai yang shih chieh.

You think, "But you just said that Patriarch Hui K'o had great anger. How could he have been without ignorance?" You are certainly more clever than I am, for I did not think of this question. But now that you have brought it up, I will answer it. His was not petty anger like yours and mine which explodes like firecrackers, "Pop! Pop! Pop." His anger was wisdom and because of it his body became *yang*. Great patience, great knowledge, great courage, and great wisdom: that's what his temper was made of.

Realizing that Hui K'o was a Bodhisattva in the flesh, the Emperor felt great shame. "A Bodhisattva came to our country," he said, "and instead of offering him protection, we killed him." Then the Emperor had all the great officials take refuge with this strange Bhikshu. Thus, even though the Second Patriarch had already been executed, he still accepted these disciples.

The Third Patriarch, Seng Ts'an of the Sui Dynasty, was of unknown family name and origin. When he first came to visit the Second Patriarch, his body was covered with repulsive sores like those of a leper.

"Where are you from?" asked the Second Patriarch. "What are you doing here?"

"I have come to take refuge with the High Master, and to study and cultivate the Buddhadharma," answered Seng Ts'an.

"You have a loathsome disease and your body is filthy. How can you study the Buddhadharma?"

Master Hui K'o was clever, but Dhyana Master Seng Ts'an was even more clever. "I am a sick man and you are a high master," he said, "but in our true minds where is the difference?"

Thereupon, the Second Patriarch transmitted the Dharma to Seng Ts'an saying, "This robe and bowl have been passed on from Bodhidharma. They certify that you have received the Dharma Seal. In order to protect it you must go into hiding, because Bodhiruci's followers will try to harm you. Be very careful and let no one know that you have received the transmission."

The Third Patriarch Seng Ts'an also feigned insanity while he taught living beings. During the persecution of Buddhism by the Emperor Wu of the Northern Chou dynasty (reigned from 561-577 A.D.), the Patriarch fled into the mountains. While he hid there, the tigers, wolves, leopards, and other fierce animals all disappeared.

After transmitting the Dharma to the Fourth Patriarch, Tao Hsin, Master Seng Ts'an invited a thousand Bhikshus to a great vegetarian feast. After they had eaten, he said, "You think that to sit in full lotus is the best way to die. Watch! I'll demonstrate my independence over birth and death!" The Master left the dining hall, followed by the thousand Bhikshus. He halted by the trunk of a tree, and after pausing for a moment, he leapt up and grabbed a big branch. Then while swinging from the tree by one hand, he entered Nirvana. No one knew his name or his birthplace.

Someone is afraid and thinks, "The First Patriarch was poisoned, the Second Patriarch was beheaded, and the Third Patriarch died hanging from a tree. I certainly do not want to be a patriarch. It's much too dangerous." With this attitude, even if you wanted to be a patriarch you could not. As long as you fear death, as long as you fear anything at all, you cannot even be a patriarch's disciple. Patriarchs are not afraid of suffering. They are not afraid of life and they are not afraid of death. Making no distinctions between life and death, they roam among people, teaching and transforming them. Like Fo T'o and Yeh She, they know that affliction is just Bodhi and that birth and death is Nirvana. So, tell me now, who is not afraid of birth and death? If there is such a one, I will make him a patriarch.

The Fourth Patriarch's name was Tao Hsin. While very young, Master Tao Hsin left home under Master Seng Ts'an and for sixty years he sat in Dhyana concentration, without lying down to rest. Although he seldom opened his eyes, he wasn't asleep. He was working at cultivation. When he did open his eyes, everyone shook with terror. Why? No one knew. Such was the magnitude of his awesome virtue.

Hearing of the Master's great virtue, in the seventeenth year of the Chen Kuan Reign of the T'ang dynasty (643 A.D.), the Emperor sent a messenger to invite him to the palace to receive offerings. Unlike we common people, who would attempt to wedge ourselves into the court without being asked, the Great Master, the Fourth Patriarch, refused the invitation saying, "I am too old and the journey would be tiring. Eating on the road would be too difficult. I cannot undergo such hardship."

When the messenger delivered the Patriarch's reply, the Emperor said, "Go back and tell him that the Emperor says that no matter how old he is or how difficult the journey, I have ordered him to come to the palace."

The messenger returned to the Patriarch and said, "Master, regardless of your health, you must come to the Emperor's court. We will carry you back, if necessary!" At that time, since there were no airplanes or cars, travel was difficult.

"No, I cannot go," replied the Patriarch. "I am too old and ill. Take my head if you must, but my heart will not go."

The messenger thought, "There is nothing to do but to go back without him. I cannot take his head to the Emperor. This Bhikshu is very strange; he is hardly human."

The messenger then hurried back to the Emperor. "Your Excellency, you may have the Master's head, but his heart will not move!"

"Very well, go get his head," replied the Emperor. He put a knife in a box and gave it to the messenger saying, "Slice off his head, but under no circumstances should you harm this Bhikshu."

The messenger understood. He returned to the Fourth Patriarch. "Venerable Master, if you refuse to come, the Emperor has ordered me to cut off your head," he said.

Patriarch Tao Hsin said, "If in this life my head gets to see the Emperor, that will be great glory. You may remove my head now." The messenger took out the knife and prepared to cut off his head. The Great Master closed his eyes and waited calmly for about ten minutes. Maybe it was ten minutes, maybe it was nine or eleven. Don't become attached. It is certainly not determined exactly how long he waited. But nothing happened, and finally Master Tao Hsin got angry, just like the Second Patriarch, and shouted, "Hey! Why don't you slice off my head!"

"The Emperor had no intention of harming you," the messenger quickly replied. "He was just bluffing."

The Patriarch heard this and laughed aloud. Then he said, "Now you know that there is still a person in the world who does not fear death."

The family name of the Fourth Patriarch was Ssu Ma and his personal name was Hsin. Ssu Ma was an honorable ancestral name. Both the Emperor Ssu Ma of the Chin dynasty and the historian and skilled writer Ssu Ma Ch'ien of the Han dynasty had this name. When the Fourth Patriarch became a Bhikshu he took the new name Tao Hsin. He lived seventy-two years, sixty of which were spent without lying down even once to sleep. The Fourth Patriarch's realm of accomplishment was inconceivable.

While Tao Hsin was cultivating, a nearby city was besieged by bandits for more than a hundred days, depriving its inhabitants of water and supplies. Seeing the lives of the people in danger, Master Tao Hsin left his mountain retreat to rescue the city dwellers. He taught them all to recite "Mahaprajna-paramita." After they had recited for a time, the bandits fled and water reappeared in the wells. This is the response based on the Way which Master Tao Hsin evoked as a result of his superior cultivation.

When the Fourth Patriarch decided to build a temple, he looked with his Buddha eye and saw Broken Head Mountain surrounded by a purple cloud of energy. Observing this auspicious sign, the Master went there to dwell, changing its inauspicious name, "Broken Head," to "Double Peak" Mountain.

The Master used expedient dharmas to teach living beings how to discard their bad habits. These stubborn living beings, however, often discarded what was good and continued doing evil. But the Master persisted and by using all kinds of skill-in-means caused these stubborn living beings to realize their mistakes. He propagated the Dharma for more than forty years, transforming living beings greater in number than seedlings of rice, stalks of hemp, shoots of bamboo, or blades of grass.

One day the Fourth Patriarch said to his disciple Dharma Master Yüan I, "You should build me a Stupa[13]. I am going to leave."

In the second year of Yung Hui, of the T'ang dynasty (651 A.D.), on the twenty-fourth day of the ninth lunar month, Patriarch Tao Hsin, who had never been ill, sat down and entered Nirvana. His disciples locked his flesh body securely in the stone Stupa. A year later the iron locks fell away and the Stupa opened by itself. Looking in, everyone saw the body of the Fourth

13. Stupas are reliquaries designed to hold the remains of Buddhas, Buddhist saints, and patriarchs

Patriarch still sitting in full lotus, appearing the same as when he was alive. The Master's body had not decayed, but the flesh had dried out. The Fifth Patriarch, Hung Jen, wrapped the body with lacquered cloth and gilded it. This "true body" still exists today.

The Fifth Patriarch, Hung Jen, also lived during the T'ang dynasty. His family name was Chou. He lived in Huang Mei County near Double Peak Mountain. When he was seven, he went to the temple on the mountain to attend upon the Fourth Patriarch. The Great Master Hung Jen cleaned the lamps and censer before the Buddha images; he swept the floor, carried water, split firewood, and worked in the kitchen. At age thirteen he took the ten novice precepts and studied under the Fourth Patriarch for over thirty years.

The Fifth Patriarch was eight feet tall and had an extraordinary appearance. When others treated him badly, he remained silent and unmoved. Because he did not give rise to discrimination, he never spoke of "right" or "wrong", and when fellow Bhikshus bullied him, he never fought back. His calm, quiet manner indicated that he had realized a state of peace.

Even after working hard all day, the Master didn't rest. Instead of sleeping, he sat in meditation, uniting body and mind in powerful samadhi.

Master Hung Jen lived in the woods of P'ing Mao Mountain slightly east of Double Peak Mountain, so his teaching is called the East Mountain Dharma Door. Once, like his master the Fourth Patriarch, he saw a horde of bandits besieging a nearby city. Their leader, a Mongol named *K'e Ta Ha Na Lu*, and his followers had so tightly cut off the communications that even the birds couldn't fly in or out. The Fifth Patriarch went down P'ing Mao Mountain toward the city. When the bandits saw him, they were terrified, for they saw not only the Patriarch, but also a retinue of golden-armored vajra king Bodhisattvas armed with jeweled weapons, manifesting awesome virtue and brightness. The thieves retreated, their siege broken.

How was the Great Master able to command these vajra king Bodhisattvas? The Fifth Patriarch had cultivated and he recited the Shurangama Mantra. *The Shurangama Sutra* says that if you are constantly mindful of the Shurangama Mantra, eighty-four thousand vajra store Bodhisattvas will protect you from all danger.

In the fifth year of the Hsien Ch'ing reign of the T'ang dynasty (660 A.D.), the Emperor invited Great Master Hung Jen to the palace. The Master declined the invitation. The Emperor sent a second invitation which the Master also declined. Finally, the Emperor sent a variety of gifts, including rare medicinal herbs, as an offering to the Great Master, the Fifth Patriarch.

In the fifth year of the Hsien Hsiang reign of the T'ang dynasty (674 A.D.), the Fifth Patriarch said to his disciple, Master Hsüan Chi, "Build me a Stupa. I am going to leave." In the second month on the fourteenth day he asked, "Is the Stupa ready?" Master Hsüan Chi replied that it was. The Patriarch said, "For many years I have taught living beings. I have taken across those whom I must take across and have transmitted my Dharma to Hui Neng, the Sixth Patriarch. Now, in addition, you ten should become Dharma Hosts, and establish Bodhimandas to preserve and spread the teaching among living beings."

The ten he addressed were: Dharma Masters Shen Hsiu, Chih Hsien, I Fang, Chih Te, Hsüan Chi, Lao An, Fa Ju, Hui Tsang, Hsüan Yao, and also Upasaka Liu Chu Pu, who had dealt with correspondence and accounting. The Fifth Patriarch sent each of these ten people to a different place to teach and transform living beings.

Shortly thereafter, he sat very still and his energy dispersed as he entered Nirvana. During the seventy-four years of his life, the Fifth Patriarch Hung Jen had accepted many disciples, and had transmitted the Dharma to the Great Master Hui Neng.

A General Introduction

Edited by Bhikshu Fa Hai of the T'ang Dynasty

What follows is not the Sutra text, but an introduction to the Sutra which was written by The Sixth Patriarch's disciple, Fa Hai. When the Sixth Patriarch taught Dharma, Master Fa Hai followed him, recording all of the things the Patriarch said. Later, he compiled and edited his notes, calling them *The Sixth Patriarch's Dharma Jewel Platform Sutra*. Had he not done this, we would have no way to study the Sixth Patriarch's Dharma. Therefore, we should certainly be grateful for such compassion as his.

Dharma Master Fa Hai's lay name was Chang, and his common name was Wen Yün. He was a native of Ch'ü Chiang, which is about ten miles from Nan Hua monastery. He was a "room-entering disciple," that is, a disciple to whom the Master had transmitted the Dharma. Though his introduction is not part of the Sutra proper, I will explain it to you, because it narrates some important events in the life of the Great Master.

Text:

The Great Master was named Hui Neng. His father was of the Lu family and had the personal name Hsing T'ao. His mother was of the Li family. The Master was born on the eighth day of the second month of the year Wu Hsü, in the twelfth year of the Chen Kuan Reign of the T'ang Dynasty (A.D. 638).

At that time, a beam of light ascended into space and a strange fragrance filled the room. At dawn, two strange Bhikshus came to visit. They addressed the Master's father saying, "Last night a son was born to you and we have come to name him. It can be Hui above and below, Neng."

The Father said, "Why shall he be called Hui Neng?"

The Monk said, "'Hui' means he will bestow the Dharma upon living beings. 'Neng' means he will be able to do the Buddha's work." Having said this, they left. No one knows where they went.

The Master did not drink milk. At night, spirits appeared and poured sweet dew over him.

Commentary:

The Great Master refers to the Sixth Patriarch, Hui Neng. The Master's merit and virtue was great, he had great wisdom and compassion and so was a master of gods and humans.

When one is alive, one has a personal name. After one dies, that name is avoided. Hence it is called a personal name, a name which is not spoken.

When the Great Master's mother gave birth to him, a fine beam of light arose, like that which the Buddha emits from his forehead. A strange, fragrant incense which had never been smelled before filled the room.

At dawn, the heavens are half dark and half light. Chü Hsi in "The Song of Household Affairs" wrote:

At dawn, get up;
Sprinkle and sweep the hall.
The inside, the outside,
You must clean it all.

In China at that time there was no linoleum. In the morning, people sprinkled water on the mud floors, waited a bit, and then swept their houses clean inside and out.

The two strange Bhikshus were quite different from ordinary people. They were like the Fourth Patriarch who, by merely opening his eyes, caused everyone to tremble in fright. These two unusual Bhikshus came to name the Sixth Patriarch. Isn't this strange? Who has two Bhikshus come to name him?

To say "above" and "below" when referring to a person's name, is a most respectful form of address.

What the newly born Patriarch ate was sweet dew.

Text:

He grew up, and at the age of twenty-four he heard the Sutra[14] and awoke to the Way. He went to Huang Mei to seek the seal of approval.

Commentary:

Some say that the Sixth Patriarch was twenty-four, others say that he was twenty-two. As the Chinese count he was twenty-four and as Westerners count, he was twenty-two. Whether he was twenty-two or twenty-four is not really important.

When the Sixth Patriarch heard the layman recite *The Diamond Sutra* and reach the line, "One should produce that thought which is nowhere supported," the Sixth Patriarch said, "Oh! Not supported anywhere!" He was immediately enlightened.

---

14. *The Vajra Prajna Paramita Sutra*, also called *The Diamond Sutra*.

This Sutra, with the Venerable Master Hua's commentary is available in translation from IITBT of SABA.

A great many people had heard *The Diamond Sutra*, but none of them had become enlightened. Now in the West, perhaps someone will hear, "One should produce that thought which is nowhere supported" and, understanding the principle, become enlightened. That is what I hope. Whether or not it will actually happen is another matter.

After becoming enlightened, he did not say, "Hah! I am enlightened." He was not like some people today who do not understand even a hair's breadth of the Buddhadharma, yet claim to be enlightened.

The ancients, even when they had become enlightened, did not recklessly say, "I am enlightened!" Even less would people who had not become enlightened claim to have done so. It is necessary to seek certification from a good knowing advisor, a person who has already awakened. That is why the Sixth Patriarch went to Huang Mei to seek the Fifth Patriarch's seal of certification.

Enlightened ancients did not attempt to certify themselves. Today, however, there are those who have not become enlightened and yet say that they have. Enlightenment and non-enlightenment are as different as heaven and earth.

Moreover, many naive young people take stupefying drugs and claim to have "gone to the void." Confused demons, posing as good knowing advisors, certify them saying, "Yes, you have attained to emptiness. However, there is no place for you to live in emptiness. Come Back. Come to my place. I have buildings and houses; I have a commune!"

The young people say, "That's not bad at all!" They take the demons as their teachers. Ultimately these "bad knowing advisors" do not know themselves if they are true or false. You and I do not know either.

But now we should use the Sutras for certification. The Sutras do not say that any foolish person has a commune in empty space. Even though rockets now go to thc moon, space settlements have not yet been built. So this kind of talk simply does not get by.

Now we are exceedingly busy. In the morning, everyone gets up at four o'clock to recite Sutras. We are busy building houses on the Earth, not in heaven. Why? We are people on earth and so our houses should be built on the earth. We are forging our bodies into indestructible vajra bodies. Our bodies are our houses, but they sometimes go bad. Now, from morning to night, we are busy constructing them, cultivating them to be in the end like indestructible vajra bodies.

With an indestructible vajra body you can go wherever you wish. You can go into empty space, up to the heavens, down into the earth, or to the dragon king's palace. It is very simple and you do not need a passport or a schedule. You are free to take off at your convenience. But first construct your indestructible body. Then you can do it.

Text:

The Fifth Patriarch measured his capacity and transmitted the robe and Dharma so that he inherited the Patriarchate. The time was the first year of the reign period Lung Shuo, cyclical year Hsin Yu (A.D. 661).

He returned south and hid for sixteen years.

Commentary:

After the Sixth Patriarch left Huang Mei, he had no safe place to live. Because Shen Hsiu's disciples and followers of non-

Buddhist religions wished to harm him, the Great Master went to live with hunters for sixteen years.

During this time no one knew that he was the Sixth Patriarch. He worked hard practicing Dhyana meditation while watching over the animals and birds the hunters had caught and secretly releasing the ones which had been only slightly injured and could still travel safely. He had much time to cultivate and perfect his skill, for no one came to trouble him.

If you do not truly cultivate, everything is easy, but if you do cultivate truly, demon-obstacles arise from the four corners and the eight directions. Unexpected circumstances prevail and things you never dreamed could happen do happen.

In his sixteen years with the hunters, the Sixth Patriarch dwelt without disturbance, living just as they did. That is genuine hiding. He did not seek fame or profit and he did not try to take advantage of circumstances. He practiced genuine cultivation.

Text:

On the eighth day of the first month in the first year of the reign period I Feng (A.D. 676), the cyclical year Ping Tsu, he met Dharma Master Yin Tsung. Together they discussed the profound and mysterious, and Yin Tsung became awakened to and united with the Master's doctrine.

Commentary:

They talked back and forth, querying each other on principle. Who asked whom? Dharma Master Yin Tsung asked the Great Master, the Sixth Patriarch. The Great Master had solved the dispute over whether the flag or the wind moved, by explaining that it was the mind that moved, and Dharma Master Yin Tsung had been astounded to hear a layman speak in such a deep and wonderful way. He got down from his Dharma seat and escorted the Sixth Patriarch to his room for a chat. "Where did you come from and what is your name?" he asked. Dharma Master Yin Tsung knew that this layman was a room-entering disciple of the Fifth Patriarch, one to whom the Fifth Patriarch had transmitted the Dharma. He immediately bowed to the Great Master. They then investigated the profound and mysterious; they talked about the wind and the flag. Until his talk with the Sixth Patriarch, Dharma Master Yin Tsung had not correctly understood the principle of the Dhyana School.

Text:

On the fifteenth day of that month, at a meeting of all the four assemblies, the Master's head was shaved. On the eighth day of the second month, all those of well-known virtue gathered together to administer the complete precepts. Vinaya Master Chih Kuang of Hsi Ching was the Precept Transmitter.

Commentary:

During the week of the eighth to the fifteenth day of the first month, Dharma Master Yin Tsung gathered the four assemblies together: the Bhikshus, Bhikshunis, Upasakas, and Upasikas. The purpose of the meeting was to shave the Master's head so that he could leave home and become a Bhikshu.

People leave home for various reasons. Some find it difficult to obtain food and clothing. They see that those who have left home are well provided for, and so they leave home so they can eat and be clothed. Others leave home because they are old and have no children. They think, "I will leave home and take a young disciple who will care for me as a son would." It is uncertain whether people who leave home for these reasons can really cultivate.

Some leave home because they are bandits or runaways. They leave home and cut off their hair so that the government won't find them and cut off their heads! Some leave home when small, but it is not certain whether they can cultivate.

Some people have "confused beliefs." Even so, they still believe, and that is good. For instance, the parents of a sick child may say, "The child may die of disease. We should give him to a temple and he can become a Bhikshu and we can go visit him. That is better than letting him die!" So out of confused belief, the parents give their child to the temple.

People of confused belief may not necessarily be bad, but people who "believe in confused principles" are definitely not good. They have faith, but it is misplaced. That is confusion within confusion and it is not good.

Some are "confused and without belief." In their confusion they do not believe in anything. Finally there are the "believing and unconfused." These people study the Buddhadharma with a faithful heart until they are no longer confused.

Of these last four types of people who have left home, one cannot say that any of them will be able to cultivate, nor can one say for sure that they cannot. Perhaps only one or two per cent can cultivate the Dharma. However, if you resolve to attain enlightenment in order to end birth and death, you can surely cultivate upon leaving home.

Again, there are those who no longer have a family and so leave their worldly homes.

Some leave the home of the three realms: the realm of desire, the realm of form, and the realm of formlessness. Once out of these three realms there are no desires, no forms, and no formless consciousness. Because of their non-attachment, these people see the three realms as empty, and so it is said that they have left the home of the three realms.

Some leave the home of afflictions. It is essential to leave afflictions behind. If you do not cut them off, you may leave home, but you cannot know the Way.

The Sixth Patriarch cannot be put into any of these categories, for he was a special case. He had attained mastery, and so whether or not he left home made no difference. Even when he appeared to be a layman, he practiced the profound conduct of a Bodhisattva and he did not behave like a layman. In this way his act of leaving home did not resemble that of others in the assembly.

The eighth day of the second month is the day when Shakyamuni Buddha left home. On that day all the illustrious, virtuous and learned Dharma Masters gathered from the ten directions. Chinese Dharma Masters and Indian Dharma Masters came to administer the complete precepts to the Sixth Patriarch.

Dharma Master Yin Tsung invited Dharma Master Chih Kuang of Hsi Ching to administer the complete precepts to the Sixth Patriarch. Hsi Ching is another name for Ch'ang An.

The person who administers the precepts is called the Precept Transmitter. Precepts have a substance and mark and a dharma. If you wish a more detailed explanation, even finer discriminations can be made.

I do not use Ting Fu Pao's commentary because it is often in error. In this case he says that three people are required to administer the precepts, while actually only one is necessary. At that time, Dharma Master Chih Kuang acted as Transmitter.

Chih Kuang was also a Vinaya Master, one who diligently studies the precepts and thoroughly understands the rules. In walking, standing, sitting and lying down, in each of these four great comportments, he must conduct himself in the awesome manner, not daring to deviate for the space of a single step. Every move a Vinaya Master makes must be in accord with the rules. Therefore the *Shurangama Sutra* says, "Severe and pure in Vinaya, they are noble models for the Triple World."

Text:

Vinaya Master Hui Ching of Su Chou was the Karmadana. Vinaya Master T'ung Ying of Ching Chou was the Teaching Transmitter. Vinaya Master Ch'i To Lo of Central India recited the precepts. Tripitaka Master Mi To of India was the Precept Certifier.

Commentary:

Ting Fu Pao writes that there should be four Karmadanas, yet the Sutra mentions only one. He says that the one mentioned was the most famous of the four. Because he didn't understand the precepts, his commentary is confused. There was only one Karmadana.

Karmadana is a Sanskrit word which means "to arrange events," or "to explain rules." The Karmadana makes certain that everything is done in accord with Dharma, in accord with the rules established by Shakyamuni Buddha. Anything not in accord with the Buddha's rules is unacceptable to the Karmadana.

When conferring the precepts, the Precept Transmitter asks the Karmadana, "May the precepts be transmitted to this person?" The question is asked three times, and each time the Karmadana must reply, "Yes."

On the precept Platform, the Karmadana and the Teaching Transmitter sit immediately to the left and right of the Precept Transmitter. The remaining seven certifiers sit on cither side. That is the arrangement of the three masters and seven certifiers. They represent the Buddhas of the ten directions in speaking Dharma and transmitting precepts. Therefore, when leaving home, receiving precepts is especially important.

The Teaching Transmitter transmits the Sutras.

Ch'i To Lo, transliterated from the Sanskrit, means "flower of merit and virtue."

Dharma Master Mi To understood the three divisions of the Tripitaka, Sutras, Sastras, and Vinaya, and so he is called a Tripitaka Master. He is closely associated with the Chinese Vinaya because he translated the Dharmagupta Vinaya from the Sanskrit into Chinese. All the precept spirits protected this intelligent master, and there are many miraculous events connected with his life. Mi To means flourishing. His full name was Ta Mo Mi To, flourishing Dharma.

Text:

Construction of the precept platform had begun in the former Sung Dynasty by Tripitaka Master Gunabhadra. He erected a stone tablet which said, "In the future, a Bodhisattva in the flesh will receive the precepts in this very place."

Commentary:

The "former Sung" was the dynasty that preceded the Sui Dynasty, not the well-known Sung Dynasty of Sung T'ai Tsu.

Gunabhadra means "a worthy of merit and virtue." This master established a precept platform at what is now called

Kuang Hsiao Monastery. His engraving foretold the coming of a Bodhisattva in the flesh: not a Bodhisattva who had gone to Nirvana, but a living Bodhisattva.

Text:

Further, in the first year of the T'ien Chien reign of the Liang Dynasty (A.D. 502) Tripitaka Master Jnanabhaishajya came by sea from West India carrying a Bodhi-tree branch, which he planted beside the platform. He, too, made a prophecy, saying, "After one hundred and seventy years, a Bodhisattva in the flesh will proclaim the Supreme Vehicle beneath this tree. Taking measureless multitudes across, he will be a true transmitter of the Buddha's mind-seal, a Dharma Host."

Commentary:

Tripitaka Master Jnanabhaishajya, "wisdom medicine," predicted that a living Bodhisattva would speak the Supreme Vehicle Dharma from beneath that Bodhi-tree, teaching the Dharma of a direct pointing to the mind to see the nature and realize Buddhahood.

As a true transmitter of the Buddha's mind-seal, this Bodhisattva would "use the mind to seal the mind." Shakyamuni Buddha held a flower in his fingers and smiling subtly, transmitted the mind seal of all the Buddhas to the First Patriarch, Mahakashyapa. Transmitters of the mind-seal are patriarchs. A Dharma Host is one who lectures Sutras and explains the Dharma.

Jnanabhaishajya brought a Bodhi-tree branch from India to China; not a whole tree, just a cutting. Bodhi-trees will grow almost anywhere. There are many such trees in China today.

The Venerable Master Jnanabhaishajya's flesh body has not decayed. It is preserved for veneration at Yüeh Hua monastery about five miles from Nan Hua Monastery. The caretaker there, who has left home, does not feed visitors, so if you wish to visit, you must bring your own food. When I was living at Nan Hua Temple, I went to see the Master Jnanabhaishajya's body and found it in excellent condition.

Text:

In keeping with the former predictions, the Master arrived to have his hair cut and to receive the precepts. He instructed the four assemblies on the essentials of the exclusive Dharma transmission.

Commentary:

The Sixth Patriarch had his head shaved and received the complete precepts. He then explained the Dharma for the four assemblies, teaching them the exclusive Dharma transmission, that is, the Dharma which has been passed down through every generation since the time of Shakyamuni Buddha.

Text:

In the spring of the following year, the Master took leave of the assembly and returned to Pao Lin. Yin Tsung, together with more than a thousand black-robed monks and white-robed layfolk, accompanied him directly to Ts'ao Hsi.

Commentary:

The Sixth Patriarch left and returned to Ts'ao Hsi.

The black-robed are those who have left home; at that time laypeople wore white robes. They all went directly to Ts'ao Hsi with the Master. Some people say that they have been to Ts'ao Hsi when they have not. They falsely claim to transmit the Ts'ao Hsi Dharma and Dhyana source, the basis of meditation. The Dharma-ending age is just that: false Buddhists with phony credentials.

Text:

At that time Vinaya Master T'ung Ying of Ching Chou and several hundred students followed the Master and came to dwell there. When the Master arrived at Pao Lin, in Ts'ao Hsi, he saw that the hall the buildings were bleak and small, insufficient to contain the multitude. Wishing to enlarge them, he paid a visit to the villager, Ch'en Ya Hsien and said, "This Old Monk comes to the Almsgiver seeking a sitting cloth's worth of ground. Is that possible?"

Commentary:

As soon as he realized that the Great Master was the Sixth Patriarch, a transmitter of the Buddha's mind-seal, Vinaya Master T'ung Ying led his disciples to Ts'ao Hsi to study the Dharma under the Great Master.

When the Sixth Patriarch arrived at Ts'ao Hsi, he saw that the buildings were too small. Wishing to enlarge them, he paid a visit to the wealthy landowner Ch'en Ya Hsien. In this passage, the Sixth Patriarch refers to himself as the "Old Monk." When he was twenty-four, he went to see Huang Mei; then he hid for sixteen years. At forty years of age, he called himself an "Old Monk," and so I am entitled to do the same. The Master told

Ch'en Ya Hsien that if he gave alms, he could transcend birth and death.

Text:

Hsien asked, "How big is the High Master's sitting cloth?"

The Master took out his sitting cloth and showed it to Ya Hsien, who thereupon agreed. But when the Patriarch unfolded and spread out his sitting cloth, it completely covered the four borders of Ts'ao Hsi. The Four Heavenly Kings[15] appeared and sat as protectors in each of the four directions.

Commentary:

The Great Master handed his sitting cloth to Ch'en Ya Hsien, who said, "If you only want that large a piece of land, fine."

But when he spread it out, the sitting cloth covered not only the area around Nan Hua Monastery, but everything within ten miles of where they stood. The Four Heavenly Kings appeared and stood guard in each of the four directions.

Text:

It is due to this occurrence that the mountain range bordering the monastery is called "The Range of the Heavenly Kings."

---

15. Catur-maharajas, the four deva kings who dwell on each side of Mount Sumeru and ward of evil influences. In the East, Dhrtarashtra, "the king who holds his country," in the South, Virudhaka, "deva of increase and growth," in the West Virupaksa, the "broad-eyed" or "ugly-eyed," and in the North Vaishravana, the king who is "greatly learned."

Hsien said, "I know that the High Master's Dharma power is vast and great. However, the burial ground of my great-great grandfather lies on this land. In the future, if you build a stupa, I hope that this area will remain undisturbed. As for the rest, I wish to give it all to be forever a treasured place. This ground has the flowing current of a living dragon and a white elephant. Level only heaven; do not level earth."

Later, the monastery was constructed according to his words. The Master roamed within these boundaries, and at places where the scenes of nature were fine he stopped to rest.

Commentary:

The area belongs to a living dragon; it has a flowing current and the mountain is like an elephant. Here, one may build a "treasured place," a Bodhimanda.

"Level only heaven; do not level earth," that is, where thc land is high, the buildings may be made lower, and where the land is low, the buildings may be made taller. But do not level the earth, for if you do you will ruin the fine conditions of wind and water and the land will lose its efficacious energies.

The Sixth Patriarch often roamed about the countryside and stopped to rest where the landscapes were especially beautiful.

Text:

Accordingly, thirteen Aranyas were erected, among them the present Hua Kuo Hall. The site of the Pao Lin Bodhimanda was decided upon long ago by Indian Tripitaka Master Jnanabhaishajya, who, during his journey from Nan Hai, passed through Ts'ao Hsi, where

he cupped up the water with his hands and found it to be delicious. Surprised, he told his disciples. "This water is not different from that in India. Its source would surely be an excellent site on which to build a monastery."

He followed the water and looked in the four directions. The mountains and waters encircled one another and the peaks were impressive. He sighed and said. "This is just like Jewelled Wood Mountain in India."

Commentary:

Why is the area around Nan Hua Monastery called Pao Lin? Pao Lin means "jewelled wood." When the Venerable Jnanabhaishajya drank the water at Ts'ao Hsi, its taste was identical to that of the water in a certain place in India. He knew that the source of the spring was indeed an efficacious spot on which to build a temple. At dusk, he reached the site of Nan Hua Monastery. Gazing up at the mountain, he said, "This mountain looks just like Jewelled Wood Mountain in India. We shall call this 'Jewelled Wood Bodhimanda.'"

Master Jnanabhaishajya was not alone; many of his disciples were travelling with him. He said to them, "The source of this stream is certainly a good site for building a temple." Monastic buildings are called Aranyas, a Sanskrit word meaning, "silent place." They are pure, quiet places for cultivation.

The clear blue waters reflected the bright shining mountain peaks. The area was particularly beautiful.

Text:

He said to the villagers of Ts'ao Hou, "A pure dwelling may be built here. After one hundred and

seventy years, the Unsurpassed Dharma Jewel will teach here. Those who attain the Way in this place will be as numerous as the trees of this forest. It should, therefore, be called 'Pao Lin.'"

At that time Magistrate Hou Ching Chung of Shao Chou reported these words to the Emperor who assented and conferred upon it the name 'Pao Lin Bodhimanda.' The construction of the pure halls began in the third year of the T'ien Chien reign of the Liang dynasty (A.D. 504).

Commentary:

The village was called Ts'ao Hou, "descendents of Ts'ao," because its inhabitants were descendents of General Ts'ao Ts'ao of the Period of the Three Kingdoms.

One hundred and seventy years after Master Jnanabhaishajya made this prediction, the Sixth Patriarch received the precepts and taught living beings at Pao Lin. The "Unsurpassed Dharma Jewel" refers to the Sixth Patriarch.

Sangha and laypeople who were to attain enlightenment at this place would be as numerous as the trees in a forest. It was therefore to be called "Jewelled Wood."

Text:

In front of the hall was a pond in which a dragon often swam, bumping and scraping the trees of the forest. One day he appeared, larger than ever, covering the area with a thick mist. The disciples were afraid, but the Patriarch scolded him, saying, "Hah! You can only make yourself appear in a large body, not in a small one. If you were a divine dragon, you could transform the great into the small and the small into the great."

Commentary:

The dragon was so big that you could only see the dragon; you couldn't see the pond at all. He danced on top of the water, splashing it everywhere in waves which were ten feet, twenty feet, and even thirty feet high. He was showing off.

"Incredible!" said the disciples. "This dragon certainly intends to harm us."

The Sixth Patriarch shouted at the dragon. He said, "If you really had spiritual powers, you could transform nothing into something and something into nothing; you could transform yourself or not be transformed, just as you wished, manifesting the great within the small and the small within the great."

Text:

The dragon suddenly disappeared, but returned an instant later in a small body, skipping about on the surface of the pond. The Master held out his bowl and teased him, saying, "You don't dare climb into the old Bhikshu's bowl." At that moment the dragon swam in front of the Master, who scooped him out of the water with his bowl. The dragon couldn't move. Holding the bowl, the Master returned to the hall and explained the Dharma to the dragon.

Commentary:

When the dragon heard the Sixth Patriarch dare him to manifest a small body, he disappeared. Strange? Think about it. Suddenly he wasn't there. Then, in the time it takes to feel a hunger pang, a little dragon appeared, dancing on top of the water. The Great Master said, "You have a little body now, but you wouldn't dare get into my bowl, would you? You wouldn't dare. Dragon! I dare you to get into my bowl!"

The dragon flew across the water and swam up before the Patriarch. The Patriarch didn't wait for the dragon to jump into his bowl, but reached right down and scooped him out of the water.

In Manchuria, where I am from, there is a saying, "Before there were people in Manchuria, you could scoop up the fish with a bucket and chickens fell into the cooking pot." As for rabbits, you could just step outside, swing a stick, and knock over a few. This is what is meant by "scooped." Catching the dragon was as easy as scooping for fish in Manchuria.

Text:

The dragon then shed his skin and left. His bones, only seven inches long and complete with head, tail, horns, and claws, were preserved in the temple. Later the Master filled in the pond with earth and stones. Now, in that place, in the front of the hall on the right side is an iron stupa.

Commentary:

Dharma Master Fa Hai's introduction says that the pond was on the left side of the hall, but it was actually on the right. One commentator, Ting Fu Pao, had never been there and consequently did not realize that the direction of the pond should have been determined from the Patriarch's position when sitting in the hall, that is, on the right side.

CHAPTER I

ACTION AND INTENTION

Commentary:

In this first chapter of the Sutra, the Sixth Patriarch gives his disciples a biographical sketch of himself. "Action" refers to the Sixth Patriarch's activities and "intention" is that upon which he based his cultivation. "Action and Intention" refers to the source–where it all began.

Sutra:

At one time the Great Master arrived at Pao Lin. Magistrate Wei Ch'ü of Shao Chou and other local officials climbed the mountain and invited the Master to come into the city to the lecture hall of the Ta Fan Temple to speak the Dharma to the assembly.

When the Master had taken his seat, the Magistrate and over thirty other officials, more than thirty Confucian scholars, and more than one thousand Bhikshus, Bhikshunis, Taoists, and laypeople, all made obeisance at the same time, wishing to hear the essentials of Dharma.

Commentary:

For every Sutra, six requirements must be met. Commonly explained in the opening sentences, they are: faith, hearing, time, host, place, and assembly. Only when these six are fulfilled is the orthodox Dharma being spoken.

To conduct a Sutra session, there must be an *assembly*; Magistrate Wei Ch'ü and the gathering of disciples and followers fulfills this requirement.

Then there must be a *place* to speak the Dharma; Pao Lin Mountain fulfills this requirement. A Dharma Master who thoroughly understands the Dharma must be present as *host*; here it is the Great Master the Sixth Patriarch. "At one time" suffices for the *time* requirement, and that "all made obeisance at the same time" fulfills the *faith* requirement. They came "wishing to hear the essentials of Dharma," and that fulfills the requirements of *hearing*.

Wei Ch'ü and the officials climbed Pao Lin Mountain which is about ten miles from Shao Chou where Ta Fan Temple, now called Ta Chien Temple, is located. I lived there for a while. This is where the Sixth Patriarch spoke *The Dharma Jewel Platform Sutra*.

Sutra:

The Great Master said to the assembly, "Good Knowing Advisors, the self-nature of Bodhi is originally clear and pure. Simply use that mind, and you will straightaway accomplish Buddhahood. Good Knowing Advisors, listen while I tell you about the actions and intentions by which Hui Neng obtained the Dharma."

Commentary:

The Great Master spoke to the assembly; "You are people with good roots and much wisdom. The self nature of Bodhi is one's own originally enlightened clear and pure nature. It cannot be produced or destroyed, defiled or purified, increased or decreased. Use this mind. Don't use your false-thinking mind."

Using his own name, in the formal style, the Sixth Patriarch calls himself "Hui Neng," saying, "Now I will tell you how Hui Neng obtained the Dharma. Listen!"

Sutra:

"Hui Neng's stern father was originally from Fan Yang. He was banished to Hsin Chou in Ling Nan, where he became a commoner. Unfortunately, his father soon died, and his aging mother was left alone. They moved to Nan Hai and, poor and in bitter straits, Hui Neng sold wood in the market place."

Commentary:

From his native district of Fan Yang, Hui Neng's father was sent to Ling Nan. Because the father is more apt to discipline the children, he is respectfully called "stern." The mother ordinarily offers loving kindness to her children, and so she is spoken of as "compassionate."

Hui, (惠), "kind," means that he was kind and compassionate, bestowing Dharma upon living beings. Neng, (能), "able," means that he was able to do the Buddha's work. The Sixth Patriarch's family name was Lu.

Hui Neng's father was banished to Ling Nan, a frontier region during the T'ang Dynasty inhabited by government exiles. The Sixth Patriarch's father, an official, may have been convicted of an offense and thus banished to Ling Nan.

Hui Neng had an unfortunate and unlucky life. His father died when the Master was between the ages of three and five years, leaving him alone with his widowed mother. He and his mother moved to Nan Hai where they endured the hardships of poverty. How did they survive? Master Hui Neng hiked into the mountains and chopped wood, returned and sold it in the market place, using the money to buy rice for his mother and himself.

Sutra:

Once a customer bought firewood and ordered it delivered to his shop. When the delivery had been made, and Hui Neng had received the money, he went outside the gate, where he noticed a customer reciting a Sutra. Upon once hearing the words of this Sutra: "One should produce that thought which is nowhere supported." Hui Neng's mind immediately opened to enlightenment.

Commentary:

Because the Sixth Patriarch's family was poor, he received little formal schooling and could not read. At that time in China one needed money to go to school. But in spite of his illiteracy, the Sixth Patriarch's disposition was extremely sharp; and as soon as he heard the line of the Sutra which says that one should have a true mind which is nowhere attached, he immediately became enlightened. He understood what he had never understood before.

Many will hear the sentence; "One should produce that thought which is nowhere supported." Are there any who will open to enlightenment?

Someone exclaims, "Why, I have!"

I ask you, what is the enlightenment you have opened? What is the enlightenment unopened? Ask yourself.

Sutra:

Thereupon he asked the customer what Sutra he was reciting. The customer replied, "*The Diamond Sutra*."

Then again he asked, "Where do you come from, and why do you recite this Sutra?"

The customer said, "I come from Tung Ch'an Monastery in Ch'i Chou, Huang Mei Province. There the Fifth Patriarch, the Great Master Hung Jen dwells, teaching over one thousand disciples. I went there to make obeisance and heard and received this Sutra."

Commentary:

The Great Master the Fifth Patriarch lived in Tung Ch'an Monastery with more than a thousand disciples whom he taught and transformed. At that time in China the study of the Dharma was so fervently pursued that it was not unusual to have a thousand people on one mountain studying the Buddhadharma together.

Where in America are there a thousand Buddhist disciples studying the Dharma together? Such a large country yet there is no such place. It is possible, however, that later there will be more than ten thousand people studying the Buddhadharma, but this is not assured. We will have to watch my disciples and see how hard they work.

Most Americans are intelligent, but there are some whose intelligence surpasses itself. Everyday from morning to night they are caught up in taking confusing drugs. By taking these drugs they may attain small and different states of consciousness which they cannot obtain without drugs. These people try drugs again and again until one day they see that it is useless. They think, "I've been taking drugs for such a long time now and I still have not become enlightened." When they realize this, they may turn toward the truth.

I teach you the Buddhadharma so in the future you can speak the Dharma to teach and transform living beings. Do not be careless, but work well and without confusion and then many will come to study.

You who are now studying this *Sixth Patriarch's Sutra* must know the origin of your learning. When people ask, "Where did you study the Buddhadharma?" you can reply, "We studied at the Buddhist Lecture Hall of the Sino-American Buddhist Association." This is just what is meant by this passage of text.

Sutra:

"The Great Master constantly exhorts the Sangha and laity only to uphold *The Diamond Sutra*. Then, they may see their own nature and straightaway achieve Buddhahood."

Hui Neng heard this and desired to go and seek the Dharma, but he recalled that his mother had no support.

From past lives there were karmic conditions which led another man to give Hui Neng a pound of silver, so that he could provide clothing and food for his aging mother. The man instructed him further to go to Huang Mei to call upon and bow to the Fifth Patriarch.

Commentary:

You should be clear that the "Great Master" referred to here is the Fifth Patriarch not the Sixth Patriarch.

When Hui Neng heard that there was a place where over one thousand people were studying the Buddhadharma together, he became very excited. "What am I to do? I really want to study there!" he exclaimed to the customer. "I heard you recite *The Diamond Sutra* and I understood the principles. I want to go seek the Buddhadharma, but I have an aging mother who has no one to care for her. What can I do?"

Since Bodhisattvas do not seek fame, the Sixth Patriarch did not say which great Bodhisattva helped him at this time. The Sutra simply says that, because of former karmic conditions, a customer gave Hui Neng a pound of silver. This was certainly a valuable offering. The yield of a day's work chopping firewood was worth only a few copper pennies in the market place so even if Hui Neng had sold all the wood gathered in a thousand days, its value would not have equaled the gift of silver.

The silver provided for his mother's food and lodging. Maybe the man said, "You are poor and yet you want to study the Buddhadharma. Here, I will help you a bit," and gave him an offering that he might go and seek Dharma. The merit and virtue of this offering was great, and in the future this man will certainly be a flesh body Bodhisattva. Now, perhaps one of us is doing this kind of work; think to yourself, "Have I done this kind of meritorious deed?" You don't remember? It doesn't matter, there's no need to have false thinking about it.

The man urged him on, saying, "You have such great faith that as soon as you heard this Sutra you opened to enlightenment and understood the principle. Hurry! Go right away to see the Great Master at Huang Mei! It will surely be worth your while. Do not delay, go at once!"

Sutra:

After Hui Neng had made arrangements for his mother's welfare, he took his leave. In less than thirty days he arrived at Huang Mei and made obeisance to the Fifth Patriarch, who asked him, "Where are you from and what do you seek?"

Hui Neng replied, "Your disciple is a commoner from Hsin Chou in Ling Nan and comes from afar to bow to the Master, seeking only to be a Buddha, and nothing else."

The Patriarch said, "You are from Ling Nan and are therefore a barbarian, so how can you become a Buddha?"

Hui Neng said, "Although there are people from the north and people from the south, there is ultimately no north or south in the Buddha nature. The body of the barbarian and that of the High Master are not the same, but what distinction is there in the Buddha nature?"

The Fifth Patriarch wished to continue the conversation, but seeing his disciples gathering on all sides, he ordered his visitor to follow the group off to work. Hui Neng said, "Hui Neng informs the High Master that this disciple's mind constantly produces wisdom and is not separate from the self nature. That, itself, is the field of blessing. It has not yet been decided what work the High Master will instruct me to do."

The Fifth Patriarch said, "Barbarian, your faculties are too sharp. Do not speak further, but go to the back courtyard." Hui Neng withdrew to the back courtyard where a cultivator ordered him to split firewood and thresh rice.

More than eight months had passed when the Patriarch one day suddenly saw Hui Neng and said, "I think these views of yours can be of use but fear that evil people may harm you. For that reason I have not spoken with you. Did you understand the situation?"

Hui Neng replied, "Your disciple knew the Master's intention and has stayed out of the front hall, so that others might not notice him."

Commentary:

As soon as the Sixth Patriarch made arrangements for his mother's welfare, he left. Some thirty days later he arrived at the east side of Shuang Feng mountain, at Tung Ch'an Monastery. During his journey he had had no false thoughts and so he was unaware of how much time had passed before he arrived at Huang Mei. The Master was twenty-two years old at the time.

When the Great Master asked from where he had come, Hui Neng told him that he was from the south, from Hsin Chou. "I don't want anything at all!" he said, "I only want to be a Buddha. All the rest is irrelevant."

The Fifth Patriarch said, "You are a southerner, and southerners are all barbarians." The word "barbarian" is, in Chinese, "ke liao."[16] "Ke" is dog-like animal with an extremely short snout. "Liao" refers to the coarse people of the borderlands. Basically, this means that those who cannot understand the principles of being human belong to the category of animals. "And how can you become a Buddha?" asked the Fifth Patriarch.

The Sixth Patriarch answered him promptly: "Although people are from the north and from the south," he said, "the Buddha nature is one and is everywhere the same."

The Fifth Patriarch's disciples were gathered all around, so he said no more. He simply told the Sixth Patriarch, "Good, you have come. Now, go to work with the others. Hurry off!"

Hui Neng said his own mind always produced wisdom. This wisdom is produced from one's own self-nature, and the fields of blessings[17] are not separate from it. "I do not yet know what the Master wants me to do," he said.

---

16. 獦獠–"ke liao"

The Patriarch heard Hui Neng talking this way and said, "This barbarian has sharp roots!"[18] He cautioned Hui Neng to be more discreet and not talk so much. "Speak no more!" he said. "Go to the back courtyard!"

In the back courtyard a cultivator told Hui Neng what to do. When people first come to a place, they are always bullied. This disciple, who had not yet left home said to Hui Neng, "You! Every day you must cut wood, build the fire and cook the food. Here's an axe, and be sure to cut kindling too! Besides that, every day you must thresh the rice."

Over eight months later, the Patriarch saw Hui Neng working on the threshing ground and said to him, "I think that your wisdom and opinions can be used, but fearing jealous people might harm you, I have not spoken with you too much. Did you know that?"

Hui Neng said, "I understand. I have not dared go into the front Dharma hall to speak with the Master lest others notice my actions or the Master's compassion toward me."

Sutra:

One day the Patriarch summoned his disciples together and said, "I have something to say to you: for people in the world, the matter of birth and death is a great one.

---

17. Fields of blessings refer figuratively to the meritorious deeds one does before the Triple Jewel (the Buddha, the Dharma, and the Sangha). Also, the robes worn by members of the Sangha are sewn in patches which resemble fields. By revering and making offerings to the Sangha, one "plants" seeds of merit and virtue in a place where they will certainly "ripen" and bear blessed fruit.

18. Roots refer to one's capacity to hear, believe, understand, accept and maintain the Buddhadharma. People may be endowed with superior, ordinary or inferior roots.

"All day long you seek fields of blessings only; you do not try to get out of the bitter sea of birth and death. If you are confused about your self-nature, how can blessings save you?"

Commentary:

The Fifth Patriarch said, "Regardless of whether you are extremely rich or bitterly poor, you cannot avoid birth and death. Consequently, you should know how you were born. If this question of birth and death is not resolved, life is dim and confused, and you are confused with coming and going.

"You do nothing but seek merit among the gods and among humans; you do not know how to seek wisdom. Thus, you swirl and drift in the suffering sea of birth and death."

It is said that one who cultivates wisdom and does not cultivate merit is like an Arhat with an empty begging-bowl; he is very wise, but no one makes offerings to him. But if one cultivates merit and neglects wisdom, he is just like a big elephant wearing a pearl necklace; beneath the adornments of blessing, he is stupid and will never solve the problem of birth and death.

Sutra:

"Each of you go back and look into your own wisdom and use the Prajna-nature[19] of your own original mind to compose a verse. Submit it to me so that I may look at it.

"If you understand the great meaning, the robe and Dharma will be passed on to you and you will become the sixth patriarch. Hurry off! Do not delay! Thinking and

19. "Transcendental wisdom." See Chapter II.

considering is of no use in this matter. When seeing your own nature it is necessary to see it at the very moment of speaking. One who does that perceives as does one who wields a sword in the height of battle."

Commentary:

"Verse" here is the Sanskrit word "gatha." A gatha is composed of lines of uniform length, though the length may vary from gatha to gatha.

"Go quickly!" said the Fifth Patriarch. "Go as if a fire were about to overtake you. Do not dawdle and procrastinate saying, 'Oh, I cannot do it today. I will do it tomorrow instead,' and then the next day saying, 'Not today either, perhaps tomorrow...' Do not keep putting it off and do not try to think about it. It is useless to use your discriminating mind. If you have deep prajna wisdom, you understand the moment you hear the words spoken. Just as one grabs a weapon and confronts the oncoming enemy, so do you perceive. You can see your nature in the same immediate way.

Sutra:

The assembly received this order and withdrew, saying to one another, "We of the assembly do not need to clear our minds and use our intellect to compose a verse to submit to the High Master. What use would there be in this?"

"Shen Hsiu is our senior instructor and teaching transmitter. Certainly he should be the one to obtain it. It would be not only improper for us to compose a verse, but a waste of effort as well."

Hearing this, everyone put his mind to rest, and said, "Henceforth, we will rely on Master Shen Hsiu. Why vex ourselves writing verses?"

Commentary:

They went away to other courts, other gardens, and other buildings, saying to themselves, "Why worry about writing this verse? We do not need to waste the effort."

I believe the people who spoke this way were of Shen Hsiu's party. Why did they not write verses? Because Shen Hsiu's followers were trying to make him the patriarch; all his followers, disciples, Dharma brothers, friends, and relatives contrived to set up the position for Shen Hsiu. They convinced everyone else not to write verses, because if anyone else wrote verses, then perhaps Shen Hsiu might not get to be the next patriarch.

They secretly passed it around and whispered behind the scenes, like friends of a candidate for President who say, "Hey! Vote for this one! He can be President!" They spread it about and stuffed the ballot box.

Convinced that they had no learning, the assembly decided it was useless to write verses. Swayed by the rumors, they said, "The Senior-Seated Shen Hsiu is second to the Abbot. His literary skill is good, his virtue is high, he lectures on the Sutras and speaks Dharma for us. Certainly he should become the sixth patriarch."

When the assembly heard Shen Hsiu's followers saying things like, "If we write verses, they will be very unpolished and certainly not good enough to submit," they all decided not to write verses themselves. They didn't want to compete with Shen Hsiu, their superior.

Sutra:

Shen Hsiu then thought, "The others are not submitting verses because I am their teaching transmitter. I must compose a verse and submit it to the High Master.

"If I do not submit a verse, how will the High Master know whether the views and understanding in my mind are deep or shallow?

"If my intention in submitting the verse is to seek the Dharma, that is good. But if it is to grasp the patriarchate, that is bad, for how would that be different from the mind of a common person coveting the holy position? But, if I do not submit a verse, in the end I will not obtain the Dharma. This is a terrible difficulty!"

Commentary:

The Fifth Patriarch had announced that in order to obtain the Dharma, one must compose a verse. Shen Hsiu knew that if he did not submit one, the Fifth Patriarch would not know whether Shen Hsiu had wisdom and he could not transmit the Dharma to him. Shen Hsiu fretted and worried, "What shall I do? This is very hard; it is just too difficult!"

Sutra:

In front of the Fifth Patriarch's hall were three corridors. Their walls were to be frescoed by Court Artist Lu Chen with stories from the *Lankavatara Sutra* and with pictures portraying in detail the lives of the five patriarchs, so that the patriarchs might be venerated by future generations.

Commentary:

A court artist is one appointed as an official to the Imperial Court because of his talent.

The title of *The Lankavatara Sutra* has two meanings: "city" and "cannot be gone to." This city, located behind Malaya Mountain, is inaccessible to those without spiritual powers. Shakyamuni Buddha used his spiritual powers to go there and speak *The Lankavatara Sutra* for the benefit of those who had spiritual powers. The court artist was to depict the miraculous, inconceivable, wonderful transformations which took place in the assembly on Lanka Mountain.

The court artist was also to paint pictures illustrating the flow of the Dharma from Great Master Bodhidharma, the First Patriarch, to the Great Master Hui K'o, the Second Patriarch, and onward from generation to generation, to the Fifth Patriarch, Great Master Hung Jen. The paintings would remain in the world so that future generations might receive benefit from respecting and making offerings to them.

Sutra:

After composing his verse, Shen Hsiu made several attempts to submit it. But whenever he reached the front hall, his mind became agitated and distraught, and his entire body became covered with perspiration. He did not dare submit it, although in the course of four days he made thirteen attempts.

Commentary:

Shen Hsiu's students were not greedy to become patriarch, but Shen Hsiu had a great desire for the position.

Whenever he tried to submit his verse, he went a little crazy. "What am I going to do? Is this verse right or not? Can I submit it?" He did not know if it was right or wrong. "Ah, maybe...is it this way or is it that way? Maybe it isn't. Maybe it is...more or less." Endless questions flooded his mind, making him extremely nervous. Every time he tried to hand it in, he broke out in a heavy sweat. Why? It was a huge gamble; if he failed, he would not be a patriarch, but if he passed, he would. Fear of failure caused his extreme agitation.

It was really suffering, really hard work! It is not easy to be a patriarch. Look at how much effort he expended. For four entire days and nights he never shut his eyes. He just kept trying to submit his verse. At night he would go as far as the Fifth Patriarch's hall, peer around, break out in a sweat, and flee back to his room. During the day he tried again. In the periods in between, he could not sit, lie down, or sleep, and when he tried to eat, he couldn't swallow.

He went before the Patriarch's hall thirteen times and still did not submit the verse. Now, when I give you a quiz, you write the answers very promptly and hand them in. Suppose I were to give you a patriarch test! I think your hands would tremble so that you could not write out the answers. Finally, after so many attempts, when Shen Hsiu had almost worried himself to death, he thought, "Hey! Get hold of yourself. Calm down and think this thing over. Meditate and enter samadhi!"

Sutra:

Then he thought, "This is not as good as writing it on the wall so that the High Master might see it suddenly. If he says it is good, I will come forward, bow, and say, 'Hsiu did it.' If it does not pass, then I have spent my

years on this mountain in vain, receiving veneration from others. And as to further cultivation–what can I say?"

That night, in the third watch, holding a candle he secretly wrote the verse on the wall of the South corridor, to show what his mind had seen.

Commentary:

"That's it!" he said with relief. "I will write it on the wall and when he sees it he will say, 'This is truly a fine verse, truly wonderful!' and I will admit that I wrote it. But if he says, 'This is too confused. It is nothing but useless trash!' then I will know that I have wasted my time here on the mountain."

He crept stealthily, like a thief in the night He carried just a little candle, for if the light were too bright, someone might have seen him.

Sutra:

Verse:

The body is a Bodhi tree,
The mind like a bright mirror stand.
Time and again brush it clean,
And let no dust alight.

After writing this verse, Shen Hsiu returned to his room, and the others did not know what he had done.

Then he thought, "If the Fifth Patriarch sees the verse tomorrow and is pleased, it will mean that I have an affinity with the Dharma. If he says that it does not pass, it will mean that I am confused by heavy karmic obstacles[20] from past lives, and that I am not fit to obtain

the Dharma. It is difficult to fathom the sage's intentions."

In his room he thought it over and could not sit or sleep peacefully right through to the fifth watch.

Commentary:

He bounded back to his room two steps at a time, as if he were being chased, but quietly, taking great, silent leaps like an expert military spy. He was afraid that if anyone saw him, they would know he wrote the verse. But no one saw him, no one knew–not even the ghosts and spirits. "If he likes this verse," thought Shen Hsiu, "then I must have conditions with the wonderful mind-to-mind seal of the Buddhas, and it is my destiny to be patriarch. But if it does not pass, my confusion from the karma created in past lives must be a heavy obstruction. It is hard to figure out what he will say. There is just no way to know."

Actually, his verse was not bad, but he had not fully understood. So after he returned to his room, he was still uneasy.

Sutra:

The Patriarch already knew that Shen Hsiu had not yet entered the gate and seen his own nature. At daybreak, the Patriarch called Court Artist Lu Chen to fresco the wall of the south corridor. Suddenly he saw the verse and said to the court artist, "There is no need to paint. I am sorry that you have been wearied by coming so far, but *The Diamond Sutra* says, 'Whatever has marks

---

[20]. The results of bad deeds done in the past manifest as various kinds of hindrances which impede one's cultivation and detain one's enlightenment.

is empty and false.' Instead leave this verse for people to recite and uphold. Those who cultivate in accordance with this verse will not fall into the evil destinies and will attain great merit."

He then ordered the disciples to light incense and bow before it, and to recite it, thus enabling them to see their own nature. The disciples all recited it and exclaimed, "Excellent!"

Commentary:

"If you cultivate according to the principles contained in this verse," said the Fifth Patriarch, "you will not fall into rebirth in the three evil paths of the hells, animals, or hungry ghosts, and you will receive many benefits."

Sutra:

At the third watch, the Patriarch called Shen Hsiu into the hall and asked him, "Did you write this verse?"

Shen Hsiu said, "Yes, in fact, Hsiu did it. He does not dare lay claim to the position of Patriarch, but hopes the High Master will be compassionate and see whether or not this disciple has a little bit of wisdom."

The Patriarch said, "The verse which you wrote shows that you have not yet seen your original nature but are still outside the gate. With such views and understanding you may seek supreme Bodhi, but in the end will not obtain it. Supreme Bodhi must be obtained at the very moment of speaking. In recognizing the original mind, at all times, in every thought, you yourself will see that the ten thousand Dharmas are unblocked; in one truth is all truth and the ten thousand states are of

themselves 'thus,' as they are. The 'thusness' of the mind, just that is true reality. If seen in this way, it is indeed the self nature of supreme Bodhi."

Commentary:

The Patriarch chose the same hour at which Shen Hsiu had written the verse on the wall the night before. He secretly called him in and said, "Psst! Was it you who wrote that verse?"

"Yes, yes," Shen Hsiu whispered back, "yes, in fact, I, Hsiu, wrote it. I do not dare seek the status of the patriarch, but..."

"Your verse shows that you are still an outsider," said the Fifth Patriarch. "You have not yet seen your nature. As soon as you speak the words, know your original nature!"

When you understand the mind and see your own nature, you know that the nature is not produced and not destroyed; for at all times, all dharmas are perfectly fused, without the slightest bit of obstruction. There is no place where all dharmas are not identical.

When you understand one truth, all truth is understood. The ten thousand externals are all produced from the state which is "thus, unmoving," and within the mind which is "thus, thus, unmoving," true reality is to be found. Seen in this way, this state is the original nature exactly; it is the highest enlightenment. And so, in response to Shen Hsiu, I wrote a verse myself:

Because of the Way,
ten thousand things are born.
One who obtains it
penetrates the mystery oneself;
Awakened, the basic substance is
fathomed:
Bodhi does not decrease or increase.

Sutra:

"Go and think it over for a day or two. Compose another verse and bring it to me to see. If you have been able to enter the gate, I will transmit the robe and Dharma to you."

Shen Hsiu made obeisance and left. Several days passed, but he was unable to compose a verse. His mind was agitated and confused and his thoughts and mood were uneasy. He was as if in a dream; whether walking or sitting down, he could not be happy.

Commentary:

After the Great Master had explained that the Bodhi self-nature cannot be sought with the mind that wants to take advantage of things, he told Shen Hsiu, "If you obtain the original substance, become enlightened and understand the mind and see your self-nature, entering the gate of the Buddhadharma so that you are no longer on the outside, I will transmit the Dharma to you." "Enter the gate" means "understand the mind and see your own nature."

As the days passed, Shen Hsiu gradually went insane. Neither his mood nor his thoughts would calm down. Although he was unable to fall asleep he was as if in a dream. He didn't know what he was doing because his desire to become patriarch was so great. I believe that, after he failed the initial test and then was unable to compose another verse, he even considered suicide.

Sutra:

Two days later, a young boy chanting that verse passed by the threshing room. Hearing it for the first

time, Hui Neng knew that the writer had not yet seen his original nature. Although he had not yet received a transmission of the teaching, he already understood its profound meaning. He asked the boy, "What verse are you reciting?"

"Barbarian, you know nothing," replied the boy. "The Great Master has said that birth and death are a profound concern for people in the world. Desiring to transmit the robe and Dharma, he ordered his disciples to compose verses and bring them to him to see. The person who has awakened to the profound meaning will inherit the robe and Dharma and become the Sixth Patriarch. Our senior, Shen Hsiu, wrote this 'verse without marks' on the wall of the south corridor. The Great Master ordered everyone to recite it, for to cultivate in accord with this verse is to avoid falling into the evil destinies and is of great merit."

Commentary:

A young lad ventured close to the threshing floor where the Sixth Patriarch was working, singing as he walked,

The body is a Bodhi tree.
The mind like a bright mirror-stand.
Time and again, brush it clean;
Let no dust alight.

The youth was chanting Shen Hsiu's verse because he wished to obtain great benefit, avoid the three evil destinies of rebirth, and see his nature.

When the Sixth Patriarch asked the boy what he was reciting, the boy replied, "You barbarian! Don't you know that the Fifth

Patriarch said that of all the problems people face, the problem of birth and death is the most grave?"

A "verse without marks" is one which reveals that its author is not attached to marks.

"You really have no good roots!" the boy said to the Sixth Patriarch. "After so many days, you still don't know? You are useless, capable only of toiling at bitter work; all you can do is pound rice. You shouldn't let such a fine opportunity slip by. Listen closely, and I will tell you what has happened and teach you this verse so that you too can become enlightened and see your nature. Pay attention and rely on this verse as you cultivate so that in your next life you won't have to endure such suffering as you endure now. You won't have to be a horse or a cow or fall among the other animals or into the hells. At the very least you'll be a wealthy and respected person of good fortune."

The youth's heart wasn't bad at all.

Sutra:

Hui Neng said, "I, too, would like to recite it to create an affinity. Superior One, I have been pounding rice here for over eight months and have not yet been to the front hall. I hope that the Superior One will lead me before the verse to pay homage." The boy then led him to the verse to bow.

Hui Neng said, "Hui Neng cannot read. Please, Superior One, read it to me." Then an official from Chiang Chou, named Chang Jih Yung, read it loudly. After hearing it, Hui Neng said, "I, too, have a verse. Will the official please write it for me?"

The official replied, "You, too, can write a verse? That is strange!"

Commentary:

The boy said, "Listen to me and I will teach you: 'The body is a Bodhi tree.' Can you remember that? 'The mind is like a bright mirror-stand.' You should remember that! Don't forget! 'Time and again brush it clean; let no dust alight.' If you remember that verse clearly and study as you chant, you'll certainly receive an efficacious response."

Because the lad had been so considerate, the Sixth Patriarch referred to him as "Superior One," a title which is ordinarily reserved for one's master. People who have left home often call their teachers, "Superior One," acknowledging their high achievement.

Then the Sixth Patriarch said, "The layman Hui Neng is truly useless, for he can't read a single word. Superior One, would you please recite it for me? Having heard the verse, he said, "Well, I have a verse, too, but I'm unable to write it. What can I do? Please, good official, Layman Chang, will you write it out for me?"

The official was wide-eyed with surprise. He looked scornfully at the barbarian and said, "Ha! You can write a verse? This is very strange. In my whole life I have never heard of an illiterate who can write verses!"

Sutra:

Hui Neng said to the official, "If you wish to study the supreme Bodhi, do not slight the beginner. The lowest people may have the highest wisdom; the highest people may have the least wisdom. If you slight others, you create limitless, unbounded offenses."

The official said, "Recite your verse and I will write it out for you. If you obtain the Dharma you must take me across first. Do not forget these words."

Hui Neng's verse reads:

Originally Bodhi has no tree,
The bright mirror has no stand.
Originally there is not a single thing:
Where can dust alight?

When this verse had been written, the followers all were startled and without exception cried out to one another, "Strange indeed! One cannot judge a person by his appearance. How can it be that, after so little time, he has become a Bodhisattva in the flesh?"

Commentary:

Originally, Layman Lu had not planned to say a thing, but if he had remained silent, no one would have helped him write a verse. So in reply to the mocking of Layman Chang, the Master said, "If you wish to study the highest Bodhi, do not ridicule those who are studying the Buddhadharma for the first time."

It may well be that those who appear to be the lowest and stupidest have the highest wisdom, for those who have truly great wisdom may act as if they have no wisdom at all. No matter what they are asked, they reply, "I don't know," This is an example of the great wisdom which is like stupidity. For instance, when I ask a question of my disciples they often say, "I don't know." When they first came to study, they said, "I know everything!"

Once I met a person who said he knew everything. I asked, "How can you know everything? If you know all there is to know, I'll ask you a question."

He said, "What is your question?"

I replied, "Do you know how many grains of rice you swallowed at lunch today?"

"No, I didn't count them," he admitted.

"Your 'not counting' is just 'not knowing,'" I said.

Those who do the most menial work often have wisdom excelling that of people in high positions. Then again, those who ordinarily have great wisdom may have times when their wisdom is suffocated by thoughts of desire.

"O.K., O.K.," said the official, "that's right. You certainly speak with principle. Now, what is your verse? Recite it and I will write it out. You don't have to say another word. But you must remember to take me across first because if I don't write your verse no one will know of it."

Originally Bodhi has no tree. Bodhi is just the Way of enlightenment, and that's all there is to it; how can there be a tree? If there is a tree, Bodhi becomes a mere thing, a place of attachment. Originally Bodhi doesn't have anything. If you say you are enlightened, what is enlightenment like? Is it green or yellow? Is it red or white? Can you speak of the appearance of Bodhi when it has no appearance?

The bright mirror has no stand. You may say the mind is like a bright mirror stand, but there is actually no stand at all. If you have a stand, you have a place where you can dwell. But you should "produce a thought which is nowhere supported;" how can you have a stand? If you have a stand, then you have a dwelling place, a place where you are attached; therefore, the bright mirror has no stand. What is the appearance? No appearance.

Originally there is not a single thing. Basically there is nothing at all: no style; no picture; no shape or mark. Originally there is nothing at all.

Where can dust alight? Since there isn't anything, where does the dust come from? Basically you have no dwelling place. The essential meaning of the verse is this: You should "produce a thought which is nowhere supported." There should be no attachment at all. This was precisely the Buddha's meaning when, upon becoming enlightened, he said, "All living beings have the wisdom and virtuous characteristics of the Thus Come One. It is merely because of false thinking and attachment that they are unable to certify to the attainment of them." This was spoken specifically to instruct people to put aside attachment, to produce an unsupported thought.

If you are attached, what are you up to? Huh? Now you are attached, but in the future will you die, or not? What will you be attached to when you die?

All the Bhikshus, laymen, and assembled disciples stood in astonishment and whispered among themselves, "Hey! Hey! Does he have a verse, too? Oh! It's really true, you can't judge people by appearances. This rice-thresher, Layman Lu, can compose verses. We can no longer slander him and call him a barbarian."

"Why he hasn't been here very long," they continued, "but how can you deny that he's a flesh body Bodhisattva?" Actually, some were mocking the Sixth Patriarch, babbling, "Don't look down on him. He's a flesh body Bodhisattva." Perhaps there were Arhats[21] in the assembly who intentionally made such

21. The highest level of sagehood in the Lesser Vehicle, as contrasted with the Great Vehicle Bodhisattva. "Arhat" has three meanings: "worthy of gifts," "slayer of the thieves of affliction," and "not to be reborn."

comments so that people would look closely and clearly recognize that he actually was a flesh body Bodhisattva. Again there were those who said, "This is truly a flesh body Bodhisattva," but meant it only as sarcasm and lighthearted ridicule, for they still didn't know if the verse was correct.

Everyone was chattering, exchanging comments, making such a racket that the Fifth Patriarch came to the hall and demanded, "What are you doing? What are you up to?"

"This rice-thresher, this barbarian, can write verses!" they stammered.

Sutra:

The Fifth Patriarch saw the astonished assembly and feared that they might become dangerous. Accordingly, he erased the verse with his shoe saying, "This one, too, has not yet seen his nature."

The assembly agreed.

Commentary:

The gathering was so excited the Fifth Patriarch feared that someone might even try to assassinate Layman Lu. This sentence of text proves that people with twisted hearts, followers of Shen Hsiu, were already locked in a fierce battle for positions of power. If the Dharma and the Patriarchate were transmitted publicly to anyone other than Shen Hsiu, that person would have been murdered on the spot. But they didn't know that the Fifth Patriarch was a bright-eyed one who read their scheming minds. So to protect the Sixth Patriarch he erased the verse and said, "This man's verse is also incorrect."

Perhaps some of you are thinking, "The Fifth Patriarch lied! First he said that if one cultivated in accord with Shen Hsiu's verse, he would not be subject to the three evil destinies, but would gain great benefit and see his own nature. Then the Fifth Patriarch told everyone that Layman Lu had not really seen his nature when, in truth, he had. Isn't that false speech?

No. This is a provisional teaching, not false speech. The Fifth Patriarch spoke to protect the new patriarch; he would not allow the others to harm him. In this way, the Buddhadharma could remain long in this world and be transmitted far and wide.

"Yes," said the followers, "he has not seen his nature." Although they agreed, no one knew whether the verse was right or not. The first verse said, "Bodhi is a tree;" the second said, "Bodhi has no tree." The first verse said, "The bright mirror has a stand," and the second said, "There is no mirror stand." Which was right? Which was wrong? No one understood. None of them had become enlightened, so they couldn't recognize an enlightened verse. It is like the judging of a doctoral dissertation: if you only have a Master's Degree, you cannot judge a doctoral dissertation. It is the same with the enlightened and the unenlightened: since they were not enlightened themselves, the followers did not understand, and so they simply agreed with the Master and said, "No, this one has not yet seen his nature."

Sutra:

The next day the Patriarch secretly came to the threshing floor where he saw Hui Neng pounding rice with a stone tied around his waist, and he said, "A seeker of the Way would forget his very life for the Dharma. Is this not the case?"

Commentary:

The next day everyone was quiet and no longer worrying about who was enlightened and who was not. The Fifth Patriarch secretly left his room and went quickly to the threshing floor to see the Great Master Hui Neng. As he went he peered about to see if anyone was looking; just like Shen Hsiu when he had finished writing the verse, he ran silently, darting glances over his shoulder to make sure no one saw him.

When the Fifth Patriarch got to the threshing floor, he saw Hui Neng pounding rice. He had tied a stone around his waist and pounded rice so that others could eat. What was he doing? He was practicing the Bodhisattva Way, forgetting others and having no notion of self. He did not think, "Why should I pound rice for you to eat? You don't work. You don't do anything at all! I pound rice all day and it is very difficult!" He did not think that way. Instead, he thought, "You do not work? Fine, I will do it myself," just like one of my disciples who is so busy that when he is called to lunch he says, "Wait a minute, wait a minute!" I really like that kind of disciple, but not everyone can be that way.

"Isn't that so?" the Fifth Patriarch said. Remember this. It ought, it must be this way! You must give up being afraid of difficulty to the point of forgetting to eat. No one knows how many days the Sixth Patriarch went without eating. No one called him to eat, and he himself forgot about it until he had no strength. He tied a heavy rock around his waist to add weight to his body so that he could pound the rice. I think he used the stone to add to his weight because he had not eaten for some time; however, you should not get attached and think, "It was definitely like that." On the other hand, do not think, "It definitely wasn't like that." The profound insight comes from precisely that kind of non-attachment.

Sutra:

Then the Fifth Patriarch asked, "Is the rice ready?"

Hui Neng replied, "The rice has long been ready. It is now waiting only for the sieve."

Commentary:

This passage in *The Sixth Patriarch's Sutra* is extremely important. The Fifth Patriarch found the Great Master Hui Neng toiling on the threshing floor and asked him, "Is the rice ready?" On one level the question means, "Have you finished threshing the rice?" On another level, the meaning is: "Have your efforts been successful? Has your work taken you up the road?"

Why does the Sutra say, "rice"? Because rice is made up of many grains, perfectly shaped, so symbolizing the precious *mani*[22] jewel of the self nature. "Is the *mani* jewel of your nature ready? Is the light of your mind full? Is the light of your nature full? Is the light of your body full?"

When the raw grain is boiled in water it becomes edible. The Patriarch's question means, "How is your cultivation of the Way? You have been pounding rice and cultivating Dhyana meditation. How is your skill?" There are many levels of meaning here. The Sixth Patriarch, of course, understood the Fifth Patriarch's question, for it is said,

One who has gone through,
knows one who has gone through;
Those who do,
know those who do.

22. A jewel, a pearl, symbol of perfection and purity.

"The rice has long been ready. My skill was perfected long ago," the Sixth Patriarch answered. "It is now waiting only for the sieve." In threshing rice, a sieve is used to sift out the husks. Here, the sieve represents getting rid of the filth. The fourth chapter of *The Lotus Sutra* tells of the poor son who spent twenty years getting rid of the filth of the delusions of views and delusions of thoughts[23].

Although the Sixth Patriarch's spiritual skill was perfected, it still waited for the sieve; he still had to sweep out the filth of the delusions of views and thought. Do you understand now why Sutras must be explained? If they were not explained, you would not even know enough to sweep away the filth, and you would be utterly useless.

Sutra:

The Patriarch rapped the pestle three times with his staff and left. Hui Neng then knew the Patriarch's intention, and at the third watch he went into the Patriarch's room.

Commentary:

The Fifth Patriarch rapped the pestle three times with his staff and left. Old monks who have left the home life to become Bhikshus often carry a walking stick. Sometimes these staffs are made of twisted vines. The Great Master Hsü Yün[24] said:

---

23. There are 88 categories of view-delusions, which arise when greed and love are produced with respect to externals, and there are 81 categories of thought-delusions, which arise when, confused about principles, one gives rise to discrimination.

24. The seventeenth Buddhist patriarch in China (1839–1959)

We go to pick the ivy,
Lively like a dragon,
Beating wind and rain,
Beating empty space.

The ivy vine curves and twists like a dragon who by attacking the wind and rain attacks empty space. That is certainly a case of going out to look for trouble. If that vine were as busy as my disciples it would have no time to beat space and wind.

"Knock, knock, knock," went the Fifth Patriarch's staff, and how do you think he left? If you know, then you know. If you don't know, then you must wait until I tell you. He went out with his two hands behind his back, holding his crooked staff.

Why did the Patriarch rap three times? Do you understand the meaning of that? The Sixth Patriarch understood right away. The rapping meant, "Come to my room at the third watch, at midnight." This is called "speaking the Dharma without words." Here in the meditation hall, for example, when the wooden fish[25] is hit twice, it means "Walk;" hit once, it means "Stop and sit down;" hit three times, it means, "Meditate! Work hard!" All that is "speaking the Dharma without words."

Why did the Fifth Patriarch carry his staff behind his back? Now you are going to ask me, "How do you know he carried it behind his back since it doesn't say so in the Sutra?" Well, how do you *not* know? I know that you don't know. He carried it behind his back to indicate that the Sixth Patriarch should come in by the back door. "Do not let the others see you come in!"

If the Fifth Patriarch had said openly, "Come to my room at the third watch and we'll have a little talk," I am sure that the

25. A wooden percussion instrument shaped like a fish, use in monasteries to accompany chanting and to give signals.

word would have spread like fire to Shen Hsiu's ears and Shen Hsiu and his disciples would not have been very kind to the Sixth Patriarch. The Fifth Patriarch tested the Sixth Patriarch's wisdom by rapping his staff three times and putting it behind his back.

The Sixth Patriarch understood but no one else did. They were all as if deaf and dumb, without any idea as to what had transpired in this wordless exchange of Dharma.

At midnight, as soon as the Sixth Patriarch entered the room, there was a quick exchange. "What are you doing here?" demanded the Fifth Patriarch.

"But the Patriarch told me to come at the third watch!" came the reply.

"Really? Did I tell you that? How could I have forgotten? What do you think you are doing? Why did you come in the back door instead of the front door?"

"Did the Master not tell me to use the back entrance?"

The Fifth Patriarch laughed and said, "You are not bad, really not bad. You are all right!"

You, ask how I know that? I ask, "How do you not know it?"

Sutra:

The Patriarch covered them with his precept sash so they could not be seen, and he explained *The Diamond Sutra* for him down to the line, "One should produce a thought that is nowhere supported."

Commentary:

The Fifth Patriarch was afraid that someone might have seen the Great Master Hui Neng enter his room and might be outside the window eavesdropping. At that time the windows were made of paper; so, to insure privacy, the Fifth Patriarch pulled his robe over both their heads.

The Fifth Patriarch's explanation of *The Diamond Sutra* was not a public one, such as I have given you. His was a secret and very difficult explanation, telling the Sixth Patriarch how to forge an indestructible vajra body. When he heard the words, "One should produce a thought which is nowhere supported," Hui Neng achieved the great enlightenment and knew that all the ten thousand dharmas are not separate from the self-nature. He suddenly experienced that even greater enlightenment

Although the Sixth Patriarch knew the method, his afflictions of views and thought had not yet been completely eliminated. That he was waiting for the sieve can mean, also, that no one had certified him. Even though, in his intense vigor, he had reached a high peak, and the fire in the censer was pure green, he had not yet been certified by a good knowing advisor. So when the Fifth Patriarch heard him say that the rice was ready and merely waiting for the sieve, he prepared to certify the Sixth Patriarch.

Because I have a kind of radar, I was able to record their conversation and I shall now replay it for you. Keep in mind that this is a T'ang Dynasty recording, not a present-day one:

"Do you want to reach Buddhahood?" asked the Fifth Patriarch.

"Yes," said the Sixth Patriarch, "I just want to become a Buddha. I do not seek anything else. I only want to attain Buddhahood."

"Your resolution is extremely firm," replied the Fifth Patriarch, "but if you want to realize Buddhahood you must first cut off ignorance, for it is ignorance which produces the afflictions of delusion, brought on by false views and false thought. If you want to cut off these afflictions, you must first cut off ignorance.

"For example, the cycle of birth and death is based on the state of emotional love. When you break through ignorance, then the delusions of false views and false thoughts which are tied to birth and death cease to exist, for ignorance is the root of birth and death. If you want to cut off ignorance and thereby put an end to birth and death, then, as *The Diamond Sutra* says, "produce a thought which is nowhere supported." That means do not dwell in emotional love, get rid of desire, and cast out craving. Then you can bring an end to birth and death.

The Sixth Patriarch heard this and suddenly became enlightened. He saw through to his original face and said, "Ah! It is basically just like this! It is not difficult at all! In fact, it's very easy!" Thus he became enlightened.

This has been a T'ang Dynasty recording which has just been played for you to hear.

In cultivating and studying the Buddhadharma, you should produce an unsupported thought. That means to dwell neither in emotion nor love. If you dwell in emotion and love, you dwell in ignorance, and thus in birth and death. If you do not dwell in emotion or in love, if you do not dwell in existence or non-existence, you know the Middle Way. The Middle Way is not separate from existence and is not separate from emptiness, nor does it exist elsewhere. The ability to transform emotion and love into genuine Prajna wisdom is enlightenment. Not changing them is confusion. It is said, "Although the sea of suffering is inexhaustible, a turn of the head is the other shore." The difference between confusion and enlightenment is just in knowing how to turn. If you accept emotion and love and run after desire, then the more you run, the more confused you become. If you can turn your head, you arrive at Nirvana, the other shore. If you do not turn your head, you become more and more confused. The more confused, the farther away you are and the deeper you sink into confusion. But although you are extremely far off, one turn can be sudden enlightenment. Sudden enlightenment is awakening. Awakening is the Buddha.

You may be thinking, "If I become a Buddha, there won't be any work for me to do. Wouldn't I just sit in a lotus flower all day and wait for people to come and light incense and bow before me? Frankly, I don't think that sounds the least bit interesting!" If that is what you think, you can go on being a living being, but you can be a living being who is a friend to others, taking them across to Buddhahood.

You need not worry about Buddhahood being uninteresting. Yesterday I talked about the ghost who had no trouble and as a consequence did not want to become a person:

I've been a ghost for three thousand years,
Without happiness, without fears.
Shen Kung tells me to go be a man,
But I really just don't think I can!

The ghosts have no fears, but they only come out at night, because they belong to the *yin*, the darkness principle. The Buddha is totally *yang*, like the light of the sun. So, you decide. Do you want to be a ghost or a Buddha? If you want to be a ghost, then it is all right to have emotion and love. But if you want to be a Buddha, you must "produce a thought which is nowhere supported."

Sutra:

At the moment he heard those words, Hui Neng experienced the great enlightenment and he knew that all the ten thousand dharmas are not separate from the self-nature. He said to the Patriarch:

How unexpected! The self-nature is
originally pure in itself.
How unexpected! The self-nature is
originally neither produced nor destroyed.
How unexpected! The self-nature is
originally complete in itself.
How unexpected! The self-nature is
originally without movement.
How unexpected! The self-nature
can produce the ten thousand dharmas.

Commentary:

Great enlightenment penetrates to the beginning and to the end: it is a complete understanding of the deep Prajna wisdom. Because the Sixth Patriarch understood Prajna wisdom he said, "The ten thousand dharmas are not separate from the self-nature, for the mind produces the ten thousand dharmas."

The Sixth Patriarch exclaimed that the self-nature is pure. Why, then, does the Sutra say earlier that the self-nature is neither defiled nor pure?

The term "pure" represents the appearance of the original substance, because the concept cannot be represented any other way. Here, "pure" means "originally pure" and does not refer to the purity which is the opposite of defilement.

Production and destruction, birth and death, occur because living beings become attached. Without attachments, where would birth and death come from? Where would they go? There is no such thing as birth and death!

The Sixth Patriarch realized that the self-nature is originally complete in itself, with nothing lacking and nothing in excess. It cannot be added to or depleted. In the final analysis the Buddha is not greater than ordinary living beings. Why do living beings fail to understand that? Because they turn their backs on enlightenment and unite themselves with the "dust" of external objects. With their backs turned, they cannot recognize the precious things that are originally theirs. They cast the root aside and grasp at the branches seeking pleasurable sensations which are false. They grasp at fame and profit, stupidly.

Living beings are upside-down; they have no concentration power. But, nevertheless, their self-nature is without movement. Not only is that true of the Sixth Patriarch's self-nature, but the self-nature of all living beings is unmoving, too. All are equal.

The ten thousand dharmas are produced from the self-nature, and the self-nature includes all of existence. The Master hadn't comprehended that before, but now at last he understood the wonderful principles.

Sutra:

The Fifth Patriarch knew of Hui Neng's enlightenment to his original nature and said to him, "Studying the Dharma without recognizing the original mind is of no benefit. If one recognizes one's own original mind and sees one's original nature, then one is called a great hero, a teacher of gods and humans, a Buddha."

Commentary:

The Fifth Patriarch knew that the Sixth Patriarch had become enlightened, and that he recognized his original face and knew whether his nostrils faced up or down. When he held his hand over his head, the Sixth Patriarch knew whether it was upside-down or right-side up. Recently, I asked you all, "When your hand hangs at your side, is it upside-down and when you raise it up over your head, is it right-side up? Or is it that when it hangs at your side it is right-side up and when you raise it over your head it is upside-down?" None of you understood this principle. Why? Because there is basically no such thing as upside-down or right-side-up! The Sixth Patriarch was especially clear about such questions. The Fifth Patriarch knew that he understood and so he covered them both with his robe and said, "Unless you recognize your original mind, it is useless to study the Dharma."

It is said, "If one recognizes one's own mind, the great earth doesn't have an inch of dirt." It changes into yellow gold, adorned with the seven precious things–gold, silver, lapis lazuli, crystal, mother-of-pearl, red pearls, and carnelian.

You say, "It doesn't look like that to me." Of course it doesn't. You haven't recognized your original mind. When you recognize it, you will see things differently. It's like wearing tinted glasses. If you wear red glasses, people look red, and if you wear green glasses, they look green. If your glasses are yellow, then everyone looks yellow. Because you haven't recognized your original mind, the great earth appears to be covered with dirt. This is because the dirt within you is so great. What is the dirt? It is simply your scattered thoughts, for without them, the great earth doesn't have an inch of dirt.

Studying the Buddhadharma is of no benefit unless you recognize your original mind. Look at it! What color is it? Is it green, yellow, red, white, or black? Is it long or short, square or round? What does it look like? What is its appearance? To say it has an appearance is an analogy, because fundamentally it has no appearance. When you recognize this "no appearance" you will understand. But before you have recognized it, do not speak about it in a confused way.

Recognize your original mind and see your nature. At that point you are a Buddha, because in the final analysis living beings are the Buddha and the Buddha is a living being. We now have the opportunity to realize Buddhahood. Not recognizing, not seeing, however, you still must study the Buddhadharma.

Sutra:

> **He received the Dharma in the third watch and no one knew about it. The Fifth Patriarch also transmitted the Sudden Teaching and the robe and bowl saying, "You are the Sixth Patriarch. Protect yourself carefully. Take living beings across by every method and spread the teaching for the sake of those who will live in the future. Do not let it be cut off."**

Commentary:

At midnight, the Fifth Patriarch transmitted the wonderful Dharma to the Sixth Patriarch, using the mind to seal the mind, and no one at all knew about it. The insiders didn't know, the outsiders didn't know, not even the ghosts and spirits knew.

The Fifth Patriarch transmitted the Teaching of Sudden Enlightenment which points directly to the mind to see the nature and realize Buddhahood. "Think this over," he said. "You are the Sixth Patriarch. As you cultivate the Buddhadharma, you must walk the true path. Do not simply talk about enlightenment. Do not use 'head-mouth zen' and say 'I have studied the Dharma to the point that when there is no principle, I can make one up. I can prove that there is no truth or falsehood, and that to understand that by itself is to understand the ultimate meaning of the Middle Way.' Don't talk that way. It is just head-mouth zen because it comes not from real cultivation but from jealousy and obstructions and an obsession to be number one. If you are like that, you certainly can't be a Patriarch.

The Fifth Patriarch gave the Dharma to Hui Neng because Hui Neng always practiced the Bodhisattva Way. He pounded rice for everyone to eat and so helped them in their cultivation. That same Bodhisattva conduct is practiced here in the kitchen of this temple by the cooks. They make extremely fine food! However, when I eat I don't notice whether it is good or not because I don't have time to investigate eating-dharmas. Today, at lunch, didn't I say that one who tastes his food and thinks it's good or bad has no spiritual skill?

Bodhisattvas help others at every level, not obstructing them, but, like the superior man, mentioning their good points instead. For instance, when I announced that several people were going to leave home and asked if anyone objected, no one did. You said, "I commend those who want to leave home." Your not objecting is practicing the Bodhisattva Way.

Late at night, the Sixth Patriarch easily obtained the Patriarchate. The Fifth Patriarch approved, but he didn't consult anyone because he knew they would have protested.

"Go out into the world," said the Fifth Patriarch. "Protect the robe and bowl, for they have been handed down from Shakyamuni Buddha from generation to generation. Take everyone across and spread the Dharma into the future. Do not let it be cut off!"

The Fifth Patriarch, sad and worried, was on the verge of tears. How do I know he wanted to cry? The Second Patriarch, at his execution, had wept as he said, "During the time of the Fourth Patriarch, *The Lankavatara Sutra* will become a mere name and appearance. No one will understand it." Now, in the same way, the Fifth Patriarch's heart welled up within him as he said, "Don't allow the Dharma to be cut off. Be careful. Pay attention, Don't be muddled or take your job lightly. It is extremely important that the Dharma not be cut off."

Sutra:

Listen to my verse:

> ***With feeling comes the planting of the seed.***
> ***Because of the ground, the fruit is born again.***
> ***Without feeling there is no seed at all.***
> ***Without that nature there is no birth either.***

Commentary:

"With feeling comes the planting of the seed." I have a feeling of loving kindness and so I have come to plant a seed. "Feeling" can mean compassion. I have a compassionate feeling and so I have come to plant the seed, to transmit the Buddhadharma to you.

"Because of the ground, the fruit is born again." This transmission is like putting a seed into the ground so that the plant can grow and bear fruit.

"Without feeling there is no seed at all." Without feeling, no seed is planted. If no one transmits the Buddhadharma to you, then there is no Bodhi-seed.

"Without the nature there is no birth either." Where there is no nature, there is no birth. That is one way to explain this verse. There is another way:

"With feeling comes the planting of the seed." The feeling is an emotional feeling of love. The seed is planted because of this feeling of love and people study the Dharma because of it. If they are not relatives, they are friends. Relatives have relative's emotional feelings and friends have friend's emotional feelings.

Because you have these emotional feelings you come to study the Dharma; you come to plant the seed.

"Because of the ground the fruit is born again." Emotional feeling plants the seed of Bodhi because of the ground which is the place where one can reap the fruit. On this piece of ground, you can grow the Bodhi-fruit.

"Without feeling there is no seed at all." If there is no feeling or emotion, there is no seed. That is, if no one came to this Bodhimanda to study the Dharma, there would be no feeling and no seed planted.

"Without that nature, there is no birth either." You cannot realize Buddhahood without the Buddha nature. Now, the Buddha nature is here and you should realize Buddhahood.

The verse may be explained in many ways, so long as the explanation is in accord with principle.

Sutra:

The Patriarch further said, "In the past, when the First Patriarch Great Master Bodhidharma first came to this land and people did not believe in him yet, he transmitted this robe as a symbol of faith to be handed down from generation to generation. The Dharma is transmitted from mind to mind, leading everyone to self-awakening and self-enlightenment.

"From ancient times, Buddha only transmits the original substance to Buddha; master secretly transmits the original mind to master. Since the robe is a source of contention, it should stop with you. Do not transmit it, for if you do, your life will hang by a thread."

Commentary:

Didn't I say before that Chinese people have no respect for Indian people? When Bodhidharma arrived in China everyone said, "He's a hick." No one knew who he was. Even after five years in China, he was not recognized as the Patriarch.

True patriarchs accept the robe and bowl as certification of their rightly inherited position, while impostors may try to steal the robe and take the Dharma by force. Shen Hsiu thought a forced inheritance would be real; but it could only be false.

During the time of the Fourth Patriarch, three attempts were made to steal the robe and bowl, and another three attempts were made during the time of the Fifth Patriarch. But the thieves always failed because the Bodhisattvas came to the Patriarchs' aid.

When the Sixth Patriarch was guarding the robe, six attempts were made. Later the robe and bowl were taken by Empress Wu Tse T'ien. It is not certain who it was entrusted to afterward.

The Fifth Patriarch cautioned Hui Neng: "If you suspend a hundred-pound rock from a thread, it is certain to snap; so with your life if you continue to transmit the robe."

Sutra:

"You must go quickly for I fear that people might harm you."

Hui Neng asked, "Where shall I go?"

The Patriarch replied, "Stop at Huai and hide at Hui."

Hui Neng received the robe and bowl in the third watch. He said, "Hui Neng is a Southerner and does not know these mountain roads. How does one reach the mouth of the river?"

The Fifth Patriarch said, "You need not worry. I will accompany you."

The Fifth Patriarch escorted him to the Chiu Chiang courier station and ordered him to board a boat. The Fifth Patriarch took up the oars and rowed. Hui Neng said, "Please, High Master, sit down. It is fitting that your disciple take the oars."

The Patriarch replied, "It is fitting that I take you across."

Hui Neng said, "When someone is deluded, his master takes him across, but when he is enlightened, he takes himself across. Although the term 'taking across' is the same in each case, the function is not the same."

Commentary:

The Fifth Patriarch instructed the Sixth Patriarch to leave quickly, for he knew that Shen Hsiu's followers would certainly want to kill him when they realized he had inherited the patriarchate. "Do not stay here," the Fifth Patriarch said. "Stop at Huai and hide at Hui." Huai is a district in Kuang Hsi, Wu Chou, and Hui is Szu Hui, now called Hsin Hui.

High Master is a respectful form of address used for a teacher or an Abbot, so the Sixth Patriarch used it to address the Fifth Patriarch "High Master, it is only proper that your disciple take the oars."

"Hey!" said the Fifth Patriarch, "Let me take you across the river." The Master and disciple exchanged courtesies, but although they each used the same term "taking across," it meant something different in each case. For the teacher to take the disciple across is not the same thing as for the disciple to take the teacher across. Hui Neng understood. "When the student is confused," he said, "the teacher must save him. But when the student becomes enlightened, he must save himself."

Before becoming enlightened and obtaining the original substance of the self-nature, the disciple is confused and lost. His teacher advises him to work hard: "Do not be afraid of the pain in your legs when you sit in meditation. If you are afraid of suffering you cannot become enlightened." The Sixth Patriarch, when he hung a stone around his waist so he could pound the rice harder, was not afraid of suffering. The rock which the Layman Lu, the Sixth Patriarch, used to tie around his waist when he pounded rice is still on P'ing Mao Mountain at Tung Shan Ch'an Monastery and carved on the rock is the inscription: "The rock Hui Neng, the former Layman Lu, tied around his waist."

Sutra:

"Hui Neng was born in the frontier regions and his pronunciation is incorrect, yet he has received the Dharma transmission from the Master. Now that enlightenment has been attained, it is only fitting that he take his own nature across."

The Patriarch replied, "So it is, so it is. Hereafter because of you, the Buddhadharma will be widely practiced. Three years after your departure I will leave this world. Start on your journey now and go south as fast as possible. Do not speak too soon, for the Buddhadharma arises from difficulty."

Commentary:

Because he was from the south, the Sixth Patriarch spoke Cantonese rather than Mandarin, so few people understood him.

Nevertheless, he inherited the mind seal of the wonderful Dharma.

Master Hui Neng was truly enlightened, unlike some people who are not enlightened but cheat and say that they are, who have not testified to the fruit of enlightenment but lie and say that they have.

The Fifth Patriarch thought, "This disciple knows my heart." He said to Hui Neng, "Yes, it is just that way."

One should take one's own nature across. Remember that. For example, someone must teach you to recite the Shurangama Mantra, but once you know how, you must recite it on your own. People should not have to say, "It is time for you to recite the Shurangama Mantra." Again, someone must teach you to recite Sutras, but then you must do it yourself. That is what is meant by "taking one's own nature across."

A teacher shows you how to remove afflictions. He says that anger is harmful, and that one should transform one's nasty temper into Bodhi. Once taught, the nature cannot be taken across unless the method is applied. The Master says, "Don't get upset. When faced with a crisis, proceed as if nothing has happened. All things are like flowers in the sky or the moon's reflection in water–unreal, illusory, like a dream or a dewdrop. Remember that and there will be no affliction." If, when faced with a situation, or a state of mind, you see through it and put it down, you have taken your nature across.

Smoking can be a problem. The teacher says, "Stop smoking! Smoking hinders cultivation." When I said that to one disciple he said, "Stop smoking? I'll give it a try," and he stopped. He took his nature across.

Another disciple is fond of drinking. Having studied the Buddhadharma, he ought to have quit drinking, but he says, "I'm confused. I'm not enlightened." If you stop you become enlightened; if you don't, you sink into confusion. Whether or not you become enlightened is entirely up to you.

Cutting off all unwholesome activities is to become enlightened and to take your nature across. Not understanding, you may think, "The Dharma Master says that drugs are bad, so I'll take some more. I'll take a double dose. No, I'll take five times as much! I'll keep getting high until I am enlightened." Continue to take drugs and you will poison yourself and die instead. Confused by drugs, you cannot take your nature across.

Before studying the Buddhadharma, you should not do confused and wicked things. After you have studied the Buddhadharma, the prohibition is even stronger. If you continue to misbehave, you commit the crime of "knowing and intentionally violating the Dharma," and you are certain to fall into the hells. There is nothing polite about these matters. If you do confused and wicked things, you will fall into the hells. If I do them, I will fall into the hells. If someone else does them, he will fall into the hells. No one can avoid this.

In a hundred thousand ages,
The karma made is not destroyed;
When the causes and conditions rebound,
You undergo the retribution by yourself.

No one can suffer for you in the hells. Karma refers to acts of killing, stealing, sexual misconduct, lying, and drinking, all of which bear retribution in the future. Your karma does not get lost, and it is you, and you alone, who must suffer the consequences. However,

If you end your confusion
and get rid of the dirt,

You can easily take
your own nature across.

The dirt in your nature is your upside-down actions, your false thinking, your ignorance, your outflows[26], and your bad habits. Eliminate these and you have taken your nature across.

When I lectured this Sutra in another place, I said, "If you create offense-karma, you will go to the hells; if someone else creates offense-karma, he will go to the hells, if I create offense karma, I will go to the hells." One person who was there objected:

"Dharma Master," he said "I have never seen these hells. Where are they? I would like to take a look at them because I simply don't believe they exist."

I said, "It is easy enough to fall into the hells, and if you try to fall into them you will fall even more quickly and not escape for a very long time." I hope that those who wish to try out the hells will reconsider.

What kind of person can take his own nature across? A person with wisdom. Deluded people, on the other hand, cannot take their nature across, and what is more, even if a teacher tries to help them, they refuse to listen. It is like trying to teach a dog. You say, "Don't bite people," and, the first chance it gets, the dog bites someone. So you hit it and it still bites people. Why? Because it has a stupid nature. Cats are just the same. You can tell a cat, "Do not kill mice, do not take life, but nevertheless the cat kills the first mouse it sees. You may try to teach a mouse not to steal, but still it sneaks off and steals.

26. Refer to the discharge of energy through the six sense organs; hence, defilement, affliction; that which obstruct cultivation.

Smoking and drinking are done by those who do not know any better. People with true and proper understanding do not do mixed-up things. People with mixed up understanding do not do true and proper things. You must correct your own faults. Your teacher shouldn't have to watch your every move and follow you around to make sure that you behave. You must take your own nature across.

This is a general explanation, for if I were to speak in detail, I would not finish until the exhaustion of the boundaries of the future.

"I have transmitted my Dharma, and in three years I will complete the stillness and go to Nirvana," said the Fifth Patriarch. "Go well, and whatever you do, don't be lazy. Go well, don't go bad. Don't go the wrong way. Don't take drugs and ruin your body, for your body is your means of cultivation. If you ruin your body, how will you be able to cultivate? Go well, go well, do your best. Quickly head south." That is certainly the kind of advice the Fifth Patriarch gave.

"But don't speak of the Dharma too soon. Hide your light and store up your potential, as troops are fed well so that they may conquer every enemy and capture every city. The Buddhadharma is hard to bring forth. It arises from difficulty."

Sutra:

After Hui Neng took leave of the Patriarch, he set out on foot for the South. In two months he reached the Ta Yü Mountains.

The Fifth Patriarch returned to the monastery but for several days he did not enter the hall. The assembly was concerned and went to ask: "Has the Master some slight illness or problem?"

"There is no illness," came the reply, "but the robe and Dharma have already gone south."

"Who received the transmission?" they asked.

"The Able One obtained it," said the Patriarch.

The assembly then understood, and soon several hundred people took up pursuit, all hoping to steal the robe and bowl.

Commentary:

The Sixth Patriarch left the Fifth Patriarch, no longer attending upon the High Master or making offerings to him. He walked south from P'ing Mao Mountain and in a little over two months, he finally reached the Ta Yü mountain range which forms the border between Nan Hsiung and Kuang Tung.

The Fifth Patriarch returned to his room. For many days he did not go into the hall to speak Dharma or take his meals. The assembly was curious. "High Master," they said, "you're not ill, are you?"

"You may all disperse," said the Fifth Patriarch, "because I no longer have the Buddhadharma. The robe and Dharma have gone south. I intend to rest now, I am going to retire."

"Who received the transmission?" they asked.

"The Able One," said the Patriarch. "He who was able obtained it. Whoever the able one is, he got it."

When this announcement was made there were those in the assembly who had keen intelligence, one of them being Dharma Master Fa Ju. He was one of the ten people to whom the Fifth Patriarch gave instructions before he entered Nirvana, telling them, "Each of you go to a different direction and be a Dharma Host." But now, when Fa Ju heard the Fifth Patriarch say that the Able One had obtained the transmission, he cried out, "No! That must mean the southern barbarian has got the Dharma! How strange." The "Able One" refers to Hui Neng: "Able" (*neng*) was his name.

Word spread, and soon everyone knew. They all objected violently. "No! No!" they shouted, "How can it be? Let's go take it from him right now." Several hundred powerful people ran after Hui Neng. Consider the situation: the Fifth Patriarch had transmitted the Dharma to a barbarian, and the entire assembly was resentful. "How could you give it to him?" they said. "We have been following you for so many years. Why didn't you give it to us?" They thought to themselves, "The Patriarch's brain must be addled. How else could he give the Dharma to such a hick? How can he become the Sixth Patriarch? We should get back the robe and bowl–by force!"

Sutra:

One Bhikshu, Hui Ming, a coarse-natured man whose lay name had been Ch'en, had formerly been a fourth class military official. He was intent in his search and ahead of the others. When he had almost caught up with Hui Neng the latter tossed the robe and bowl onto a rock, saying, "This robe and bowl are tokens of faith. How can they be taken by force?" Hui Neng then hid in a thicket.

When Hui Ming arrived, he tried to pick them up, but found he could not move them. He cried out, "Cultivator, Cultivator, I have come for the Dharma, not for the robe!"

Hui Neng then came out and sat cross-legged on a rock. Hui Ming made obeisance and said, "I hope that the Cultivator will teach the Dharma for my sake."

Hui Neng said, "Since you have come for the Dharma, you may put aside all conditions. Do not give rise to a single thought and I will teach it to you clearly." After a

time, Hui Neng said, "With no thoughts of good and with no thoughts of evil, at just this moment, what is Superior One Hui Ming's original face?" At these words, Hui Ming was greatly enlightened.

Commentary:

Bhikshu Hui Ming was coarse and uneducated. He never opened his mouth unless it was to scold someone, and if they refused to listen, he beat them. He could smash a rock of several hundred pounds with one blow. With this extraordinary strength he became a fourth class army officer.

Hui Ming had one peculiar trait. His feet were covered with feathers which enabled him to run fast. He could travel sixty miles a day, compared to the ordinary man's thirty. His feathered feet and great strength carried him far ahead of the others. As he flew along, his mind raced, "I'll get the robe and bowl and then it will be mine! It belongs to the strongest man."

When Hui Neng saw this big crude feather-footed pursuer, he was a bit frightened. Although he had obtained the Dharma, he had just begun to cultivate and did not yet have great spiritual power. He shouted into empty space: "This robe and bowl are symbols of the faith. How can you take them by force? How can there be any dispute?"

What do you think?

Hui Ming had actually intended to grab the robe and bowl and run. But he could not move them. Why do you suppose he couldn't move them? After all he was so strong he could have smashed the bowl to smithereens with a single blow and have ripped the robe to shreds. Yet for all his strength and as light as the robe was, he couldn't budge it. This indicates that there were Dharma protectors–gods, dragons, and others of the eight divisions present guarding the robe and bowl. Since he couldn't grab them, he thought, "That's strange. I can't use force here. Ah! I'll ask for the Dharma instead." Had he truly been seeking the Way he wouldn't have first tried to grab the robe and bowl but would immediately have said, "Cultivator, Cultivator, I come for the Dharma, not for the robe and bowl." Don't you think my opinion about this is logically sound?

Hui Neng emerged and sat in lotus position on a rock. Hui Ming bowed to the Sixth Patriarch. He understood now that the Dharma of the Buddhas and Bodhisattvas cannot be taken by force. "You say you've come for the Dharma." said Hui Neng. "Really? Did you really come for the Dharma and not to steal the robe and bowl? Fine. Put aside all conditions. Put your mind to rest. Stop grasping at conditions and then I will explain the Dharma clearly for you."

For seven or eight minutes the Great Master sat waiting. Neither he nor Hui Ming gave rise to a single thought. Everything stopped. Not even the ghosts and spirits knew what was happening. Everything was empty.

Hui Ming was not giving rise to thought. He was not thinking north, south, east, or west. So Hui Neng said, "With no thoughts of good and no thoughts of evil, at just that moment, what is Superior Ming's original face?" Since the Sixth Patriarch was at that time still a layman he respectfully addressed Hui Ming as "Superior One."

The word "what" means "who". In the Dhyana School we meditate on the question, "Who is reciting the Buddha's name?" When Hui Ming heard the word "what" he became enlightened. "Oh!" he said, "originally it's just this way!"

Hearing these words, have you become enlightened?

Sutra:

Hui Ming asked further, "Apart from the secret speech and secret meanings just spoken, is there yet another secret meaning?"

Hui Neng said, "What has been spoken to you is not secret. If you turn the illumination inward, the secret is with you."

Hui Ming said, "Although Hui Ming was at Huang Mei he had not yet awakened to his original face. Now that he has been favored with this instruction he is like one who drinks water and knows for himself whether it is cold or warm. The cultivator is now Hui Ming's master."

"If you feel that way," said Hui Neng, "then you and I have the same master, Huang Mei[27]. Protect yourself well."

Hui Ming asked further, "Where should I go now?"

Hui Neng said, "Stop at Yüan and dwell at Meng."

Commentary:

All of the Sixth Patriarch's pursuers were greedy, but Hui Ming was the worst. He had just seen his original face, he had just become enlightened, but he wasn't satisfied. He wanted to know if he had missed anything. "Are there any more secrets?" he asked. "Is there something even more wonderful?"

"What I have said is not the most miraculous and wonderful thing," said the Sixth Patriarch, "What is most important is that you turn the light back around and illuminate inward so that you

27. i.e., The Fifth Patriarch. The Masters are often referred to honorifically by the place where they lived and taught.

may see the wonderful secret which is within you. It is all within you; it is not here with me."

"Great Master," said Hui Ming, "I wish to take you as my teacher."

"If that is how you feel," said the Sixth Patriarch, "we have the same teacher, Huang Mei. We both have the Fifth Patriarch's Dharma transmission and are Dharma brothers. That is fine! Now, take good care of the Dharma and don't allow it to become extinct."

It was not until three years after this encounter with the Patriarch that Hui Ming went to Meng Mountain in Yüan District. There he met a ghost who, in his last life, had been a top-ranking scholar under the imperial examination system. The ghost composed a poem and sang it to Hui Ming:

Still, still, barren waste–a dream.
Then, now, triumph, loss lazy thought measures.
Wild grass, idle flowers picked, how many?
Bitter rain, sour wind, how many broken hearts?

At night, with firefly light I come and go.
At dawn, the cock crows; I hide away my form.
Regret from the first not tilling the mind ground:
Two streams are caused to fall–green mountain tears.

Seeing the ghost's plight, Hui Ming explained the Dharma to the ghost and took him across. Ever since then there has been the "ceremony of Meng Mountain" which is performed to take ghosts across and liberate them.

Sutra:

Hui Ming bowed and left. Reaching the foot of the mountain, he said to the pursuers. "Up above there is only a rocky, trackless height. We must find another path." The pursuers all agreed. Afterwards, Hui Ming changed his name to Tao Ming to avoid using Hui Neng's first name.

Commentary:

After receiving instruction from the Sixth Patriarch, feather-footed Hui Ming went down the mountain and told the pursuers that he had not seen the Sixth Patriarch.

Hui Ming usually told the truth, and so everyone believed him now, even though he was lying. Actually this was not a lie, but an expedient device used to protect the Sixth Patriarch from those who, unlike Hui Ming, had not received the Dharma and therefore still wished to kill the Sixth Patriarch.

Hui Ming dared not presume to be his Master's equal. He changed his name from Hui Ming to Tao Ming to avoid using the Patriarch's first name.

Sutra:

Hui Neng arrived at Ts'ao Hsi where he was again pursued by men with evil intentions. To avoid difficulty, he went to Szu Hui and lived among hunters for fifteen years, at times teaching Dharma to them in an appropriate manner.

The hunters often told him to watch their nets, but whenever he saw beings who were still living he released them. At mealtime he cooked vegetables in the pot

alongside the meat. When he was questioned about it, he would answer "I only eat vegetables alongside the meat."

Commentary:

Shen Hsiu still wanted to kill the Sixth Patriarch and steal the Patriarchate. Hui Neng escaped to Szu Hui, the present Hsin Hui, where he lived with a band of hunters for fifteen years. Who would have suspected that a Buddhist would choose to live with hunters? No one. Shen Hsiu's party searched far and wide, but they never found him.

Some say the Great Master lived with the hunters for sixteen years, but their calculation includes the time he spent coming and going. He actually lived with them for only fifteen years.

For lunch, the Great Master gathered wild vegetables on the mountain and cooked them in the pot beside the meat. If someone asked him, "Why are you doing that?" he said, "I only eat the vegetables. I don't eat meat."

Sutra:

One day Hui Neng thought, "The time has come to spread the Dharma. I cannot stay in hiding forever." Accordingly, he went to Fa Hsing Monastery in Kuang Chou where Dharma Master Yin Tsung was giving lectures on *The Nirvana Sutra.*

At that time there were two bhikshus who were discussing the topic of the wind and a flag. One said, "The wind is moving." The other said, "The flag is moving." They argued incessantly. Hui Neng stepped forward and said, "The wind is not moving, nor is the flag. Your minds, Kind Sirs, are moving." Everyone was startled.

Dharma Master Yin Tsung invited him to take a seat of honor and sought to ask him about the hidden meaning. Seeing that Hui Neng's exposition of the true principles was concise and to the point and not based on written words, Yin Tsung said, "The cultivator is certainly no ordinary man. I heard long ago that Huang Mei's robe and bowl had come south. Cultivator, is it not you?"

Hui Neng said, "I dare not presume such a thing."

Yin Tsung then made obeisance and requested that the transmitted robe and bowl be brought forth and shown to the assembly.

Commentary:

The Great Master went to Kuang Chou, to Fa Hsing Monastery, now called Kuang Hsiao Monastery, where Dharma Master Yin Tsung was lecturing on *The Mahaparinirvana Sutra*, which the Buddha spoke just before entering Nirvana. At the monastery the Master met the two monks arguing over the topic of the wind and a flag. One said the wind moved, the other said the flag moved, and he told them, "You are both wrong. Neither the wind nor the flag is moving. Your minds are moving. If your minds were not moving, then neither the wind nor the flag would move."

Everyone was astonished to hear this layman speak in such a wonderful and mysterious way. Yin Tsung asked him, "Aren't you the holder of Huang Mei's robe and bowl?"

"I am unworthy of such a title," the Master said modestly.

Yin Tsung knew, however, that the Great Master was only being polite. Yin Tsung recognized Layman Lu as the Sixth Patriarch.

Sutra:

He further asked, "How was Huang Mei's doctrine transmitted?"

"There was no transmission," replied Hui Neng. "We merely discussed seeing the nature. There was no discussion of Dhyana samadhi or liberation."

Yin Tsung asked, "Why was there no discussion of Dhyana samadhi or liberation?"

Hui Neng said, "These are dualistic dharmas. They are not the Buddhadharma. The Buddhadharma is a Dharma of non-dualism."

Yin Tsung asked further, "What is this Buddhadharma which is the Dharma of non-dualism?"

Hui Neng said, "The Dharma Master has been lecturing *The Nirvana Sutra* which says that to understand the Buddha-nature is the Buddhadharma which is the Dharma of non-dualism. As Kao Kuei Te Wang Bodhisattva said to the Buddha, 'Does violating the four serious prohibitions, committing the five rebellious acts, or being an icchantika and the like cut off the good roots and the Buddha-nature?'

"The Buddha replied, 'There are two kinds of good roots: the first, permanent; the second impermanent. The Buddha-nature is neither permanent nor impermanent. Therefore it is not cut off.'

"That is what is meant by non-dualistic. The first is good and the second is not good. The Buddha-nature is neither good nor bad. That is what is meant by non-dualistic. Common people think of the heaps[28] and realms[29] as dualistic. The wise man comprehends that they are non-dualistic in nature. The non-dualistic nature is the Buddha-nature."

Hearing this explanation, Yin Tsung was delighted. He joined his palms and said, "My explanation of Sutras is like broken tile, whereas your discussion of the meaning, Kind Sir, is like pure gold."

He then shaved Hui Neng's head[30] and asked Hui Neng to be his master. Accordingly, under that Bodhi tree, Hui Neng explained the Tung Shan Dharma-door.

Commentary:

The four serious prohibitions are killing, stealing, lying, and sexual misconduct. The five rebellious acts are matricide, patricide, killing an Arhat, shedding the blood of a Buddha, and breaking up the harmony of the Sangha. What happens to the good roots and the Buddha-nature of one who commits such offenses?

Icchantika is a Sanskrit word which may be explained as meaning "of incomplete faith." Are the good roots and the Buddha-nature of icchantikas cut off?

Kao Kuei Te Wang Bodhisattva asked the Buddha these questions because he mistook good roots for the Buddha-nature itself. In his answer, the Buddha makes it clear that good roots are not the Buddha-nature.

---

28. What appears to be the "self" or "personality" may be broken down into five impersonal components called heaps: a)form, b)feelings, c)perceptions, d)impulses, e)consciousness.

29. There are eighteen realms of sense, i.e. the six sense organs (eye, ear, nose, tongue, body, and mind), the six objects of the sense organs (forms, sounds, smells, tastes, touchables, and mind objects [dharmas]) plus the six consciousnesses which arise between the organs and the objects (eye-consciousness, ear-consciousness, etc.)

30. thus accepting him into the Sangha.

Because the Great Master obtained the Dharma from the Fifth Patriarch at Tung Shan, "East Mountain," it is called the Tung Shan Dharma-door.

Sutra:

"Hui Neng obtained the Dharma at Tung Shan and has undergone much suffering, his life hanging as if by a thread.

"Today, in this gathering of the magistrate and officials, of Bhikshus, Bhikshunis, Taoists, and laymen, there is not one of you who is not here because of accumulated ages of karmic conditions. Because in past lives you have made offerings to the Buddhas and planted good roots in common, you now have the opportunity to hear the Sudden Teaching, which is a cause of obtaining the Dharma.

"This teaching has been handed down by former sages; it is not Hui Neng's own wisdom. You who wish to hear the teaching of the former sages should first purify your minds. After hearing it, cast aside your doubts, and that way you will be no different from the sages of the past."

Commentary:

Thus, the Sixth Patriarch concludes the narrative of his life. We in America who are so fortunate to hear this Sutra explained have also for ages established common karmic conditions by making offerings to the Buddhas.

"The Dharma is transmitted from former sages, Buddhas, and Bodhisattvas. It is not my own wisdom," said Hui Neng. "If you listen to me carefully, it will be just as if you were listening to the Buddhas and Bodhisattvas speaking."

Sutra:

Hearing this Dharma, the entire assembly was delighted, made obeisance, and withdrew.

CHAPTER II

PRAJNA

Sutra:

The following day, at the invitation of Magistrate Wei, the Master took his seat and said to the great assembly, "All of you purify your minds and think about Maha Prajna Paramita."

Commentary:

This second chapter of the Sutra is an explanation of Prajna, given by the Master upon the request of Magistrate Wei.

Prajna is a Sanskrit word which means "wisdom." There are three kinds of Prajna: literary Prajna, contemplative Prajna, and real mark Prajna.

Because the word Prajna encompasses these three meanings, it has a fuller connotation than the word "wisdom." Therefore the Chinese translators of Sutras did not translate it, but instead transliterated it.[31]

The Sixth Patriarch took his seat and said, "All of you should quit daydreaming. Listen to the Dharma with a pure mind and a united heart. Be mindful of Maha Prajna Paramita."

---

31. There are five kinds of terms which the Great Master Hsüan Tsang of the T'ang Dynasty transliterated: a) the esoteric terms; b) terms with many meanings; c) terms for things which did not exist in China; d) the honorific terms, e) terms which should be used following the example of the Ancients.

Maha Prajna Paramita is called "great wisdom." Maha means great; Prajna means wisdom; Paramita means arrived at the other shore.

Sutra:

He then said, "Good Knowing Advisors, the wisdom of Bodhi and Prajna is originally possessed by worldly people themselves. It is only because their minds are confused that they are unable to enlighten themselves and must rely on a great Good Knowing Advisor who can lead them to see their Buddha-nature. You should know that the Buddha-nature of stupid and wise people is basically not different. It is only because confusion and enlightenment are different that some are stupid and some are wise. I will now explain for you the Maha Prajna Paramita Dharma in order that each of you may become wise. Pay careful attention, and I will explain it to you.

"Good Knowing Advisors, worldly people recite 'Prajna' with their mouths all day long and yet do not recognize the Prajna of their self-nature. Just as talking about food will not make you full, so, too, if you only speak of emptiness you will not see your own nature in ten thousand ages. In the end you will not have obtained any benefit.

"Good Knowing Advisors, Maha Prajna Paramita is a Sanskrit word which means 'great wisdom which has arrived at the other shore.' It must be practiced in the mind, and not just recited in words. When the mouth recites and the mind does not practice, it is like an illusion, a transformation, dew drops, or lightning. However, when the mouth recites and the mind practices,

then mind and mouth are in mutual accord. One's own original nature is Buddha; apart from the nature there is no other Buddha."

Commentary:

The Master said, "Worldly people recite 'Prajna, Prajna, Prajna,' but they do not know the Prajna of their own original nature, or their own inherent wisdom. You may recite recipes from a cookbook from morning to night saying, 'This is delicious!' but you will never fill your stomach that way. Saying 'Prajna is empty' is not to do anything about it. In the end it is of no benefit. It is nothing more than 'head-mouth zen' and will not help you to see your own inherent Prajna."

Instead, see everything as empty and put it aside: see it, smash it, and put it down. Empty everything. Then you need not recite it all day long with your mouth. If your mouth recites but your mind does not practice, your recitation is a worthless illusion. If you see the Prajna wisdom of your own nature, you will not become entangled in stupid affairs. You will not be ignorant. If you remain ignorant, your mind is not practicing.

If you use your mind as well as your mouth in cultivating Prajna, you will see that your own fundamental nature is itself the Buddha.

Everyone can realize Buddhahood. You need only cultivate. What should you cultivate? Your nature. Do not seek outside yourself, but turn the light inward; reverse the illumination and look within.

Sutra:

"What is meant by Maha? Maha means 'great.' The capacity of the mind is vast and great like empty space,

and has no boundaries. It is not square or round, great or small. Neither is it blue, yellow, red or white. It is not above or below, or long or short. It is without anger, without joy, without right, without wrong, without good, without evil, and it has no head or tail.

"All Buddha-lands are ultimately the same as empty space. The wonderful nature of worldly people is originally empty, and there is not a single dharma which can be obtained. The true emptiness of the self-nature is also like this.

"Good Knowing Advisors, do not listen to my explanation of emptiness and then become attached to emptiness. The most important thing is to avoid becoming attached to emptiness. If you sit still with an empty mind you will become attached to undifferentiated emptiness."

Commentary:

Because the mind first thought of going there, we now send rockets to the moon. The mind has no limits or boundaries. You can't say that it is big or small, for there is nothing bigger and nothing smaller.

The self-nature is the Middle Way. Your true mind is neither right nor wrong, true or false. In your true mind there are no thoughts of good or evil. Therefore the Sixth Patriarch asked Hui Ming, the ex-soldier who had come to steal the robe and bowl, "With no thoughts of good and with no thoughts of evil, at just this moment, what is the Superior One Hui Ming's original face?" He posed this question to reveal that there is neither good nor evil in the true mind. As they say in philosophy, "It has no head or tail!"

There is not even one single dharma. It is empty.

The self-nature is like empty space;
It contains within itself both truth and falsehood.
Enlighten yourself to the original substance;
In one penetration, penetrate all.

"When you hear me say that Prajna is empty, do not become attached to undifferentiated emptiness. If you do you will sit as if dead," continued the Sixth Patriarch.

We should cultivate true emptiness, which is wonderful existence, not vacuity. In true emptiness everything is known and everything is not known.

Understanding, complete and clear,
Like water reflecting the moon.
The mind in samadhi, like the sky,
For ten thousand miles, not a cloud.

Sutra:

"Good Knowing Advisors, the emptiness of the universe is able to contain the forms and shapes of the ten thousand things: the sun, moon, and stars; the mountains, rivers, and the great earth; the fountains, springs, streams, torrents, grasses, trees, thickets, and forests; good and bad people, good and bad dharmas, the heavens and the hells, all the great seas, Sumeru[32] and all mountains–all are contained within emptiness. The emptiness of the nature of worldly men is also like this.

"Good Knowing Advisors, the ability of one's own nature to contain the ten thousand dharmas is what is

32. The central mountain of every world system. Translated into Chinese as 妙高–miao kao, "wonderfully high."

meant by 'great.' The myriad dharmas are within the nature of all people. If you regard all people, the bad as well as the good, without grasping or rejecting, without producing a defiling attachment, your mind will be like empty space. Therefore it is said to be 'great,' 'Maha.'"

Commentary:

Empty space not only holds all good things, it includes all bad people as well. Empty space would never say, "You bad person! Get out of my empty space! Good people, come on in!"

In the same way, you should see good and bad people without being attached to the good or repulsed by the bad. As I have told you before, bad people have something in them which is extremely good. You should hope that they reform. I have many disciples who do not obey me. I tell them to go south and all day long they run north; I tell them to go east and they go west. Although they disobey, I wait patiently because I know the time will come when they will change.

All good and all bad are included within the self-nature; you should neither grasp it nor cast it aside. Grasping and rejecting are defiling attachments.

Sutra:

"Good Knowing Advisors, the mouth of the confused person speaks, but the mind of the wise person practices. There are deluded men who sit still with empty minds, vainly thinking of nothing and declaring that to be something great. One should not speak with these people because of their deviant views.

"Good Knowing Advisors, the capacity of the mind is vast and great, encompassing the Dharma realm. Its

function is to understand clearly and distinctly. Its correct function is to know all. All is one; one is all. Coming and going freely, the mind's substance is unobstructed. That is Prajna."

Commentary:

The deluded person does not do what must be done. He merely talks. A wise person, on the other hand, always puts principle into practice, not with head-mouth zen, but with constant cultivation.

The Great Master said, "You are all very wise. The vast mind pervades the all-inclusive Dharma realm. It is like a mirror; when things come, it reflects them; when things go, it is empty. The true mind knows everything when it is used. To have Prajna is to have complete understanding and be free of all stupidity."

Sutra:

"Good Knowing Advisors, all Prajna wisdom is produced from one's own nature; it does not enter from the outside. Using the intellect correctly is called the natural function of one's true nature. One truth is all truth. The mind has the capacity for great things, and is not meant for practicing petty ways. Do not talk about emptiness with your mouth all day and in your mind fail to cultivate the conduct that you talk of. That would be like a common person calling himself the king of a country, which cannot be. People like that are not my disciples."

Commentary:

Do not seek Prajna outside your self-nature. Do not make the mistake of using the intellect, the discriminating mind. The self-nature is not meant for small things.

The Great Master said, "Do not say, 'Empty, empty, empty, Prajna, Prajna, Prajna...' People who do that are not my disciples." Why? Because they don't listen. I tell them not to get attached to emptiness, and they get attached to emptiness. I tell them not to get attached to existence and they get attached to existence. I tell them not to have sexual desire, and they still do not cut it off. "Oh, no problem," they say, "Slowly, slowly."

Sutra:

"Good Knowing Advisors, what is meant by 'Prajna?' Prajna in our language means wisdom. Everywhere and at all times, in thought after thought, remain undeluded and practice wisdom constantly; that is Prajna conduct. Prajna is cut off by a single deluded thought. By one wise thought, Prajna is produced. Worldly men, deluded and confused, do not see Prajna. They speak of it with their mouths, but their minds are always deluded. They constantly say of themselves, 'I cultivate Prajna!' and though they continually speak of emptiness, they are unaware of true emptiness. Prajna, without form or mark, is just the wisdom mind. If thus explained, just this is Prajna wisdom."

Commentary:

If you have Prajna, then in thought after thought you clearly understand; in thought after thought you are not confused; in thought after thought you have no ignorance.

"Prajna is cut off by a single deluded thought." To speak of it as "cut off" is merely an analogy. Actually it is not cut off. How could proper wisdom, which is without production or destruction, be cut off? "Cutting off" merely describes the moment of delusion, because at that moment Prajna is not apparent.

"By one wise thought Prajna is produced." When you are not deluded or confused, Prajna is produced. I will give you an example of how confusion cuts off Prajna: When people say that drinking is harmful, smoking is not good, and taking confusing drugs is bad, and you do not believe it, you cut off Prajna. If you change, you give rise to Prajna and true intelligence. When someone tries to teach you, but you refuse to understand or believe, that is delusion. In short, delusion is to know clearly that something is wrong, but to go ahead and do it anyway. Such delusion cuts off Prajna. The great majority of people in this world are deeply deluded, for they do not see Prajna and they do not know how to cultivate it.

Their mouths speak about wisdom, but their actions betray their stupidity. They talk about Prajna saying, "Emptiness is Prajna. There are twenty kinds of emptiness related to Prajna. You should empty everything." But they do not know true emptiness. Perhaps they understand a little of the Sutras, or recite a few lines of a mantra, but even though they speak they do not change their own faults and therefore do not recognize true emptiness.

You must give up ignorance, bad habits, faults, and obstructions, if you are to understand true emptiness.

"Prajna, without form or mark, is the wisdom mind." Wisdom has no form or characteristic. Didn't the Sixth Patriarch just say that Prajna is neither long nor short, neither square nor round, neither big nor small? Nor is it green, yellow, red, white or black. What is it, then? It is the wise mind, free from ignorance, which knows right dharmas from wrong dharmas.

Sutra:

What is meant by Paramita? It is a Sanskrit word which in our language means 'arrived at the other shore,' and is explained as 'apart from production and extinction.' When one is attached to states of being, production and extinction arise like waves on water. That is what is meant by 'this shore.' To be apart from states of being, with no production or extinction, is to be like freely flowing water. That is what is meant by 'the other shore.' Therefore it is called 'Paramita'.

Commentary:

To reach the other shore is to be separated from birth and death. This shore is birth and death; the other shore is Nirvana. To go from this shore to the other, you must cross the great sea of afflictions. Because there are afflictions, there is also birth, death, and Nirvana. If you have no afflictions, then birth and death *are* Nirvana and Nirvana *is* birth and death. Birth, death, and Nirvana are nothing more than names.

The absence of birth and death is Nirvana. If you have no afflictions, then in the midst of birth and death you have no birth and death. We are born and we die because of affliction. This is very important and you should all remember it: birth and death exist because of afflictions; affliction exists because of ignorance; and ignorance is simply whatever you don't understand.

What don't you understand? What *do* you understand? Knowing you do not understand is ignorance. Knowing you do understand is Prajna. There is just that small difference.

"When one is attached to states of being, production and extinction arise like waves on water." What is meant by the other shore? What is Nirvana? Nirvana is like water without waves. When the wind rises, the waves swell. The wind of ignorance, the waves of affliction are "this shore."

"To be apart from states, with no production or extinction, is to be like freely flowing water." The principle is clear: the nature is like water, the water of wisdom. When there are no waves, there is no birth and death.

We should work hard to understand why our minds have so many extraneous thoughts. These thoughts are like so many waves. Without them there would be no production or extinction, no birth or death. With production and extinction you are on this shore, but if you separate yourself from production and extinction you are like freely flowing water, permeating the universe with wisdom. That is what is meant by 'the other shore.'

That section of text is very useful. Use a little effort and you will understand it and derive from it inexhaustible benefit.

Sutra:

"Good Knowing Advisors, deluded people recite with their mouths, but while they recite they live in falsehood and in error. When there is practice in every thought, that is the true nature. You should understand this dharma, which is the Prajna dharma; and cultivate this conduct, which is the Prajna conduct. Not to cultivate is to be a common person, but in a single thought of cultivation, you are equal to the Buddhas."

Commentary:

In each thought, avoid doing stupid things. If you understand this dharma, you realize that Prajna is to refrain from stupidity. What is stupidity? Doing what you absolutely should not do. Most important is the matter of sexual desire. You absolutely should not give rise to sexual desire, for when it arises you get confused and forget everything. You forget Prajna, you forget Paramita. At that time you cannot even recite their names. You become involved in it and no longer pay attention to principle. Although it is the stupidest thing one can do, people still like to do it. They want to be stupid instead of wanting to cultivate the Prajna dharma. If you want to cultivate and practice Prajna for even a single thought, you must cut off desire and cast out love. The absence of sexual desire is the practice of Prajna and "in a single thought of cultivation, you are equal to the Buddhas."

Sutra:

"Good Knowing Advisors, common people are Buddhas and affliction is Bodhi. Past thoughts deluded are the thoughts of a common person. Future thoughts enlightened are the thoughts of a Buddha. Past thoughts attached to states of being are afflictions, and future thoughts separate from states of being are Bodhi."

Commentary:

Where does the Buddha come from? He starts out as a common person. Yes, the Buddha was a common person who cultivated and eventually achieved Buddhahood. Why are we common people? Simply because we do not cultivate the Prajna dharma. Our nature flows out and becomes emotion; our emotions flow out and become desire. Common people are that way. But the returning of desire to one's own nature, so that one is unmoved by ignorance: that is the Buddha.

"Affliction is Bodhi." Without affliction there is no Bodhi. So you say, "Then I will not get rid of my afflictions. I will keep them." If you keep them, they are still afflictions, and afflictions are just afflictions. You should use a scientific method to temper your afflictions. How? Actually, this change is no change, it is merely a returning to your original nature.

My hand, for example, has a palm and a back to it. The back of the hand represents affliction and the palm represents Bodhi. All you need to do is flip it over and everything is all right. There is no addition or subtraction required. Just turn it over! If you do not turn it over, you are off by just that margin, and affliction is affliction and Bodhi is Bodhi. But as soon as you turn it around, affliction is Bodhi and birth and death is Nirvana. I have often spoken of this. At Berkeley I said:

Affliction is Bodhi, ice is water,
Birth and death and Nirvana are empty dharmas.

If you understand, then dharmas are also empty. If you do not understand, then there are still dharmas. You should understand that people and dharmas are both empty.

"Past thoughts deluded are the thoughts of a common person. Future thoughts enlightened are the thoughts of a Buddha." With stupid thoughts, you are common person; with wisdom and enlightenment, you are a Buddha.

"Past thoughts attached to states of being are afflictions, and future thoughts separate from states of being are Bodhi." When thought is attached to states, affliction arises. You may think, "This is San Francisco. It surely isn't the same as New York!" Fundamentally San Francisco and New York are the same. They are both big cities. But you make distinctions. "In San

Francisco," you say, "there is no snow, but New York has lots of snow." This is just the discriminating mind. Basically the two cities are the same.

If you are unattached to states of being, you will not have so much affliction. If you do not use your discriminating mind, there is no affliction. Past thoughts, which were attached to states, discriminated between San Francisco and New York, and therefore affliction arose. A later thought, which is unattached, makes you say, "They are empty! San Francisco and New York are the same. Why bother to discriminate one from the other?" If you do not discriminate, that is Bodhi.

It is easy to speak that way, but putting down all discrimination is another matter. That is difficult. When you understand that kind of state, there is no home and no country. There is nothing at all. This is to "produce that thought which is nowhere supported." It is also to "produce that body which is nowhere supported." Not dwelling anywhere, you can manifest a body that can go everywhere. Is this not wonderful dharma? It is nothing less than Bodhi. There's no need to sigh. If you can be enlightened, then you are enlightened. If you can't be yet, then slowly, slowly, you can be.

Nature in samadhi,
Demons defeated:
Everyday–happiness.

False thought
not arising:
Everywhere–peace.

When your mind is in samadhi, there is not so much false thinking. Everyday you are happy and at peace. Why are you unhappy now? Because of false thoughts. Without false thoughts, every place is the Land of Ultimate Bliss[33], and you can "produce that body which is nowhere supported."

Sutra:

"Good Knowing Advisors, Maha Prajna Paramita is the most honored, the most supreme, the foremost. It does not stay; it does not come or go. All Buddhas of the three periods of time emerge from it. You should use great wisdom to destroy affliction, defilement, and the five skandhic heaps. With such cultivation as that you will certainly realize the Buddha Way, transforming the three poisons into morality, concentration, and wisdom.

Commentary:

The Great Master again addressed the assembly, saying, "In the self-nature of each of you there is limitless wisdom. Maha Prajna Paramita is originally fully present within your self-nature. You need not seek it outside.

"It does not stay; it does not come or go." The Prajna wisdom of your self-nature is unattached. All Buddhas of the three periods of time, the past, present and future, issue from Maha Prajna Paramita–the highest, most supreme, most honored, number one dharma.

"You should use this great wisdom, not small wisdom, to destroy affliction, defilement and the five skandhic heaps of form, feelings, perceptions, impulses and consciousness. Without Prajna you cannot see that the five heaps are empty, and therefore you have affliction and are unable to cut off defilement. If you wish to have genuine Prajna, you must

33. Paradise, the pure land of Amitabha Buddha.

'illumine and view the five skandhas all as empty,' as Avalokiteshvara did when deeply practicing the Prajna Paramita. Avalokiteshvara Bodhisattva worked a long time practicing the deep Prajna Paramita. He could not, in just a short time, illumine and view the five heaps as empty. If you practice the deep Prajna Paramita, you can see the five heaps in this way, and when you destroy all affliction and attachment to sense-objects, the original Prajna nature manifests itself.

"With such cultivation as that, you will certainly realize the Buddha Way, transforming the three poisons into morality, concentration, and wisdom." There is no doubt that you will realize the Way, turning greed, hatred, and stupidity into morality, concentration, and wisdom. Let's see whether or not you can change. If you change, you will dwell in Prajna; if you do not change, you will wander among the deluded.

Sutra:

"Good Knowing Advisors, my Dharma-door[34] produces 84,000[35] wisdoms from the one Prajna. Why? Because worldly people have 84,000 kinds of defilement. In the absence of defilement, wisdom is always present, since it is not separate from the self-nature.

"Understand that this dharma is just no-thought, no-remembrance, non-attachment, and the non-production of falsehood and error. Use your own true-suchness nature, and, by means of wisdom, contemplate and illuminate all dharmas without grasping or rejecting

---

34. The Dharma doors are the doctrines, discourses, and wisdom of the Buddhas, the cultivation of which lead to enlightenment.

35. This term is used in the general sense for a great number.

them. That is to see one's own nature and realize the Buddha Way.

"Good Knowing Advisors, if you wish to enter the extremely deep Dharma realm and the Prajna samadhi, you must cultivate the practice of Prajna. Hold and recite *The Diamond Prajna Sutra* and that way you will see your own nature."

Commentary:

The Sixth Patriarch said, "From one kind of wisdom, measureless Prajnas are produced." These 84,000 kinds of wisdom are just 84,000 kinds of Prajna. If you change the defilement of external objects, it becomes wisdom.

Do not use your discriminating consciousness to contemplate and illuminate all dharmas. Use wisdom.

If you wish to enter the Sutra store and have wisdom like the sea, if you wish to master all dharmas and the Prajna Samadhi, you must cultivate the Prajna conduct. How do you practice the Prajna Dharma-door? Hold and recite *The Diamond Prajna Sutra*. Because the Sixth Patriarch became enlightened upon hearing *The Diamond Sutra*, he tells everyone, "You should all recite *The Diamond Sutra*. Hold it in your mind. Do not be distracted or forgetful. Hold *The Diamond Sutra* and you will see your own nature."

In reciting Sutras it is essential to avoid giving rise to false thinking and extraneous thoughts. Once there was a man who recited *The Diamond Sutra* every day. One night he dreamt that a ghost asked him to take him across to a more favorable rebirth just as we perform the Ullambana ceremony on the fifteenth day of the seventh month in order to take across parents from this and past lives. The ghost said, "Please recite a Sutra to take me across."

"How many times shall I recite it?" the man asked.

The ghost said, "One recitation will be enough."

The next day, halfway through the recitation, one of the man's servants brought him a cup of tea. He pushed the cup aside, thinking, "I do not want it," and continued to recite.

That evening the ghost returned. "You promised to recite the Sutra for me," he said, "but you only recited half of it."

"What do you mean?" the man replied, "I recited the whole Sutra."

The ghost said, "You recited the whole Sutra, but halfway through you thought, 'I do not want it,' so the merit from the second half of the recitation was lost."

The man then realized what happened. "Yes," he replied "I did think, 'do not want,' but it was tea I did not want, not the Sutra's merit."

It took only these words "I do not want" halfway through the recitation to convince the ghosts and spirits that he did not want the merit. Probably the ghosts took the merit for themselves. The man said, "I will recite it again." This time he recited without interruption and the next evening the ghost happily bowed to him in thanks for the compassionate recitation.

So when you recite *The Diamond Sutra* do not think, "I do not want." Reciting "Subhuti[36], Subhuti, I don't want Subhuti," Subhuti will probably run away.

Sutra:

> **"You should know that the merit and virtue of this Sutra is immeasurable, unbounded, and indescribable, as the Sutra text itself clearly states.**

---

36. It was Subhuti, the foremost of the Buddha's disciples in understanding emptiness, that the Buddha addressed when he spoke *The Diamond Sutra*.

"This Dharma-door is the Superior Vehicle, taught for people of great wisdom and superior faculties. When people of limited faculties and wisdom hear it, their minds give rise to doubt.

"Why is that? Take for example the rain which the heavenly dragons shower on Jambudvipa[37]. Cities and villages drift about in the flood like thorns and leaves. But if the rain falls on the great sea, its waters neither increase nor decrease.

"If people of the Great Vehicle, the Most Superior Vehicle, hear *The Diamond Sutra*, their minds open up, awaken, and understand. They then know that their original nature itself possesses the wisdom of Prajna. Because they themselves use this wisdom constantly to contemplate and illuminate, they do not rely on written words.

"Take for example the rain water. It does not come from the sky. The truth is that the dragons cause it to fall in order that all living beings, all plants and trees, all those with feeling and those without feeling may receive its moisture. In a hundred streams it flows into the great sea and there unites in one substance. The wisdom of the Prajna of the original nature of living beings acts the same way."

Commentary:

People without good roots say, "*The Diamond Sutra* is meaningless! What good points does reciting it have? If you

---

37. Every world system contains one sun, one moon, and one Mount Sumeru as well as four great continents. Jambudvipa is the continent located south of Mount Sumeru; it is the continent upon which we live.

recite it every day, can you go without eating and still live? Keep reciting and we will see if you can go without eating." People of shallow roots and wisdom do not believe in this Sutra.

The great sea represents people of great roots and energy. As soon as they hear this dharma, they realize that Prajna is originally complete within the self-nature, and so they believe it. People of small roots and wisdom, however, are like grass and leaves which float on the surface of the water and sink as soon as it rains. They doubt the Great Vehicle Dharma.

Reflecting within, it is not necessary for those of great wisdom to be highly literate in order tc understand Prajna wisdom.

The Prajna wisdom of the self-nature of living beings is just like the rain from the heavens which flows into the great sea. The sea represents our inherent wisdom. No matter how much rain falls, the sea neither increases nor decreases.

The Buddhadharma is like a great sea;
Only those with faith can enter.

It may also be said, "Only those with wisdom can enter," because without wisdom it is difficult to enter this sea.

Sutra:

"Good Knowing Advisors, when people of limited faculties hear this Sudden Teaching, they are like the plants and trees with shallow roots which, washed away by the great rain, are unable to grow. But at the same time, the Prajna wisdom which people of limited faculties possess is fundamentally no different from the Prajna that men of great wisdom possess.

"Hearing this Dharma, why do they not become enlightened? It is because the obstacle of their deviant views is a formidable one and the root of their afflictions is deep. It is like when thick clouds cover the sun: if the wind does not blow, the sunlight will not be visible.

"Prajna wisdom is itself neither great nor small. Living beings differ because their own minds are either confused or enlightened. Those of confused mind look outwardly to cultivate in search of the Buddha. Not having awakened to their self-nature yet, they have small roots.

"When you become enlightened to the Sudden Teaching, you do not grasp onto the cultivation of external things. When your own mind constantly gives rise to right views, afflictions and defilement can never stain you. That is what is meant by seeing your own nature."

Commentary:

Deluded people do not become enlightened because their deviant views are too strong and too formidable an obstruction, and cause them to disbelieve. Their ignorance is great and they give rise to much affliction, which is like thick clouds covering the sun. The sunlight is simply the Prajna of your self-nature and the clouds are your deviant views and afflictions. If no wind blows the clouds away, the sunlight will not shine through.

Some living beings are heavily afflicted by bad habits. Having created a great deal of bad karma, they are confused. Those with fewer bad habits and lighter karma can become enlightened. The confused person seeks the Dharma outside his own mind. Seeking outwardly, he does not recognize the originally complete Buddha of his own self-nature. The more he seeks the Buddha outside the farther away he goes.

You should enlighten yourself and not seek outside. If you hear the Sudden Teaching you may become enlightened right away. Understand the Prajna of your own nature and always hold to right knowledge and vision. You will then be without affliction or defilement.

Sutra:

"Good Knowing Advisors, the ability to cultivate the conduct of not dwelling inwardly or outwardly, of coming and going freely, of casting away the grasping mind, and of unobstructed penetration, is basically no different from *The Prajna Sutra*."

Commentary:

Inside there is no body and mind, outside there is no world. But this is not dull emptiness. It is not to say, "My body and mind do not exist; the world does not exist!" and then to fall into vacuity. What is spoken of here is non-attachment: non-attachment to the body, to the mind, and to the world. Then you may "come and go freely."

Coming here, going there, coming back to the body and mind, going out into the Dharma Realm, you are free if you are unattached to the coming and the going. If you are attached, you are in bondage.

Unattached, you are free with respect to life and death. "If I want to live, I live. If I want to die, I die." You asked, "Is this suicide?" No. You need simply sit down, enter Dhyana Samadhi, and go. You need not take poison to make sure than you will die. Isn't this freedom? If it were not freedom, you would not be able to go. How was the Third Patriarch, Seng Ts'an, able to reach up and grasp the limb of a tree and, while hanging there, die? How could he enter Nirvana in this way? He could do this because he was free to live or die, free to come or go.

If I wish to live, then I may never die.
If I wish to die, I die right now.

This is what is meant by "coming and going freely."

If you are free to come and go, you can end your life even while in the midst of talking, just like the Great Master Tao Sheng. He was really a good sport. The first part of *The Mahaparinirvana Sutra* said that the icchantikas, those of little faith, do not possess the Buddha nature, but Tao Sheng disagreed: "I say that icchantikas *do* have the Buddha nature!"

Everyone said, "He's crazy! He's mentally ill! He knows what the Sutra says, yet he deliberately contradicts it." They scolded him, they shunned him. "Get out of here," they said.

Master Tao Sheng then made a vow. He said, "If my explanation of Dharma is in agreement with the Buddha's Sutras and the Buddha's Mind, then in the future I shall end my life while lecturing from the Dharma seat. But if I have spoken contrary to the Buddha's Mind, this vow will not be fulfilled."

He then went into the mountains and lectured on Sutras to the rocks and ragged boulders. When the rocks heard him, they nodded their heads in acceptance of his principles.

When Sheng, the Venerable,
spoke the Dharma,
Even the rocks
bowed.

He continued to lecture on Sutras until once when, mysteriously and wonderfully, he paused while lecturing and died sitting in the Dharma seat. The assembly looked up and cried, "He has gone to rebirth!"

Wasn't he a good sport? This is what is meant by "coming and going freely."

You say, "Dharma Master, I quite agree with you. I don't want to be attached. In fact, I don't want to follow the rules. After all, the rules are just an attachment." Wrong! If you can "cast away your grasping mind" and be unattached, you should be unattached to what is wrong, but you should not be unattached to what is right. For example, if you follow the rules you can become a Buddha. But if you think, "I am not attached. I don't have to follow the rules," then you cannot become a Buddha.

Go down the right road.
Retreat from the wrong one.

Do not become attached to principles which are in opposition to the Way, but grasp and hold tightly to those principles which are in accord with it. Holding to and reciting may be an attachment, but holding to and reciting *The Diamond Sutra* is cultivation.

Do not say, "I am attached. I have a small fault which I do not want to give up. What is more, I do not want anyone to know about it." That is to be even more attached. "All right then," you say, "I don't care if anyone knows about it. If people say I am wrong, I will be unattached and pay no attention." That is deviant knowledge and deviant views. The more you cultivate that way, the farther you drift from the Buddhadharma.

Once you have left attachments behind, you can penetrate and understand without obstruction and be without obstacles to your progress. The ability to cultivate this conduct "is basically no different from *The Prajna Sutra*." If you cannot cultivate this conduct, you will be in opposition to the principle of *The Diamond Sutra*, but if you can cultivate, it is Prajna wisdom manifest.

Sutra:

"Good Knowing Advisors, all Sutras and writings of the Great and Small Vehicles, the twelve divisions of Sutras, have been devised because of people and established because of the nature of wisdom. If there were no people the ten thousand dharmas would not exist. Therefore you should know that all dharmas are originally postulated because of people, and all Sutras are spoken for their sakes."

Commentary:

On the higher plane, a Sutra tallies with the principles of all the Buddhas, and below, it tallies with the opportunities for teaching living beings; for that reason the word Sutra took on the meaning "to tally."

The twelve divisions of Sutra text are:

1. Prose;
2. Verse;
3. Transmitting of Predictions;
4. Interpolations;
5. The speaking of Dharma without its having been requested;
6. Discussion of causes and conditions;
7. Analogies;

8. Events of the past lives of the Buddhas;
9. Events of the past lives of the Bodhisattvas and disciples;
10. Writings which explain principle in an especially expansive way;
11. Dharma which has never been spoken before;
12. Commentaries.

Sutras exist because people exist. If there were no people, the Sutras would be useless. In the same way, troubles exist only because there are people to have them. The Dharma teaches people how to end their troubles; to get rid of the 84,000 kinds of defilement and trouble, the Buddha teaches 84,000 Dharma-doors But if there were no people, the troubles would never have arisen.

The Buddha spoke all Dharmas
For the minds of human beings.
If there were no minds
Of what use would Dharmas be?

Sutra:

"Some people are deluded and some are wise; the deluded are small people and the wise are great people. The deluded question the wise and the wise teach Dharma to the deluded. When the deluded people suddenly awaken and understand, their minds open to enlightenment and they are no longer different from the wise.

"Good Knowing Advisors, unenlightened, the Buddha is a living being. At the time of a single enlightened thought, the living being is a Buddha.

Therefore you should know that the ten thousand dharmas exist totally within your own mind. Why don't you, from within your own mind, suddenly see the true suchness of your original nature?

"*The Bodhisattva-shila Sutra* says, 'Our fundamental self-nature is clear and pure.' If we recognize our own mind and see the nature, we shall all perfect the Buddha Way. *The Vimalakirti Nirdesha Sutra* says, 'Just then, suddenly regain your original mind.'"

Commentary:

If, in the very shortest space of time, the space of a thought, you suddenly understand, you wake up and become a Buddha. Confused, you are a living being; enlightened, you are a Buddha.

One confused thought:
you are a living being.
Thought after thought confused:
thought after thought, a living being.
One enlightened thought:
you are a Buddha.
Thought after thought enlightened:
thought after thought, a Buddha.

What does it mean to be enlightened? Ask yourself! Ultimately, what advantage do emotion and desire have? Emotion and desire harm your body; that is a serious problem. They rob you of your life; they make you stupid. If in thought after thought you have desire, then thought after thought you are deluded. It is said,

Karma ended, emotion emptied,
is the true Buddha.
Karma heavy, emotion turbid,
is the living being.

Enlightenment is here: put down defiled thoughts and pick up the pure. What are defiled thoughts? Thoughts of desire are defiled thoughts. I will make it even clearer: thoughts of sexual desire are defiled thoughts. You should clearly recognize your thoughts of sexual desire. Should you give way to sexual desire with your body, then the action of your body, your body-karma, is impure. If you talk about sex, the action of your mouth is impure. If you constantly think about sex, your mind-karma is impure. However, if you are without offense in body, mouth, and mind, you are not far from Buddhahood.

Most people turn their backs on enlightenment and unite themselves with the dust of external objects and states. Falling into states of emotion and desire they become defiled. Leaving emotion and desire behind and turning your back on the dust, you are united with enlightenment. You are clear and pure and can realize Buddhahood. However, as long as you have the slightest trace of defilement, you cannot realize Buddhahood; you remain a living being. One confused thought makes you a living being for the space of that thought. If every thought is confused, you are continually a living being. One enlightened thought makes you a Buddha for the space of that thought. If every thought is enlightened, you are always a Buddha.

Do you see? It is very simple. Still, you need the help of a Good Knowing Advisor who will teach you that, in order to be clear and pure, it is of the utmost importance to be unselfish. Not working for your own benefit and being without greed, hatred, stupidity, and a view of self, you may attain purity. That is enlightenment.

Some people hear, "One enlightened thought; you are a Buddha," and they say, "Everyone is a Buddha!" Right. All living beings are Buddhas, but they must first wake up to it. To say, "Everyone is a Buddha" when you are not enlightened is to be like the common person mentioned earlier in the Sutra who called himself the king. The real king would throw that man in prison.

Heaven cannot hold two suns;
The citizens cannot serve two kings.

Why don't you cultivate your own mind? Get rid of the defilement and then you can see your own nature as it truly is. See it right now. Do not say, "Wait a minute, wait a minute." See it immediately!

If you see your nature, you realize Buddhahood. If I see my nature, I realize Buddhahood. If someone else sees his nature he realizes Buddhahood. There is no inequality here. This principle is completely democratic: whoever sees his nature realizes Buddhahood.

You need not wait. See right through it, and suddenly, you don't know how, you are enlightened. Strange and unspeakably wonderful. You return to yourself and regain your original mind.

Sutra:

"Good Knowing Advisors, when I was with the High Master Jen, I was enlightened as soon as I heard his words, and suddenly saw the true suchness of my own original nature. That is why I am spreading this method of teaching which leads students of the Way to become

enlightened suddenly to Bodhi as each contemplates his own mind and sees his own original nature."

Commentary:

"All of you of great knowledge, hear me!" said the Sixth Patriarch. "I have explained so much Dharma to you. Have you become enlightened yet? When I was with the High Master Jen, the Fifth Patriarch, I awoke as soon as I heard him speak.

"I, the Sixth Patriarch, an illiterate barbarian, a stupid country person, met the High Master Jen." The Master did not say the Fifth Patriarch's full name, but merely said "Jen" as a gesture of respect. "The High Master Jen" he said, "endured the temper of many." Those below him tried to pressure him into transmitting the Dharma to Shen Hsiu. The Fifth Patriarch was not even free to transmit the Dharma, but was forced to endure the tyranny of his own disciples. His name, *Jen*, means "to endure." He endured, practicing the perfection of patience until, one day, the barbarian arrived. "I will give the Dharma to the barbarian," the Fifth Patriarch thought, "and forget about all of you. Do you think you can bully a Patriarch? I will transmit the Dharma to someone who can't even read. What use is your education now?" Thus, the High Master Jen ceased enduring and transmitted the Dharma to the Sixth Patriarch.

The Sixth Patriarch was a friend who understood. "High Master," he said, "you have suffered greatly!" Then he told the assembly, "I was enlightened as soon as I heard his words."

Why did the Fifth Patriarch transmit the Dharma to this barbarian? It was not just because he wanted to defy Shen Hsiu. Rather it was because this barbarian was so intelligent that, as soon as he heard the Fifth Patriarch speak, he said in reply, "So that's how it is! My self-nature is originally pure. My self-nature is originally bright and light. My self-nature is originally unmoving. How wonderful it is!"

"Yes," said the Fifth Patriarch, "you are right. It is just that way."

The Sixth Patriarch told the assembly, "I propagate this Sudden Teaching in order to cause all students of the Way to become enlightened suddenly to their own mind and see their own nature."

Sutra:

"If you are unable to enlighten yourself, you must seek out a great Good Knowing Advisor, one who understands the Dharma of the Most Superior Vehicle and who will direct you to the right road.

"Such a Good Knowing Advisor possesses great karmic conditions, which is to say that he will transform you and guide you and lead you to see your nature. It is because of the Good Knowing Advisor that all wholesome Dharmas can arise. All the Buddhas of the three periods of time, and the twelve divisions of Sutra texts as well, exist within the nature of people, originally complete within them. If you are unable to enlighten yourself, you should seek out the instruction of a Good Knowing Advisor who will lead you to see your nature."

Commentary:

If you can't enlighten yourself, you must seek out a bright-eyed knowing one, one who has "gone through."

Wishing to travel the mountain tracks,
Ask someone who has taken the trip.

Ask him, "Where does this road lead?" If you do not ask someone who has traveled the road before, but instead ask a blind man for directions, the blind man will say, "Just keep walking. Go wherever you wish." If you ask the blind man, "Is this emptiness?" he will say: "It certainly is. No one can hinder you here!" But is it really emptiness?

The great Good Knowing Advisor understands the Dharma of the Superior Vehicle and directs you to the right road.

If there is a great affinity between you, you may meet a bright-eyed knowing one who will teach you to understand your mind and see your nature. All good dharmas arise because of him. Your good roots flourish because he watches over their growth. He explains the Dharma to you every day and causes your good roots to grow.

All the Buddhas of the past, present, and future and the twelve divisions of Sutra text are originally complete within your own nature. But if you cannot understand that, you should seek out the instruction of a Good Knowing Advisor. He will teach you to behold the pure and wonderful substance of your self-nature.

Sutra:

"If you are one who enlightens himself, you need not seek a teacher outside. If you insist that it is necessary to seek a Good Knowing Advisor in the hope of obtaining liberation, you are mistaken. Why? Within your own mind there is self-enlightenment which is a Knowing Advisor.

"But if you give rise to deviant confusion, false thoughts, and perversions, although a Good Knowing Advisor external to you instructs you, he cannot save you."

Commentary:

If you seek outside yourself, you will not obtain it. You must enlighten yourself, by recognizing the Prajna of your self-nature. Your true Good Knowing Advisor is within your self-nature; he is simply your own wisdom.

"Deviant" means "not right." "Confusion" means, "lack of understanding." Not understanding what? Not understanding what is right. For example, people have certain fondnesses. Some have the deviant confusion of sex. You should not regard these confusions as unimportant, for when you do, your confusion deepens and the small confusions become large ones. Thinking the large confusions to be unimportant, you arrive at old age with old confusions and go to your death with death-confusions. Even at the time of death you are confused and unclear. How pitiful!

"False thoughts" are untrue thoughts. They are vain and unreal. "Perversions" occur when you clearly know that something is wrong, but do it anyway. You understand perfectly well that it is not right, but you say, "It is right! It is right!"

If you continue to do things contrary to Dharma, you are perverted. You are perverted when you not only do these things yourself, but influence others to do them as well. To discuss this thoroughly would take a long time. To have success, students of the Buddhadharma must not be perverted. If you have deviant confusion, false thoughts, and perversions, although a Good Knowing Advisor external to you, such as your good teacher or good friend, instructs you, he cannot save you.

Your good teacher and worthy friend may try to help you, but if you refuse to obey him he can do no more. Your Good Knowing Advisor is not a policeman! If you break his laws, he cannot put you in jail. He can only hope that you will gradually change your faults. If living beings obey, the master is certainly pleased, but if they do not, although he cannot get angry, he is unhappy in his heart because he has no way to help them.

Sutra:

> **"If you give rise to genuine Prajna contemplation and illumination, in the space of an instant all false thoughts are extinguished. If you recognize your self-nature, in a single moment of enlightenment you will arrive at the stage of a Buddha."**

Commentary:

"Genuine" means "not deviant and confused." "Prajna" is genuine wisdom. To "contemplate and illuminate" is to slice off deviant confusion, false thought, and upside-down actions with the sword of wisdom. If you do not swing the wisdom-sword and cut through your deviant confusion, your false thinking, and your upside-down actions, you are deluded, lack wisdom and do upside-down things.

Recognize your own original nature. Understand it once, and, in that one moment of enlightenment, you will go to the Buddha realm. On the other hand, where do you go in one moment of confusion? To the ghost realm.

Enlightened,
a Buddha.
Confused,
a living being.

In the space of an instant all false thoughts are extinguished, destroyed by your wisdom-sword like ice melted by the sun.

Sutra:

> **"Good Knowing Advisor, when you contemplate and illuminate with the wisdom which brightly penetrates within and without, you recognize your original mind.**
>
> **"The recognition of your original mind is the original liberation. The attainment of liberation is the Prajna Samadhi, is no-thought."**

Commentary:

Using your inherent wisdom, observe inwardly the mind and body and outwardly the world. Completely understand both, as you would look through a pane of glass: from the outside seeing in and from the inside seeing out. Inwardly, there is no body and mind, and, outwardly, there is no world. But, although there is no body nor mind nor world, the body and mind and the world function in accord with one another. Although they function together, they are not attached to one another. This is called "recognizing your own original mind." The original self-nature, the true mind, clearly penetrates within and without.

The recognition of your original mind is liberation. When you are not attached to sense objects or false thought, you obtain liberation. This is the Prajna Samadhi of your self-nature and is simply no-thought.

I previously spoke about non-recollection, no-thought, and non-falseness. Non-recollection is morality, no-thought is Samadhi, and non-falseness (i.e. being without false thought) is wisdom. When morality, Samadhi, and wisdom all manifest, greed, hatred, and delusion disappear.

Sutra:

"What is meant by 'no-thought?' No-thought means to view all dharmas with a mind undefiled by attachment. The function pervades all places but is nowhere attached. Merely purify your original mind and cause the six consciousnesses to go out the six gates, to be undefiled and unmixed among the six objects, to come and go freely and to penetrate without obstruction. That is the Prajna Samadhi and freedom and liberation, and it is called the practice of no-thought."

Commentary:

No-thought means to view all dharmas with a mind undefiled by attachment. When the mind is undefiled by attachment, dharmas are empty. If dharmas are empty, then why must you get attached to your bad habits and weaknesses?

Someone hears this and wants to try to become unattached to dharmas by ignoring his faults. He may be unattached to dharmas but he can't get rid of his faults. How can this be called "undefiled by attachment?" Since to be undefiled by attachment there must be no dharmas, there must even more emphatically be no faults. *The Diamond Sutra* says, "Even dharmas must be forsaken, so non-dharmas must be forsaken even more."

If you do not put down your bad habits and your faults, what kind of Buddhadharma do you study? I ask you! You are nothing but a fraud who cheats himself and cheats others. Students of the Dharma must definitely give up their faults. If you cannot, even though you may be able to explain a few sentences of Dharma, you are utterly useless. You are at the height of delusion.

"Prajna Samadhi pervades all places" and illuminates all places, but is nowhere attached. It is just like empty space.

"Merely purify your original mind" so that it is undefiled and unattached, and cause the six consciousnesses (visual, auditory, olfactory, gustatory, tactile and mental awareness) to go out the six gates (eye, ear, nose, tongue, body, and mind) and among the six objects (forms, sounds, smells, tastes, touchables and objects of mind), but to be undefiled and untainted to come and go freely, and to penetrate without obstruction.

If you examine this conglomeration, you will see that the six organs and six objects ordinarily unite to form a corporation. Where there is a corporation, there is defilement and mixing. Do not incorporate!

They should freely come and go:
The eyes view forms outside;
Inside there is nothing.
The ears hear sounds outside;
But the mind does not know.

What does this mean? You don't understand? Then study the Buddhadharma diligently.

At the time of unobstructed penetration, the ten thousand changes and the ten thousand transformations of the correct use are unhindered, unblocked and inexhaustible. "That is Prajna Samadhi, and freedom and liberation, and it is called the practice of no-thought."

Sutra:

"Not thinking of the hundred things and constantly causing your thought to be cut off is called Dharma-bondage and is an extremist view."

Commentary:

If you sit, saying, "I am sitting here, not thinking of anything. I am thinking of nothing!" and in this way try to cut off your thought, you still have not cut off the thought of "not thinking of anything." If you do this, you will be tied up in the dharmas, and will not obtain release. Thought, no-thought: falling into either of the two extremes is not the Middle Way.

In telling you to awaken to the no-thought dharma, it is not to say that you should be like dead ashes or rotten wood. What use are ashes without fire? They are nothing but dirt. What use is rotten wood? You can't burn it. If you sit, thinking, "Do not think! Do not think of the hundred things!" your thought of not thinking is itself a thought!

Trying not to think is like trying to prevent the grass from growing by pounding on it with a rock and shouting, "Don't come up!" You push the rock into the soil, but when you move it again the grass grows up thicker, stronger, and more dense than ever.

Then how does one attain to the no-thought dharma? It requires the samadhi power that comes from having right, not deviant, thought.

Sutra:

"Good Knowing Advisors, one who awakens to the no-thought dharma completely penetrates the ten thousand dharmas; one who awakens to the no-thought dharma sees all Buddha realms; one who awakens to the no-thought dharma arrives at the Buddha position."

Commentary:

Do you know the realms of all Buddhas? Do you know what their state is like? If you do, then you understand the no-thought dharma. "No," you say, "I do not understand the Buddha realms." Then you do not understand the no-thought dharma.

Do not be like a certain person who does not know anything at all, who cannot even explain the Five Esoteric Meanings and the Seven Sutra Title Topics, but who still runs around "lecturing" on Sutras and cheating those who do not understand the Buddhadharma. People stream in like ants to hear him. They come marching, "deng, deng, deng." What for? Who knows? Ultimately, what Buddhadharma do they study? That man reads an English translation of a Sutra aloud; he simply reads it. Anybody can read it: you can read it, he can read it–I couldn't read it. Why? Because I can't read English!

To explain Sutras, one must explain every sentence and every word, every paragraph and every chapter. You say, "He doesn't do it that way." Of course he doesn't. He doesn't know how to, so how could he?

Don't march off with the ants.

If you enlighten to the dharma of no-thought, you go to the Buddha position. Now, isn't that important?

When I explain Sutras, people come to hear, not ants. The people are few, but they come to study the Dharma, not to eat honey like ants. Here, we gather to eat bitterness; we don't come to eat candy.

Sutra:

"Good Knowing Advisors, those of future generations who obtain my Dharma should take up this Sudden Teaching Dharma door and with those of like views and

like practice they should vow to receive and uphold it as if serving the Buddhas. To the end of their lives they should not retreat, and they will certainly enter the holy position. In this way it should be transmitted from generation to generation. It is silently transmitted. Do not hide away the orthodox Dharma and do not transmit it to those of different views and different practice who believe in other teachings, since it will harm them and ultimately be of no benefit."

Commentary:

"All of you Good Knowing Advisors," continued the Sixth Patriarch, "the Dharma was transmitted from Shakyamuni Buddha to Mahakashyapa, to Ananda, and so forth to Bodhidharma, and then to the Second Patriarch, the Third Patriarch, reaching to me, the Sixth Patriarch. You should transmit the Mind-Seal Dharma-door in just that way, from generation to generation. Do not hide the orthodox Dharma and transmit deviant dharma instead."

Why was the Great Master a Patriarch? Because he never slighted the lowly. When he was at Huang Mei, everyone looked down on him because he was an illiterate country person. He knew the pain of enduring ridicule himself, and so he did not slight others. He addressed everyone as "Good Knowing Advisors" whether they were or not.

"You should not transmit this Mind-Seal to those of different views and practice," he said. Why?

Sutra:

"I fear that deluded people may misunderstand and slander this Dharma-door, and will cut off their nature

which possesses the seed of Buddhahood for hundreds of ages and thousands of lifetimes.

"Good Knowing Advisors, I have a verse of no-mark which you should all recite. Those at home and those who have left home should cultivate according to it. If you do not cultivate it, memorizing it will be of no use. Listen to my verse:

With speech and mind both understood,
Like the sun whose place is in space,
Just spread the 'seeing-the-nature way'
Appear in the world to destroy false doctrines.

Dharma is neither sudden nor gradual,
Delusion and awakening are slow and quick
But deluded people cannot comprehend
This Dharma-door of seeing-the-nature.

Although it is said in ten thousand ways,
United, the principles return to one;
In the dark dwelling of defilements,
Always produce the sunlight of wisdom.

The deviant comes and affliction arrives,
The right comes and affliction goes.
The false and true both cast aside,
In clear purity the state of no residue is attained.

Bodhi is the original self-nature;
Giving rise to a thought is wrong;

The pure mind is within the false:
Only the right is without the three obstructions.

If people in the world practice the Way,
They are not hindered by anything.
By constantly seeing their own transgressions,
They are in accord with the Way.

Each kind of form has its own way
Without hindering one another;
Leaving the Way to seek another way
To the end of life is not to see the Way.

A frantic passage through a life,
Will bring regret when it comes to its end.
Should you wish for a vision of the true Way,
Right practice is the Way.

If you don't have a mind for the Way,
You walk in darkness blind to the Way;
If you truly walk the Way,
You are blind to the faults of the world.

If you attend to others' faults,
Your fault-finding itself is wrong;
Others' faults I do not treat as wrong;
My faults are my own transgressions.

Simply cast out the mind that finds fault,
Once cast away, troubles are gone;

When hate and love don't block the mind,
Stretch out both legs and then lie down.

If you hope and intend to transform others,
You must perfect expedient means.
Don't cause them to have doubts, and then
Their self-nature will appear.

The Buddhadharma is here in the world;
Enlightenment is not apart from the world.
To search for Bodhi apart from the world
Is like looking for a hare with horns.

Right views are transcendental;
Deviant views are all mundane.
Deviant and right completely destroyed:
The Bodhi nature appears spontaneously.

This verse is the Sudden Teaching,
Also called the great Dharma boat.
Hear in confusion, pass through ages,
In an instant's space, enlightenment."

Commentary:

"With speech and mind both understood." Understanding speech is to know how to lecture on Sutras and explain the Dharma. Understanding the mind refers to the mind-ground Dharma door of Dhyana meditation. If you can lecture on Sutras, speak Dharma, and cultivate Dhyana meditation, you are "Like the sun whose place is in space;" you are like bright light which illuminates the void and yet is nowhere attached.

"Just spread the 'seeing-the-nature Way'"; the Dharma door which the Sixth Patriarch transmits teaches you to understand your mind and see your nature. Understand the mind and there are no difficulties. See your nature and there is no anxiety. When you see your original face, you understand the Buddhadharma.

"Appear in the world to destroy false doctrines." This Dharma-door exclusively speaks of transcendental principles, and destroys all heretical, non-Buddhist religions.

Dharma is neither sudden nor gradual,
Delusion and awakening are slow and quick.

Essentially, the Dharma is neither sudden nor gradual. However, confused people must be taught to cultivate gradually, while wise, enlightened people understand the sudden Dharma. If you are stupid, you become enlightened a little slower. If you are intelligent, you become enlightened a little faster.

Today I will tell you the plain truth. Everyday I lecture the sutras, but rarely do I speak plain truth. Today I'll say a little. Why? I can't speak much plain truth because you won't believe it. I say a little and you cannot believe it, so if I were to say more you would believe it even less. That's because you don't like to hear the truth, nor do you like to actually cultivate. So I have no way to speak true Dharma for you. I have to wait. I wait for an opportunity. And now an opportunity presents itself because we have come to this verse and the doctrine should be explained here. What is the Sudden Teaching? Sudden means, "cut it off." Cut what off? Cut off your sexual desire. Can you do it or not? You say, "What's the use of that?" Do you see? You don't believe. Very well, then, I will not talk about it. If I say more, you will disbelieve even more strongly. That's all there is to it. It's just this much:

Cut Off Ignorance Immediately!

Ignorance is just sexual desire. Can you cut it off? Can you? You can't cut it off, and so you don't believe in the true Dharma. When you do cut it off, you will attain the Sudden Teaching.

What is the gradual teaching? "Slowly, slowly," you say. "I can't cut it off all at once. How can I put it down? How can I let it go?" The sudden becomes gradual. That's all there is to it. Do you get the point? I give intelligent people this little bit and they cut it off. But stupid people can't put their desire down. "I don't believe this is the true Dharma," they say. "I don't believe this is the Sudden Teaching." That's why I have never spoken this way before. If you believed, you would have become a Buddha long ago. It's just because you don't believe that you are still wallowing in the mud, turning in the six paths of rebirth. If you want to turn, turn. Nobody is forcing you to stop.

It is a question of sooner or later. You may not want to cut it off now, but when you decide to become a Buddha, you will certainly have to cut it off.

But stupid people cannot comprehend
This Dharma-door of seeing the nature.

The Sudden Teaching is the Dharma-door of seeing the nature. If you cut off sexual desire you can understand your mind and see your nature.

Don't speak of this Dharma to stupid people. They cannot understand it and they won't believe it, just as now, when I told you to cut it off and you couldn't do it. Stupid people cannot comprehend, they cannot understand. If you tell them, they won't believe you.

Although it is said in ten thousand ways,
United, the principles return to one.

There are a thousand, ten thousand, millions of Dharma-doors used to explain this principle. There are 84,000 Dharma-doors to counteract just this kind of affliction, just that kind of ignorance. But when you trace them to the root, they are all just one, just the Sudden Dharma which tells you to cut off ignorance immediately and manifest the Dharma-nature.

In the dark dwelling of defilements,
Always produce the sunlight of wisdom.

Having affliction, you are in a dark room, but having wisdom, you are out in the dazzling sunlight.

The deviant comes and affliction arrives,
The right comes and affliction goes.

Today I will give you a little basic Dharma. If I never say it, you will never know. Deviant refers to the arousing of sexual desire. Do not take it as happiness; it is an affliction.

What is "right" is Prajna wisdom. Genuine wisdom breaks through ignorance and casts out affliction.

The false and true both cast aside,
In clear purity the state of no residue is attained.

This is Nirvana without residue. You say, "The verse says, 'The false and true both cast aside'–I'll ignore both of them!" If you ignore them, you are still in the dark dwelling. When you have transcended the deviant and the right, then they have no use. There is only "right" because there is "deviant;" there is only "deviant" because there is "right." When neither one exists, that is clear purity, Nirvana without residue.

Bodhi is the original self-nature;
Giving rise to a thought is wrong.

Do not seek Bodhi outside yourself. The enlightenment nature is already complete within the Prajna wisdom of your self-nature. Nevertheless you still give rise to false thoughts. Originally, in clear and pure Nirvana without residue, there is no thought, no recollection, and no falseness. It is complete in samadhi, morality, and wisdom.

The pure mind is within the false:
Only the right is without the three obstructions.

The pure mind is within the false, like water in the ice; the ice has the potential to become water.

In order to separate yourself from the three obstacles, you need only cultivate and uphold the right Dharma. The three obstacles are the karma obstacle, that is, all the karma you have created in past lives and in the present one; the retribution obstacle, that is, your body, which undergoes the obstructive effects of your karma; and the affliction obstacle, that is, all your troubles and worries.

If people in the world practice the Way,
They are not hindered by anything.

You can realize the Way by success in any Dharma-door at all. But first you must understand the true Dharma. Then you can cultivate it walking, standing, sitting, or lying down, with no obstacles whatsoever.

By constantly seeing their own transgressions,
They are in accord with the Way.

Mind your own business. Don't watch other people, like a camera which can only take pictures of what is outside, but can't take pictures of itself. You say, "That person is bad! He drinks, smokes, and takes drugs. No one can teach him. He steals! He kills! Just look at him!" You talk nothing but big talk; you only criticize others. You never ask yourself, "Did I kill today? Did I steal? Did I have deviant thoughts of lust? Did I lie or drink?" You never turn the light inward because you are too busy shining it outside.

If you wish to practice the Way, you should cultivate yourself and see your own faults. Then you will be in accord with the Way.

The Sixth Patriarch's verse is excellent. It is profound, deep, and of inexhaustible use. It is simple and clear: anyone can understand it. If you can understand the meaning, and memorize it as well, it will greatly aid your cultivation.

Each kind of form has its own way
Without hindering one another;

Everything which has a shape and an appearance is a kind of form. While dwelling in forms, if you are able to wake up and understand, to cut off desire and cast out love and be unattached to the forms, then you will naturally possess the Way. You need not look for it anywhere else.

Leaving the Way to seek another way
To the end of life is not to see the Way.

If you understand and are unconfused by forms, then there is no difficulty and no annoyance. But if you leave the Way, saying, "This is not the Way. I am going to find another way," you are just adding a head on top of a head.

If you see what happens and understand,
you can transcend the world.
If you see what happens and are confused
you fall beneath the wheel.

If you become confused and give rise to view delusion, you fall into the dust of external states and objects and to the end of your life you will not see the Way.

A frantic passage through a life,
Will bring regret when it comes to its end.
Wishing for a vision of the true Way,
Right practice is the way.

When you arrive at the Way, everything you do from morning to night is in accord with Dharma. You do right and proper things, not deviant things. If you leave your daily activities and look elsewhere for the Way, your whole life will be suffering and when you are old you will have regrets. "I have wasted my life!" you will say. "If only I hadn't drunk so much wine, I wouldn't be so stupid now. If only I hadn't gambled, I wouldn't be so poor. If someone had just told me, I could have cultivated. But I never met a Good Knowing Advisor."

You met a Good Knowing Advisor, but you didn't recognize him. His teaching passed by like the wind–in one ear and out the other. You never reformed your own faults and you never corrected your bad habits and so, at the end, you have regrets.

Cultivate properly. Do not criticize others and wash their clothes for them, saying, "This person's clothes are filthy! I'd better wash them. And look at him! He's jealous. He's afraid others are going to be better than he is." This is called, "washing other people's clothes."

If you don't have a mind for the Way,
You walk in darkness, blind to the Way.

If you only do things in darkness, if you only do things which you do not wish others to see, you are not practicing the Way.

If you truly walk the Way,
You are blind to the faults of the world.

There are those who say, "The Dharma-ending age[38] is really bad! There is no more Dharma. Cultivators do not give proof to the fruit." Why don't you give proof to the fruit? The Dharma itself has no "right," "image" or "ending" age. If you cultivate the right Dharma, you live in the right Dharma age. If you do not see the faults of the world, but see all living beings as the Buddha, then you yourself are Buddha. If you see all living beings as demons, then you are a demon.

If you attend to others' faults,
Your fault-finding itself is wrong:

Does the Buddha look at other people's faults? No. The Buddha sees all living beings as Buddhas.

Others' faults I do not treat as wrong;
My faults are my own transgressions.

---

38. After the Buddha's Nirvana, the Dharma passes through the following historical periods:
1) The first 500 years: the "right Dharma age;"
2) The following 1000 years: the "Dharma image age."
3) The following 1000 years: the "Dharma-ending age."

If he is wrong, do not follow his example. If he is wrong, do not join him and do not see his errors. Have great compassion for everyone. Be merciful. Say, "These living beings are indeed pitiful! I vow to take them all to Buddhahood."

Simply cast out the mind that finds fault,
Once cast away, troubles are gone;
When hate and love don't block the mind,
Stretch out both legs and lie down.

"I really love him!" you say. "I would gladly give up my life for him." This is all just emotion. If you truly had the compassionate heart to love and protect *all* beings, you would say, "I vow to take him to Buddhahood. If he does not realize Buddhahood, I will not realize Buddhahood."

Today someone asked to formally become a Buddhist by taking refuge in the Triple Jewel, the Buddha, Dharma and Sangha. After taking refuge you must follow the rules. Those who believe in the Buddha should not be as they were before. If they are, others will say, "He is a Buddhist, but he still has his same old life-style. He hasn't changed." Therefore I have made this vow: if those who have taken refuge with me do not realize Buddhahood, I will just wait here for them. You must realize Buddhahood before I do. I have no other method. If you take refuge, you should cultivate a little faster. Don't make me wait for you. I will wait a long time, but eventually I may dislike it and say, "I will wait no longer. I'm finished. This is it!"

"Stretch out both legs and lie down." This appeals to lazy people! However, this is not laziness or sleep. It represents freedom. Unchained, unshackled, unfettered, and free, you "leave upside-down dream-thinking far behind and attain ultimate Nirvana." Do not interpret the *Sixth Patriarch's Sutra* as saying that you should stretch out both legs and go to sleep.

If you hope and intend to transform others,
You must perfect expedient means;

To practice expedient means, one must know what Dharma should be spoken to what living being. For that one must be unattached.

Don't cause them to have doubts, and then
Their self-nature will appear.

Do not cause living beings who hear this Dharma to disbelieve, and you will then be able to use the brilliant wisdom of your own nature.

The Buddhadharma is here in the world;
Enlightenment is not apart from the world.

The Buddhadharma includes both mundane and transcendental dharma. Buddhadharma is in the midst of the world and yet transcends the world. There is no awakening and no Prajna wisdom apart from the world.

To search for Bodhi apart from the world
Is like looking for a hare with horns.

Do you think you can find a rabbit with horns? There is no such thing. If you separate yourself from worldly things to seek the transcendental dharma elsewhere, that is like looking for a rabbit with horns.

Right views are transcendental:
Deviant views are all mundane.

Right views are enlightenment. To what is one enlightened? To the fact that sexual desire must be cut off–that is transcendental dharma. Deviant views are mundane views. When you casually follow your desires, yielding to them instead of causing them to yield to you, you are holding to deviant and mundane views.

Deviant and right completely destroyed:
The Bodhi nature appears spontaneously.

When neither the deviant nor the right remain, the Bodhi nature is spontaneously manifest. You need not look for the Bodhi nature anywhere else.

This verse is the Sudden Teaching
Also called the Great Dharma Boat.

This verse is the verse of sudden enlightenment and the Dharma-door of realizing Buddhahood. It is called the Great Dharma Boat because it can ferry all living beings from the shore of birth and death across the current of affliction to the other shore of Nirvana.

Hear in confusion, pass through ages,
In an instant's space, enlightenment.

If you are deluded, many ages may pass before you become enlightened. If you are on the verge of enlightenment and can put down every one of your desires, you can suddenly become enlightened in the space of an instant. If you truly, truly understand, you can open enlightenment instantly.

Sutra:

The Master said further, "In the Ta Fan Temple I have just now spoken the Sudden Teaching, making the universal vow that all living beings of the Dharma-realm

will see their nature and realize Buddhahood as they hear these words."

Then among Magistrate Wei and the officials, Taoists and lay-people who heard what the Master said, there were none who did not awaken. Together they made obeisance and exclaimed with delight, "Good indeed! Who would have thought that in Ling Nan a Buddha would appear in the world?"

Commentary:

After they heard the markless verse, they said, "Ah! This is really fine! Who would have imagined that in Ling Nan a Buddha would appear in the world?

CHAPTER III

DOUBTS AND QUESTIONS

Sutra:

One day, Magistrate Wei arranged a great vegetarian feast on behalf of the Master.

Commentary:

The doubts referred to in the title of this chapter were those of Magistrate Wei, who did not understand how the Patriarch Bodhidharma would have told the Emperor Wu of Liang that the Emperor had no merit. Therefore the Magistrate questioned the Sixth Patriarch about it.

The Magistrate invited the Master to a great vegetarian feast. All the Bhikshus, laymen, Taoists, scholars, officials, and common people were invited to the meatless meal. Politicians like to eat meat, but because Magistrate Wei propagated the Buddhadharma, he invited them all to a vegetarian meal.

"Great" means that many people attended. In China, the Thousand Monk Vegetarian Feast occurs when a thousand Bhikshus are invited to have a meal. Among a thousand monks, there is sure to be one Arhat, so making offerings to a thousand Bhikshus is making offerings to one Arhat. Which one is the Arhat? No one knows. If you knew, you would just make offerings to the Arhat and not to the thousand Bhikshus. This great feast, however, was an offering to not just a thousand Bhikshus; I believe it was to ten thousand.

The banquet was held on behalf of the Sixth Patriarch. As one who had left home, the Master himself could not invite people to lunch. Laymen made offerings to those who have left home; those who have left home do not make offerings to laymen. Recently, I said to a visitor from Hong Kong, "Remember, lay people make offerings to the Bodhimanda, protect and support the Triple Jewel. Do not be supported by the Triple Jewel."

She replied, "I have never in my life heard a Good Knowing Advisor speak such honest words to me! This certainly has changed me. When I return, I will be different from what I was before."

Magistrate Wei was the Sixth Patriarch's disciple, and he wished to cause everyone to recognize and believe in his master. He invited them to eat vegetarian food, because it is said:

If you want to lead them
to the Buddha's wisdom
First you ought to give them
something good to eat!

In fact, one definition of the word "people" goes:

People: when they eat, they're happy.

If you feed them well, they can't forget it. "Ah!" they say, "I've got to go listen to some more Sutra lectures." They come time after time to get what they want–not Dharma, but good food. They eat and eat and soon, when they hear the Dharma, they say, "The Dharma tastes even better than these vegetables." And then they don't run away.

Magistrate Wei understood human nature. He arranged this feast on behalf of his Master. He did not do it for himself, saying,

"Look at me, making great offerings to the Triple Jewel!" He was not seeking notoriety. He probably used the technique used at today's $500-a-plate fund-raising dinners. "We are going to build Nan Hua Temple," he probably said. "You should donate five thousand dollars, or perhaps fifty thousand dollars."

Because the assembly was held for the purpose of building a temple, the Magistrate asked the Master about the merit and virtue of Emperor Wu, the great Liang dynasty Emperor who built many temples and gave sanction to many monks who left home.

Sutra:

After the meal, the Magistrate asked the Master to take his seat. Together with officials, scholars, and the assembly, he bowed reverently and asked, "Your disciple has heard the High Master explain the Dharma. It is truly inconceivable. I now have a few doubts and hope you will be compassionate and resolve them for me."

The Master said, "If you have any doubts, please ask me and I will explain."

The Honorable Wei said, "Is not what the Master speaks the same as the doctrine of Bodhidharma?"

The Master replied, "It is."

The Magistrate asked, "Your disciple has heard that when Bodhidharma first instructed the Emperor Wu of Liang, the Emperor asked him, 'All my life I have built temples, given sanction to the Sangha, practiced giving, and arranged vegetarian feasts. What merit and virtue have I gained?'

"Bodhidharma said, 'There was actually no merit and virtue.'

"I, your disciple, have not yet understood this principle and hope that the High Master will explain it."

Commentary:

Magistrate Wei represented the entire assembly in requesting the Dharma. He was extremely respectful, stern, and upright in his bearing. He didn't dare laugh or cry. The Magistrate had some small doubts; not big problems. He asked the Master to bestow great compassion on him. "Please resolve my little problem, because there are a few things I simply do not understand."

"Honorable" is a term of great respect. The Magistrate was called "honorable" because he was a high-ranking official. When my disciples go to Taiwan to take the precepts, they should call the old cultivators, the Bhikshus, "Honorable." "Honor" them once and they will be delighted. If you do not "Honor" them, they will say, "This newly-precepted one is extremely disrespectful!"

The Magistrate asked, "Don't you explain the same principle as Bodhidharma?"

The Sixth Patriarch said, "Yes, I do. It is the mind-to-mind seal transmitted by Bodhidharma, the direct pointing to the mind to see the nature and realize Buddhahood."

The Magistrate said, "I have heard that when Bodhidharma went to Nan Ching to convert the Emperor Wu of the Liang dynasty, the Emperor told him, "I have built many temples."

The Emperor Wu of Liang spent his entire life building temples. He allowed many Bhikshus to leave home and he made offerings of food and shelter to them. He would bow to anyone who left home. Wasn't this good? He gave the wealth of his country to the poor and arranged many vegetarian feasts.

"What merit and virtue have I gained?" he asked. Emperor Wu had to be number one in everything. Therefore, when he met Patriarch Bodhidharma, he did not seek the Dharma, he sought Bodhidharma's praise instead. He wanted Bodhidharma to give him a "high hat." He was afraid that Bodhidharma might not know of his merit and so he introduced himself, saying, "Look at me. I have built hundreds of temples to house thousands of monks, all of whom left home under my official sanction. What kind of merit have I gained?" What he meant was, "Look at me! I am an emperor unlike all others! Everything I do is good and meritorious." He didn't seek the Dharma to end birth and death, he wanted to put himself on display instead.

This is like a certain Dharma Protector who says, "Do you know me? I am the greatest, strongest Dharma Protector. I give all my money to the Triple Jewel." In fact, the money he uses to play around with women is several thousand times greater than the money he gives to the Triple Jewel, but he says he gives it all to the Triple Jewel. Isn't this perverse? He never speaks about the money he squanders all over heaven and earth, but when he gives a dollar to the Temple, he says, "I gave a dollar to the Temple! Do you know that?" He is certainly the Emperor Wu's disciple. With his merit and virtue he too can be an emperor someday.

Hearing the Emperor brag about "me, myself, and I," boasting and advertising his merit and in general exalting himself, Bodhidharma thought, "How can a sage go around backslapping? How can I agree with him?"

Ordinary people would have said to the Emperor, "Oh yes! Yes! Your merit is indeed great. No one in the world can match it!" Bodhidharma was a patriarch. He could not possibly have indulged in such behavior, and so he said, "No merit! Totally without merit!"

Sutra:

The Master said, "There actually was no merit and virtue. Do not doubt the words of a sage. Emperor Wu of Liang's mind was wrong; he did not know the right Dharma. Building temples and giving sanction to the Sangha, practicing giving and arranging vegetarian feasts is called 'seeking blessings'. Do not mistake blessings for merit and virtue. Merit and virtue are in the Dharma body, not in the cultivation of blessings."

The Master said further, "Seeing your own nature is merit, and equanimity is virtue. To be unobstructed in every thought, constantly seeing the true, real, wonderful function of your original nature is called merit and virtue."

Commentary:

The Sixth Patriarch replied, "Do not doubt the sage's words. There really was no merit and virtue. Emperor Wu was seeking fame; he was not seeking the orthodox Dharma."

The Great Master said, "Merit and virtue are in the Dharma body, not in cultivating blessings." What is merit then? Seeing your brilliant, wonderful, original nature is merit. With merit, you can see your own nature.

What is merit? At first, it is difficult to sit in Dhyana meditation, but after a while it becomes natural. When you begin to sit, your legs and back hurt, but after a while you defeat your legs and they no longer hurt. When your legs do not hurt, you have merit. If your legs hurt, you have no merit.

"Seeing your own nature is merit." See your original face. You ask, "What does my original face look like?" You must find out for yourself. I cannot describe it to you, and even if I did, you wouldn't know because your knowledge would have come from the outside. Enlighten yourself to your own nature. "Ah," you will say, "My original face looks just like this!"

Then you must have your vision of the self-nature certified by a Good Knowing Advisor. You cannot set yourself up as king and say, "I am the Emperor. I am a Bodhisattva!" like the hippie who had poisoned himself with drugs to the point that he claimed to be a Bodhisattva, when he actually was nothing but a demon.

"Equanimity is virtue." Without selfishness, everything is equal. There is no prejudice or partiality. If you are fair, just, and open-minded, you have virtue.

"To be unobstructed in every thought:" If you are obstructed, your thoughts flow here, stop there, and become attached. Obstruction means attachment. If you are not obstructed, you can always see your original nature. As the Sixth Patriarch said when he was enlightened, "How surprising that the self-nature is originally pure in itself! How surprising that the self-nature is originally unmoving! How surprising that the self-nature is originally not produced or destroyed! How surprising that the self-nature is so inconceivable!"

This is to "constantly see the true, real, wonderful function. It is called merit and virtue." If you do not seek within yourself, but give sanction to Bhikshus, build temples, and give to the poor instead, you accumulate blessings. Blessings, however, are not merit and virtue. You should perfect your own merit and virtue just as the Buddhas have done.

Sutra:

"Inner humility is merit and the outer practice of reverence is virtue. Your self-nature establishing the ten thousand dharmas is merit and the mind-substance separate from thought is virtue. Not being separate from

the self-nature is merit, and the correct use of the undefiled (self-nature) is virtue. If you seek the merit and virtue of the Dharma body, simply act according to these principles, for this is true merit and virtue."

Commentary:

You should not be arrogant. In all situations, you should be polite. Do not say, "Look at me! I am better than everyone else. I am so talented. I know more Buddhadharma than you." If you show off like this, you are being proud, not humble, and you have no merit. When you speak to people you should be easy and polite, not like a wooden board which smashes their heads with a single sentence. You don't have to hit people, all you have to do is say one sentence and you split their heads open, which is a fiercer thing than using an iron bar. But if you are humble, you are never impolite.

Outwardly, you should see everyone as better than you. Don't be self-satisfied.

Arrogance causes harm.
Humility brings benefit.

If you fill your cup with tea until it overflows and then keep pouring, you are being wasteful. Do not be "full of self." If you are polite, you will gain benefit. Do not say, "I am the greatest. I am number one. I am so intelligent that I understood long ago things which you still do not know!" In Buddhism you should not fear that you will not understand. Fear only that you will not practice. Whether or not you understand is not so important, but if you do not practice, you are useless.

The mind-substance should be separate from false thought, but not separate from proper thought. That is virtue. Turn the light around and reverse the illumination to see your self-nature, which constantly gives rise to Prajna. This is merit. In unimpeded, limitless transformation, the correct use of the self-nature enables you to do whatever you wish while never doing unclean things.

If you are seeking the Dharma body you should act in accord with these principles, because it is by means of such merit and virtue that the Dharma body is realized.

Sutra:

> **"Those who cultivate merit and virtue in their thoughts do not slight others, but always respect them. Those who slight others and do not cut off the 'me and mine' are without merit. The vain and unreal self-nature is without virtue, because of the 'me and mine,' because of the greatness of the 'self,' and because of the constant slighting of others."**

Commentary:

You should not slight people, animals, or any living beings. For example, whenever Sadaparibhuta Bodhisattva met someone, he immediately bowed and said, "I dare not slight you because you are going to be a Buddha." Sadaparibhuta Bodhisattva, who was a previous incarnation of Shakyamuni Buddha, realized Buddhahood because of his practice of universal respect while walking the Bodhisattva path.

"Those who slight others and do not cut off the 'me and mine' are without merit." You have no merit if, whenever you meet someone, you immediately become jealous, terrified that they will be better than you are or more intelligent or will surpass you in some other respect. Your jealousy causes you to belittle them. You see yourself as great. "See how big I am?" you say. "No one can compare with me. In the present age there is no emperor, but if there were, it would certainly be me. None of you would have a share. Why? Because I am more intelligent than all of you. I can dominate you, but you can't dominate me." "I," "myself," "me and mine" are not cut off and not put down. There is no room for merit, because you are too full of self.

You do not really cultivate, and so your self-nature is unreal. You are not basically genuine, you do not believe in yourself and you do not know whether you are true or false. I did not tell you to drink or smoke. Why are you drinking and smoking? I did not tell you to go gambling. Why did you go? You don't know why you do these mixed-up things. The self nature in this way is "vain and unreal." This happens because you have no virtue and you see yourself as too big. "Look at me!" you say, "I am a Buddha!" This is like a certain person who said, "This Dharma Master is enlightened and I am just like him!" He did not say that he himself was enlightened. He said that the Dharma Master was enlightened and that the two of them were just alike. He might as well have introduced himself by saying, "I am enlightened." This "me, myself, and I" is too big. There is no merit here.

Sutra:

"Good Knowing Advisors, continuity of thought is merit, and the mind practicing equality and directness is virtue. Self-cultivation of one's nature is merit, and self-cultivation of the body is virtue."

Commentary:

In thought after thought, without interruption, every thought should be right. In thought after thought, without stopping, every thought should be cultivation. This is merit. At first it is forced, but after a time it becomes natural, and the naturalness is merit.

Always be even-minded and impartial, direct and without deceit. That is virtue.

If you have not seen your nature, you must cultivate it. How do you cultivate it? By not giving rise to affliction. When someone hits you, think of it as if you had run into a wall. When someone scolds you, pretend that they are singing a song, or speaking a foreign language. "Oh, he's not scolding me. He's speaking Japanese: 'Chi, chi, cha, cha,' or is it Spanish?" If you think of it that way, there is no trouble at all.

If someone tries to spit at heaven, the spit just falls right back into his own face. If someone scolds you, but you take no notice, it is just as if he were scolding himself. When hit, you can think, "I have run into a wall. It certainly hurts." Can you deny that it is your own karmic retribution returning to you? If you bump your head in the dark, do you hit the wall with your fist? If you do, your fist will hurt and there will be even more pain. Pay no attention: then nothing will have happened. Maitreya Bodhisattva said,

The Old Fool wears second-hand clothes
And fills his belly with tasteless food,
Mends holes to make a cover against
The cold, and thus the myriad affairs of life,
According to what comes, are done.
Scolded, the Old Fool merely says, "Fine."
Struck, the Old Fool falls down to sleep.
"Spit on my face, I just let it dry;
I save strength and energy and
Give you no affliction." Paramita is
His style; he gains the jewel within

The wonderful. Know this news and then
What worry is there of not perfecting the Way?

This is wonderful, but not everyone can do it. The jewel within the wonderful is not easy to obtain. Cultivation of the nature is simply not getting angry.

How does one cultivate the body? Do not do bad things. Have no lust, hatred, or delusion. If you do not kill, steal, or lust, you cultivate the body. That is virtue.

Sutra:

"Good Knowing Advisors, merit and virtue should be seen within one's own nature, not sought through giving and making offerings. That is the difference between blessings and merit and virtue. Emperor Wu did not know the true principle. Our Patriarch was not in error."

Commentary:

You cannot say, "I make offerings to the Triple Jewel. I have merit." It is not merit, just blessings. Therefore blessings and merit and virtue are different. If you perform acts of blessing, you will receive the karmic retribution of blessing in future lives. But you obtain the advantages of merit and virtue now, in this life.

Bodhidharma wanted to take the Emperor across, but the Emperor's ego was too big. Therefore, in order to break the Emperor's attachment, Bodhidharma said that he had no merit and virtue. The Emperor was most displeased and from then on he ignored Bodhidharma. No matter what dharma Bodhidharma spoke, he wouldn't listen. "Why should I listen to you?" he said. He would not respond to Bodhidharma's compassionate efforts to save him and so Bodhidharma just went away. After a time, the Emperor died of starvation. Think it over: How could one with merit and virtue starve to death? He died of starvation because he had no merit and virtue. Bodhidharma had wanted to wake him up so that he would not have to die that way. What a pity that the Emperor's view of himself was so big that Bodhidharma couldn't help him.

Sutra:

The Magistrate asked further, "Your disciple has often seen the Sangha and laity reciting 'Amitabha Buddha,' vowing to be reborn in the West. Will the High Master please tell me if they will obtain rebirth there, and so dispel my doubts?"

Commentary:

The Magistrate said, "The clergy and laymen recite the name of Amitabha Buddha, the Buddha of Limitless Light. They all vow to be reborn in the Land of Ultimate Bliss[39]. High Master, will they actually be born there?"

The Magistrate himself understood the principle, but he knew that others present in the assembly did not understand and so he asked the Sixth Patriarch for an explanation. At that time, the reciters of the Buddha's name slandered the Ch'an School[40]:

---

39. For further reference see *A General Explanation of the Buddha Speaks of Amitabha Sutra by Tripitaka Master Hua*, The Buddhist Text Translation Society, San Francisco, 1974.

40. The five Buddhist schools each take a different approach to cultivation. The five are: Ch'an, Secret, Vinaya, Teaching, and Pure Land. The Pure Land sect is associated with the recitation of the name of the Buddha Amitabha in order to obtain rebirth in the Western Paradise, the Pure Land of Amitabha according to the Teaching of the *Amitabha Sutra*.

"Ch'an School people eat their fill, sit down, shut their eyes and go to sleep! What kind of work is that? Lazy work! They don't compare with those who recite the Buddha's name. Recitation is the best Dharma-door."

The Ch'an School fired back: "You recite the name of Amitabha Buddha to gain rebirth in the West. In the past, before Amitabha Buddha, what Buddha's name did you recite?"

And so they fought, saying, "You're wrong! You're wrong!" until, finally, nobody knew who was right.

Sutra:

The Master said, "Magistrate, listen well. Hui Neng will explain it for you. When the World Honored One was in Shravasti City, he spoke of being led to rebirth in the West. The Sutra text clearly states, 'It is not far from here.' If we discuss its appearance, it is 108,000 miles away, but in immediate terms, it is just beyond the ten evils and the eight deviations within us. It is explained as far distant for those of inferior roots and as nearby for those of superior wisdom."

Commentary:

Shravasti is a city in India. Translated, it means "abundance and virtue." In Shravasti, the five desires were abundant: for fame, wealth, sex, food and sleep. The people of Shravasti had the virtue of much learning and liberation: they had studied a great deal and were not attached.

In this city of abundance and virtue, the Buddha spoke of being led to rebirth in the Land of Ultimate Bliss. The Land of Ultimate Bliss appears to be 108,000 miles away, but if you discuss it in immediate terms, it is just beyond the ten evils and the eight deviations within us. Actually, *The Amitabha Sutra* says that the Western Paradise is 10,000,000,000 lands away, but the Great Master said 108,000 miles because he wanted to counter the prejudices of those in the assembly. In terms of its appearance, the Western Land is far away, but in terms of our own nature, it is just beyond the ten evils and the eight deviations.

Of the ten evils, three are committed with the body: 1) killing, 2) stealing, 3) sexual misconduct. Three are committed with the mind: 4) greed, 5) hatred, 6) delusion (or wrong views). Four are committed with the mouth, a most dirty thing: 7) foul language (talking about the affairs of men and women), 8) lying, 9) harsh speech, 10) slander.

The eight deviations are the opposite of the Eight-Fold Path. Shakyamuni Buddha taught the Eight-Fold Path of 1) right views, 2) right thought, 3) right speech, 4) right action, 5) right livelihood, 6) right vigor, 7) right recollection, 8) right concentration. The eight deviations, then, would consist of deviant views, deviant thought, deviant speech, deviant action, deviant livelihood, deviant vigor, deviant recollection, and deviant concentration.

The Buddha spoke of the Western Paradise as distant to those of common intelligence. To those of superior intelligence he spoke of the Western Paradise as being on the other side of the ten evils and the eight deviations–within their own self-nature.

Sutra:

"There are two kinds of people, not two kinds of Dharma. Enlightenment and confusion differ, and seeing can be quick or slow. The deluded person recites the Buddha's name, seeking rebirth there, while the enlightened person purifies his own mind. Therefore the

Buddha said, 'As the mind is purified, the Buddhaland is purified.'"

Commentary:

The two kinds of people are not white people and yellow people, but wise people and deluded ones. There is only one Dharma; deluded or wise, you cultivate the same Dharma.

Confused people recite the Buddha's name and expect to be reborn in the Western Paradise, while the wise recite the Buddha's name in order to purify their own minds. The pure mind is the Western Paradise. If you understand that, then it is not 10,000,000,000 lands away; it is right here. If you don't understand, you don't know how many Buddhalands beyond even that number it is. It is said,

Confused, a thousand books are few;
Enlightened, one word is too much.

When confused, you may study this Sutra, study that Sutra, investigate back and forth and still not understand. When truly awake, there is no need to study; one word is too much. But you must truly understand. Do not pretend and say, "I don't have to recite the Buddha's name." That is just laziness. Once a man who was well-read said to me, "I have read many books, and now I find that they are all wrong, so I no longer read books." He meant that he had realized Buddhahood and he no longer needed anything. This is extremely stupid behavior. Understanding nothing, he faked understanding. You may try to brew tea in cold water, forcing it to steep, but you will never get tea. How can you brew tea in cold water? There are many strange people in the world–an uncountable number.

Sutra:

"Magistrate, if the person of the East merely purifies his mind, he is without offense. Even though one may be of the West, if his mind is impure he is at fault. The person of the East commits offenses and recites the Buddha's name, seeking rebirth in the West. When the person of the West commits offenses and recites the Buddha's name, in what country does he seek rebirth?"

Commentary:

Whether you are in the East or West, you must not commit offenses. If you do, you won't be reborn in any direction except that of the hells, animals, or hungry ghosts.

If you recite the Buddha's name and hope to be reborn in the Western Paradise, you must also cultivate goodness. If you cultivate Dhyana meditation, you must also cultivate good deeds. Unless you nurture merit and virtue, you cannot become accomplished in your cultivation.

"Magistrate, if the person of the East merely purifies his mind, he is without offense." The pure mind has no confusion, no selfishness, and no profit-seeking. It is without jealousy, obstruction, greed, hatred and delusion. Purify your mind and get rid of all deviant thought. Then you will be without offense.

"Even though one may be of the West, if his mind is impure, he is at fault." This is an analogy. The Sixth Patriarch is not saying that Western people have impure minds, because those of the Western Paradise are completely different from people of this world. They do not need to purify their minds, since their minds are pure to begin with. They aren't greedy, hateful, or stupid and the three evil paths do not exist for them. Do not use this passage to try to prove that the Sixth Patriarch said people of the West have impure minds. The people of the West have neither purity nor impurity.

"The person of the East commits offenses and recites the Buddha's name to be reborn in the West. When the person of the West commits offenses and recites the Buddha's name, in what country does he seek rebirth?" This is another analogy. Those of the West never commit offenses. The Sixth Patriarch wanted to break attachments and so he asked, "If people of the East recite in order to be born in the West, then when people of the West recite, where do they seek rebirth?" If you wish to be reborn in the West, you must first have no offenses. If you have offenses, you will go nowhere but to hell.

If those of the East are reborn in the West, where are those of the West reborn? Is there some other "para"-paradise for them? Don't be so attached.

Sutra:

"Common, deluded people do not understand their self-nature and do not know that the Pure Land is within themselves. Therefore they make vows for the East and vows for the West. To enlightened people, all places are the same. As the Buddha said, 'In whatever place one dwells, there is constant peace and happiness.'

"Magistrate, if the mind-ground is only without unwholesomeness, the West is not far from here. If one harbors unwholesome thoughts, one may recite the Buddha's name, but it will be difficult to attain that rebirth.

"Good Knowing Advisors, I now exhort you all to get rid of the ten evils first and you will have walked one hundred thousand miles. Next get rid of the eight deviations and you will have gone eight thousand miles. If

in every thought you see your own nature and always practice impartiality and straightforwardness, you will arrive in a finger-snap and see Amitabha.

"Magistrate, merely practice the ten wholesome acts; then what need will there be for you to vow to be reborn there? But if you do not rid the mind of the ten evils, what Buddha will come to welcome you?"

Commentary:

Deluded people do not know how to discipline their self-nature. They do not know that purification of their own mind is the Pure Land. Sometimes they vow to be reborn in the East, sometimes in the West. Those who are enlightened know that all places are the same. For them there is no north, east, south, or west. They are comfortable everywhere, because they make no discriminations. But if you continually think evil thoughts and do evil things, you will never arrive in the West.

"Magistrate, merely practice the ten wholesome acts; then what need will there be for you to vow to be reborn there." There are people who do not dare to practice the ten good deeds[41]. They say, "If I do the ten good deeds, demonic obstacles may arise!" But they are not afraid of doing evil. They do not fear that demonic obstacles will arise when they do evil because in doing evil, they are demons themselves. People can certainly be mixed-up. They aren't afraid of doing evil, but fear doing good!

"But if you do not rid the mind of the ten evils, what Buddha will come to welcome you?" If all your life everything you do is evil and confused, if every pore from head to foot carries the monstrous karma of offensive acts, how can you be born in the

41. i.e., the opposite of the ten evils.

West? Which Buddha will come to welcome you? If you do evil, you may seek it, but you will never be born there, because you are bound by your offensive acts. Although it is said, "You may go to rebirth carrying your offenses," that is just a manner of speaking. You still must purify your own mind before you may go. What Buddha is going to welcome a criminal?

Sutra:

"If you become enlightened to the sudden dharma of the unproduced, you will see the West in an instant. Unenlightened, you may recite the Buddha's name seeking rebirth, but since the road is so long, how can you traverse it?

"Hui Neng will move the West here in the space of an instant so that you may see it right before your eyes. Do you wish to see it?"

The entire assembly bowed and said, "If we could see it here, what need would there be to vow to be reborn there? Please, High Master, be compassionate and make the West appear so that we might see it."

Commentary:

The assembly suddenly got greedy. They bowed and said, "If we can see it here, then we don't need to vow to be reborn in the West! We all want you to be compassionate and let us see the Western Paradise."

During the next lecture the Western Paradise will be moved to the Buddhist Lecture Hall, but you will have to wait until then.

Sutra:

The Master said: "Great assembly, the worldly person's own physical body is the city, and the eye, ear, nose, tongue, and body are the gates. Outside there are five gates and inside there is the gate of the mind. The mind is the 'ground' and one's nature is the 'king'. The 'king' dwells on the mind 'ground.' When the nature is present, the king is present, but when the nature is absent, there is no king. When the nature is present, the body and mind remain, but when the nature is absent, the body and mind are destroyed. The Buddha is made within the self-nature. Do not seek outside the body. Confused, the self-nature is a living being: enlightened, it is a Buddha."

Commentary:

The Sixth Patriarch said that he would move the Western Paradise to the assembly, and I agreed to move it to the Buddhist Lecture Hall. But if I were to move it, it would be a lot of work and trouble. So now we shall just change our own bodies into the Western Paradise instead.

"Good Knowing Advisors, the worldly person's own physical body is the city..." Your very own body is the Western Paradise. When your mind is pure, the Buddhaland is pure. The pure Buddhaland is bliss. In the pure mind there are no defiled dharmas, for the dharmas are purified when one is no longer turned by their defilement.

"Outside there are five gates and inside there is the gate of the mind." The mind is called a "gate" because sometimes it thinks and sometimes it doesn't. "The mind is the 'ground' and the nature is the 'king.'" The mind itself is the fine golden sand of the Western Paradise and the nature is Amitabha Buddha. "The 'king' dwells on the 'mind-ground.'" Amitabha, your nature, dwells within your own mind. "When the nature is present the 'king' is present, but when the nature is absent, there is no 'king.'" If you know that your own nature is constantly present, "such, such unmoving," finally, completely, constantly bright, then the king is present. If you understand the mind and see the nature, Amitabha Buddha manifests.

"The Buddha is made within the self-nature." The Buddha is to be cultivated within your self-nature. Your mind is the Buddha. Your nature is the Buddha. If you work on your self-nature, you can realize Buddhahood. The self-nature and the Buddha-nature are not two, but one. Therefore, if you wish to be a Buddha, you must apply effort to realize your self-nature by the purification of your mind and will, your heart and nature.

Break your bad habits and correct your faults. If you do not get rid of the ten evils, the eight deviations, and your own imperfections, you will never become a Buddha. Do not look outside!

"Confused, the self-nature is a living being." If, in confusion, you lose your self-nature, or perhaps forget about it, you are just a living being. "Enlightened, the self-nature is a Buddha." If you wake up and understand that bad dharmas should never be practiced and all good dharmas must be practiced, then you cut off bad and practice good. Just that is the Buddha.

Sutra:

"'Kindness and compassion' are Avalokiteshvara[42] and 'sympathetic joy and giving' are Mahasthamaprapta. 'Purification' is Shakyamuni, and 'equanimity and directness' are Amitabha. 'Others and self' are Mount Sumeru and 'deviant thoughts' are ocean

water. 'Afflictions' are the waves. 'Cruelty' is an evil dragon. 'Empty falseness' is ghosts and spirits. 'Defilement' is fish and turtles, 'greed and hatred' are hell, and 'delusion' is animals.

Commentary:

"'Kindness and compassion' are Avalokiteshvara..." Do you wish to be like Gwan Yin Bodhisattva? It's easy! Practice the compassionate way, practice the compassionate dharma, and be compassionate toward all living beings. One of my disciples once said to me, "Your compassion is something new. I never understood before what compassion was." Not only that disciple, who is American, but many, many other Westerners are ignorant about compassion. They are not taught compassion and so they are unfamiliar with it. It is said, "Even when right in front of you, you do not recognize Avalokiteshvara." Because you do not understand compassion, you do not know Avalokiteshvara. If you wish to know this Bodhisattva and be like him, then practice the compassionate dharma. With kindness, make people happy, and with compassion, relieve their sufferings. This is genuine happiness, not like worldly pleasures such as gambling, horse-racing, the movies, or dancing. Worldly pleasures are just a form of suffering. If you can lead others to true understanding and awakening, then you give them true happiness. To put an end to confusion, to cut off ignorance and manifest the Dharma nature, that is true happiness.

---

42. Avalokiteshvara Bodhisattva, more well-known by the Chinese, "Kuan Shih Yin," "Contemplator of the World's Sounds," is the Bodhisattva of great compassion. He stands to the left of Amitabha Buddha. Mahasthamaprapta, "The Bodhisattva Who Has Attained Great Might," stands on Amitabha Buddha's right. The three are known as the Three Sages of the Western Paradise.

"'Sympathetic joy and giving are Mahasthamaprapta.'" To delight in giving is just Mahasthamaprapta. Kindness, compassion, sympathetic joy, and giving are the four unlimited thoughts of the Buddhas. If you can give with joy, you are just like Mahasthamaprapta Bodhisattva, who practices great giving and great sympathetic joy.

"'Purification' is Shakyamuni..." Your own purification of the mind and will and heart, your own return to the original source, to your originally wonderful, bright mind, perfectly bright enlightened Tathagata store–all of that is just Shakyamuni Buddha. Shakyamuni also means "able to be humane."

"'Equanimity and directness' are Amitabha..." If you can be perfectly impartial, without the slightest prejudice, compassionate and just towards all, this is just the behavior of Amitabha. This is an analogy. Do not say, "Equanimity and directness are Amitabha!" In listening to Sutras and hearing Dharma, avoid giving rise to such attachments. To say, "I heard the Dharma Master say that equanimity and directness are Amitabha," is to slight Amitabha. If you are fair-minded, that is the conduct of Amitabha Buddha.

"But the Sixth Patriarch said this!" you say. "Can't we believe him?"

Did he really say that? Why didn't I hear him?

"'Others and self' are Mount Sumeru. This phrase is important. Nothing is higher than Mount Sumeru. You evaluate yourself and others. You have your status and they have theirs. Sumeru is a Sanskrit word which means "wonderfully high." It is wonderful because no one knows just how high it is. Arrogance and pride, notions of self and other, are like Mount Sumeru.

The analogies are to teach you to see Amitabha Buddha within your own self-nature and to recognize the imperfections there as well.

"...and 'deviant thoughts' are the ocean water." Are you afflicted? Your deviant thoughts are the salty ocean water and your afflictions are the waves. Small waves do not cause much damage, but big waves may rise tens of feet high and sink ships. How many ships lie on the bottom of the sea? No one knows. The ships were invited as guests of the dragon king and escorted to the sea's bottom by the big waves. Just so, big afflictions smother the brilliant wisdom of your self-nature. Take care not to have affliction-waves.

"'Cruelty' is an evil dragon." Cruelty: the wicked dragon king sends a wave to swamp your ship and bring you to his palace for a feast and some dragon wine.

"'Empty falseness' is ghosts and spirits." You say, "I don't believe in ghosts and spirits. If they exist, why have I never seen one?" They are empty and false; how could you see one? If you try to catch a ghost, you cannot grab him. You may see what appears to be a physical shape, but when you reach out to grab it–he remains right where he was. He is just a shadow, empty and false. He is not actually there.

I will tell you about ghosts and spirits: ghosts are black, because they belong to the *yin*. Spirits are white, because they belong to the *yang*. You may see them, but you cannot touch them. They are empty and false.

"'Defilement' is fish and turtles." Weariness of sense objects is represented by fish and turtles.

I have explained Sutras for you for a long time and I have never told you that greed and hatred *are* hell. It is not that greed and hatred are hell, but thoughts of greed and hatred will certainly send you to hell. You plant the seeds of hell now with thoughts of greed and hatred and in the future you will descend into the hells.

"'Delusion' is animals." When I explain Sutras I sometimes say, "That person is as stupid as a pig." Some people say, "Pigs are intelligent. They eat and sleep and they don't do any work." These people think that not doing anything is intelligent. Such people would like to be pigs. As soon as they eat they go to sleep and when they wake up they eat again. When the time comes, they are slaughtered for food.

Animals are stupid and yet, as meaningless as their lives are, they still wish to live. When you kill a pig, he screams, "I don't want to die! I don't want to die!" He begs for his life, but you don't understand his language. What a pity. If you understood, you might be merciful and spare him.

Sutra:

"Good Knowing Advisors, always practice the ten good practices and the heavens can easily be reached. Get rid of others and self, and Mount Sumeru topples. Do away with deviant thought, and the ocean waters dry up. Without defilements, the waves cease. End cruelty, and there are no fish or dragons. The Tathagata of the enlightened nature is on your own mind-ground, emitting a great bright light which outwardly illuminates and purifies the six gates and breaks through the six desire-heavens. Inwardly, it illuminates the self-nature and casts out the three poisons. The hells and all such offenses are destroyed at once. Inwardly and outwardly there is bright penetration. This is no different from the West. But if you do not cultivate, how can you go there?"

Commentary:

Previously, I spoke about the small waves which represent the subtle thought process which takes place in the mind. You are unaware of these thought-waves, but they are present nonetheless. The big waves represent big afflictions and the small waves the extremely subtle ignorance within your mind which runs in a current like waves on water. Are you ignorant or not? With ignorance comes greed, hatred, and stupidity. You are greedy because ignorance tyrannizes you. It says, "I want that thing. Go get it for me!" and the greedy mind goes and gets it. Beauty and wealth–if he doesn't get them, he flies into a rage, like one of my disciples who says, "I must have my way! Why isn't everything just the way I want it!" Ignorance, anger, waves... Small waves are not important, but big waves may get you an invitation to the dragon's party.

Don't be cruel; don't hurt people; don't be a venomous dragon. If you end cruelty, the fish and turtles and dragons disappear.

Your enlightened nature is the Tathagata. When you give rise to the light of great wisdom, it outwardly illuminates and purifies the six gates, so that: the eye sees forms, but is not turned by them; the ear hears sounds, but is not turned by them; the nose smells scents, but is not turned by them; the tongue tastes, but is not turned by tastes; the body feels, but is not turned by feeling; and the mind perceives dharmas, but makes them disappear.

The bright light of wisdom breaks through the six desire-heavens: 1) The Heaven of the Four Kings, 2) The Heaven of the Thirty-three, 3) the Suyama Heaven, 4) the Tushita Heaven, 5) the Nirmanarati Heaven and 6) Paranirmitavashavartin Heaven.

When the eye, ear, nose, tongue, body and mind are purified, you have broken through the six desire heavens.

The causes, the seeds, of the six desire heavens are planted within your six organs. If you are fond of beauty, you may be reborn in a heaven of beautiful goddesses. Turned by sounds, you may be born in a heaven where you listen to music all day long, much finer music than what is made by your guitars and mandolins.

"The smells in this world are so nice," you say. "Certainly the smells in the heavens are even nicer," and so you are reborn in a heaven full of good smells. When your nose is not turned by smells, you smash that desire heaven, and so forth for the remaining five organs.

You ask, "When the desire heavens are destroyed, is the earth destroyed as well?" Empty space itself disappears, how much the more so the earth.

"But where will I live?"

You can live in emptiness, and you need not return. That is the very best way.

When you turn the light around and reverse the illumination, when you investigate and awaken to the Tathagata of the enlightened nature, then the three poisons are wiped away and the offenses of the hells are destroyed. At this moment you are enlightened and understand that the nature of offenses is fundamentally empty. But unless you destroy ignorance, your offenses are not removed.

"Inwardly and outwardly there is bright penetration. This is no different from the West." Inside and out, there is bright light. Inside and out, there are no obstacles. The three evil destinies and the three obstacles exist no longer, and their absence is the Western Paradise. For this reason we do not need to move the Western Paradise to the Buddhist Lecture Hall, and we do not need to consult a travel agent for passports and visas. The Western Paradise is right here. "But if you do not cultivate, how can you go there?" Then it is very far away. It takes several days just to go to the moon. The Western Paradise is ten billion Buddhalands away, millions of times farther than the moon. Then how do you go there? You purify your mind.

Sutra:

On hearing this speech, the members of the great assembly clearly saw their own natures. They bowed together and exclaimed, "This is indeed good! May all living beings of the Dharma Realm who have heard this awaken at once and understand!"

The Master said, "Good Knowing Advisors, if you wish to cultivate, you may do so at home. You need not be in a monastery. If you live at home and practice, you are like the person of the East whose mind is good. If you dwell in a monastery but do not cultivate, you are like the person of the West whose mind is evil. Merely purify your mind; that is the 'West' of your self-nature."

Commentary:

"Fundamentally, our own bodies are the Western Paradise," the assembly exclaimed, "But we did not understand because we did not know how to use them." Those present in the assembly saw their nature: "Really good!" they exclaimed. "We have never before heard such wonderful Buddhadharma. Inconceivable! May all who hear it become enlightened immediately and certify to the fruit."

The Sixth Patriarch had made himself manifest in a layman's body in order to speak the Dharma. After his enlightenment, he did not leave home, but went to live with hunters for fifteen years instead. During that time he cultivated and worked hard. So he said that it is not necessary to be in a monastery to cultivate the Way.

Sutra:

The Honorable Wei asked further: "How should those at home cultivate? Please instruct us."

The Master said, "I have composed a markless verse for the great assembly. Merely rely on it to cultivate and you will be as if always by my side. If you cut your hair and leave home, but do not cultivate, it will be of no benefit in pursuing the Way. The verse runs:

The mind made straight, why toil following rules?
The practice sure, of what use
is Dhyana meditation?
Filial deeds support the father and mother.
Right conduct is in harmony with those above
and below.
Deference: the honored and the lowly in accord
with each other.
Patience: no rumors of the evils of the crowd.
If drilling wood can spin smoke into fire,
A red-petalled lotus can surely spring from mud.
Good medicine is bitter to the taste.
Words hard against the ear must be good advice.
Correcting failings gives birth to wisdom.
Guarded errors expose a petty mind.
Persist daily in just, benevolent deeds.
Charity is not the means to attain the Way.
Search out Bodhi only in the mind.

Why toil outside in search of the profound?
Just as you hear these words, so practice:
Heaven then appears, right before your eyes.

Commentary:

The Way must be walked.
If you do not walk it,
How is it the Way?
Virtue must be cultivated.
If you do not cultivate it,
How is it virtue?

The straight mind is without greed, hatred and stupidity. Precepts are designed to protect you from these three poisons, but if your mind is straight, what function do the precepts serve? The straight mind has no waves, no ignorance, and does not need to toil at holding the precepts.

The straight mind is Ch'an. Ch'an is used to rid you of your faults. Someone says, "The Sutra says, 'Why toil at following rules?' so I won't hold the precepts." Is that person's mind straight or not? He doesn't care whether or not his mind is straight and his "conduct sure," he just cares about not having to follow any rules. If his mind is not straight, how can he not hold precepts? If he continues to be selfish, greedy, habit-ridden, envious, and obstructive, how can his mind be straight?

Your parents gave birth to you. You should repay their kindness by being filial and good to them.

The honored and the lowly, the master and the servant, should be courteous and polite to each other.

What is patience? Refusing to speak of the shortcomings of others, not slandering, not being jealous or obstructive: all that is patience. Do not say, "This man is evil. I saw him shoplifting!" The incident never occurred, but the rumor spreads. "He took the precepts and then went out drinking!" It never happened, but someone started talking...

Do not discuss people's bad points. Bring up their good points. The impatient person never speaks of the good, only of the bad. If you have no bad points, the impatient person will create them for you.

In China, about four thousand years ago, wood drills were used to make fire. Wood was drilled and drilled until fire flared up.

If wood can make fire and the mud can grow a red lotus, then it is not absolutely necessary to leave home in order to cultivate. If you cut off your desire while still at home, you can have success.

One who criticizes you is your Good Knowing Advisor. Just as "bitter medicine" cures your disease, the critic's words may be unpleasant, but they are sound advice. "Do not be lazy," says the teacher. "Do not go to sleep!" The student says, "All you ever do is watch over me!" Americans in particular respond that way, because they are so remarkably independent. They don't listen to anyone's advice. They want to be unsurpassed and supremely honored. "Right or wrong," they say, "I listen only to myself. I don't care what anybody says. I may turn into a senseless block of wood, but nonetheless I am going to stand on my own principles." I understand Americans. They don't like to hear words which are hard against the ear.

Correcting failings gives rise to wisdom. If you do not change your faults, you are stupid. That need not be discussed in detail.

Guarded errors expose a petty mind. If you indulgently cherish your problems and make excuses, saying, "No! You don't understand. There were extenuating circumstances. It wasn't that way at all! I had to do it, you see..." you become your own lawyer and argue your defense with flashy rhetoric. I have many such disciples. They think that I am stupid and that they can deceive me.

Do what you are supposed to do every day. Be just and benevolent, always benefiting others. But do not say, "I gave $100,000. I have bought Buddhahood!" "Charity is not the means to attain the Way." You have to cultivate by searching out Bodhi only in the mind, not outside.

Although we have been discussing the Western Paradise, the verse refers to the Christian heaven as well. Heaven is not just in heaven. Heaven is right before your eyes.

Sutra:

The Master continued, "Good Knowing Advisors, you in this assembly should cultivate according to this verse to see and make contact with your self-nature and to realize the Buddha Way directly. The Dharma does not wait. The assembly may now disperse. I shall now return to Ts'ao Hsi. If you have questions come quickly and ask."

At that time, Magistrate Wei, the officials, and the good men and faithful women of the assembly all attained understanding, faithfully accepted, honored the teaching and practiced it.

Commentary:

How did the people in the assembly attain understanding? Don't pay attention to them! You must find a way to understand for yourself and leave it at that.

CHAPTER IV

CONCENTRATION AND WISDOM

Sutra:

The Master instructed the assembly: "Good Knowing Advisors, this Dharma-door of mine has concentration and wisdom as its foundation. Great assembly, do not be confused and say that concentration and wisdom are different. Concentration and wisdom are one substance, not two. Concentration is the substance of wisdom, and wisdom is the function of concentration. Where there is wisdom, concentration is in the wisdom. Where there is concentration, wisdom is in the concentration. If you understand this principle, you understand the balanced study of concentration and wisdom.

"Students of the Way, do not say that first there is concentration, which produces wisdom, or that first there is wisdom, which produces concentration: do not say that the two are different. To hold this view implies a duality of dharma. If your speech is good, but your mind is not, then concentration and wisdom are useless because they are not equal. If mind and speech are both good, the inner and outer are alike, and concentration and wisdom are equal.

"Self-enlightenment, cultivation, and practice are not a matter for debate. If you debate which comes first, then you are like a confused man who does not cut off ideas of victory and defeat, but magnifies the notion of self and

dharmas, and does not disassociate himself from the four marks."

"Good Knowing Advisors, what are concentration and wisdom like? They are like a lamp and its light. With the lamp, there is light. Without the lamp, there is darkness. The lamp is the substance of the light and the light is the function of the lamp. Although there are two names, there is one fundamental substance. The dharma of concentration and wisdom is also thus."

Commentary:

Concentration comes from holding precepts. With concentration, one can bring forth wisdom. Precepts, concentration, and wisdom are the three studies which have no outflows. If you wish to obtain concentration, you must begin by holding precepts. That is:

All evil not done.
All good respectfully practiced.

The Sixth Patriarch said, "Although you are Good Knowing Advisors, don't be attached and say that concentration and wisdom differ. In this Sudden Teaching Dharma-door of mine, concentration is wisdom and wisdom is concentration; although there are two names, there is only one substance.

What is the function of concentration? Concentration produces wisdom. When wisdom is produced, concentration is certainly within it. If you understand that concentration and wisdom are one substance with two different functions, then you understand "the balanced study of concentration and wisdom."

"If the speech is good, but the mind is not:" If your mind is full of jealousy, obstruction, insolence, conceit, deviant views, greed, hatred, and stupidity, "concentration and wisdom are useless," they are not present, "because they are not equal." But if your "mind and speech both are good," then your mouth says what is in your mind, and "concentration and wisdom are equal."

You should understand and cultivate on your own. Do not argue with people in order to show off your cultivation and advertise yourself. To debate whether concentration or wisdom comes first is to be "like a confused person who does not cut off ideas of victory and defeat:"

In debate, thoughts of victory and defeat
Stand in contradiction to the Way;
Giving rise to the mind of four marks.
How can one obtain samadhi?

Attached to the mark of self, others, living beings, and a life, how can you obtain samadhi? As soon as you argue, you have no concentration and, consequently, no wisdom. This is extremely stupid. When you argue, you give rise to the attachment to self and dharmas and then the four marks arise. With attachment to self comes attachment to others; with attachment to others comes attachment to living beings; with attachment to living beings comes attachment to life.

The analogy of the lamp and light illustrates the identical substance of concentration and wisdom. As a lamp produces light, so concentration produces wisdom. As light is the function of a lamp, so wisdom is the function of concentration. But despite the discrimination, concentration and wisdom are fundamentally one.

Sutra:

The Master instructed the assembly: "Good Knowing Advisors, the Single Conduct Samadhi is the constant practice of maintaining a direct, straightforward mind in all places, whether one is walking, standing, sitting, or lying down. As the *Vimalakirti Sutra* says, 'The straight mind is the Bodhimandala; the straight mind is the Pure Land.'

"Do not speak of straightness with the mouth only, while the mind and practice are crooked, nor speak of the Single Conduct Samadhi without maintaining a straight mind. Simply practice keeping a straight mind and have no attachment to any dharma.

"The confused person is attached to the marks of dharmas, while holding to the Single Conduct Samadhi and saying, 'I sit unmoving and falseness does not arise in my mind. That is the Single Conduct Samadhi.' Such an interpretation serves to make him insensate and obstructs the causes and conditions for attaining the Way.

"Good Knowing Advisors, the Way must penetrate and flow. How can it be impeded? If the mind does not dwell in dharmas, the Way will penetrate and flow. The mind that dwells in dharmas is in self-bondage. To say that sitting unmoving is correct is to be like Shariputra who sat quietly in the forest but was scolded by Vimalakirti."

Commentary:

You should not speak of directness, and act dishonestly. If you greet rich people with smiles and compliments, saying,

"Welcome, welcome!" when in fact it is not the person you welcome, but their money and power instead, that is flattery.

If you speak about the Single Conduct Samadhi, but you act improperly, such hypocrisy betrays a crooked mind. But if you practice keeping a direct mind, then your mind is the Bodhimanda. You should manage all your affairs with a direct mind and have no attachments.

A stupid person gives rise to a dharma-attachment. "I sit here unmoving and I have no false thinking. This is the Single Conduct Samadhi." He is completely wrong. One who thinks this way turns into a vegetable. The Way should flow without obstruction. If you stop your thought, you turn into dead ashes and rotten wood and become useless. You should "produce that thought which is nowhere supported," by attaching yourself neither to emptiness, to existence, nor to dharmas. Attachment to dharmas results in attachment to existence, and attachment to existence results in perishing in emptiness. But when you are unsupported, the Way will circulate freely.

"The mind that dwells in dharmas is in self-bondage." If you get attached to the meditation-dharma and sit without moving, you tie yourself up and become a prisoner. Shariputra, the foremost of Shakyamuni Buddha's disciples in wisdom, sat in the forest, quietly meditating, but the layman Vimalakirti reprimanded him, saying, "What are you doing? What use are you, sitting there like a corpse!"

Sutra:

"Good Knowing Advisors, there are those who teach people to sit looking at the mind and contemplating stillness, without moving or arising. They claim that it has merit. Confused men, not understanding, easily become attached and go insane. There are many such

people. Therefore you should know that teaching of this kind is a great error."

Commentary:

The deluded person does not understand the principle. They think, "I'll just sit here and not get up. This is the way to attain skill in Ch'an." They get attached to what they are doing, and they go insane. For example, many people have come here saying that they are enlightened. That is insanity.

There are many such people. Teachers from their number say, "If you certify my enlightenment, I will certify yours." That is a big mistake. In China in the T'ang dynasty, there were false Buddhist Patriarchs who practiced "intellectual zen"–they had clever answers but no foundation in actual cultivation. It is not surprising that we find such people in America today. But these imposters who falsely claim to be enlightened pave the way for those of true enlightenment. No one knew about enlightenment, so the impostors said, "We are enlightened!"

Everyone then said, "So this is enlightenment!" and they examined them closely to see what enlightenment is like. Suddenly a truly enlightened person comes and no one believes in him. They think that the truly enlightened one is the same as the impostors. You who now cultivate to become enlightened will be forced to deal with the widespread influence of such pretenders. That leads me to advise you that when you become enlightened, you should not say that you are. That is the best method.

This is the way of the world: true, true, false; false, false, true. If you are true, they say you are false. If you are false, they say you are true. Therefore you should not speak of true and false. Tell people to go and see for themselves.

Unenlightened people will say that they are enlightened. If you who have already become enlightened claim to be enlightened, then you are just like those who are not. Why? People who actually are enlightened do not introduce themselves saying, "Don't you know me? I am enlightened! I am the same as so and so, and he is enlightened. He is enlightened and I am just like him." Enlightenment and non-enlightenment are the same, not different. Do not hang out a false name. Enlightened, you are a human being. Unenlightened, you are still a human being. The enlightened and the unenlightened both can realize Buddhahood. It's a question of time.

Do not advertise yourself. If no one knows you, that is the very best! Then your straight mind is the Bodhimandala.

Sutra:

The Master instructed the assembly: "Good Knowing Advisors, the right teaching is basically without a division into 'sudden' and 'gradual.' People's natures themselves are sharp or dull. When the confused person who gradually cultivates and the enlightened person who suddenly connects each recognize the original mind and see the original nature, they are no different.

"Therefore, the terms sudden and gradual are shown to be false names.

"Good Knowing Advisors, this Dharma-door of mine, from the past onwards, has been established from the first with no-thought as its doctrine, no-mark as its substance, and no-dwelling as its basis. No-mark means to be apart from marks while in the midst of marks. No-thought means to be without thought while in the midst of thought. No-dwelling is the basic nature of human beings.

"In the world of good and evil, attractiveness and ugliness, friendliness and hostility, when faced with language which is offensive, critical, or argumentative, you should treat it all as empty and have no thought of revenge. In every thought, do not think of former states. If past, present, and future thoughts succeed one another without interruption, it is bondage. Not to dwell in dharmas from thought to thought is to be free from bondage. That is to take no-dwelling as the basis.

"Good Knowing Advisors, to be separate from all outward marks is called 'no-mark.' The ability to be separate from marks is the purity of the Dharma's substance. It is to take no-mark as the substance.

"Good Knowing Advisors, the non-defilement of the mind in all states is called 'no-thought.' In your thoughts you should always be separate from states; do not give rise to thought about them."

Commentary:

Basically, real Buddhism has no sudden or gradual Dharma. Stupid people cultivate it bit by bit, whereas enlightened people immediately cut off false thinking, bad habits, and involvement with external objects and so understand the mind and see their own nature.

From the time of Shakyamuni Buddha right up until the present, the Sudden Teaching Dharma-door which the Sixth Patriarch transmitted established no-thought, no-mark, and no-dwelling as its doctrine, its substance, and its basis.

Thoughts of the past, present, and future are continuous like waves on water. To be attached to such thoughts is to tie yourself up, to lock yourself up so that you cannot be free. You should not be attached to any dharmas.

In your own clear, pure thoughts, keep constantly separate from states and do not think about the external environment.

Sutra:

"If you merely do not think of the hundred things, and so completely rid yourself of thought, then as the last thought ceases, you die and undergo rebirth in another place. That is a great mistake, of which students of the Way should take heed.

Commentary:

While you should not produce thoughts with regard to external states, that does not mean that you should completely rid yourself of thought.

Attached to marks,
whatever you do is wrong;
But in non-activity
you fall into emptiness.

"What should I do?" you ask. It is just at this point that the greatest difficulty arises, but if you handle it, just that is no-thought.

If you want to have no-thought, then die. That is to have no-thought. But if you die here, you will be reborn somewhere else. That is really wrong! If you want to cultivate the Way, you should pay special attention and take heed!

Sutra:

"To misinterpret the Dharma and make a mistake yourself might be acceptable, but to exhort others to do the same is unacceptable. In your own confusion you do

not see, and, moreover you slander the Buddha's Sutras. Therefore no-thought is established as the doctrine.

"Good Knowing Advisors, why is no-thought established as the doctrine? Because there are confused people who speak of seeing their own nature, and yet they produce thought with regard to states. Their thoughts cause deviant views to arise, and from that all defilement and false thinking are created. Originally, not one single dharma can be obtained in the self-nature. If there is something to attain, or false talk of misfortune and blessing, that is just defilement and deviant views. Therefore, this Dharma-door establishes no-thought as its doctrine.

Commentary:

You may be stupid yourself and not understand your mind and nature. What is more you may slander the Buddha's Sutras and say that they are incorrect. For that reason, no-thought is set up as the doctrine.

Some people say that they have seen the nature. They say they are enlightened, but they have all kinds of thoughts about externals, deviant views, and defilements.

But your own clear, pure origin, the wondrous, bright enlightenment nature has not one single dharma within it. It is the clear, pure, source, the wondrous, bright, true nature. Originally, there is not one single thing.

Some people speak of misfortune and blessing, saying, "Tomorrow you are going to die, unless, of course, you buy great merit today by giving me a million dollars." Hearing such talk, the victim immediately buys some merit and, naturally, he does not die. He claims that the prediction was certainly efficacious, but does not mention the fact that he was cheated out of a million dollars.

Or someone says, "You have great blessings, but you are off by just a little bit. If you create a million dollars worth of merit, next term you can be president."

"The presidency is certainly cheap. If I buy it for a million, I'll still have several billion left," says the victim, and he buys the presidency. That is false talk of misfortune and blessings. It is defilement and deviant views.

I will speak to you more about no-thought, no mark, and no-dwelling. Without a mark, where do you dwell? Without thought, what mark do you have? Isn't that right? No-thought, no mark, and no-dwelling: no-thought is no production, no mark is no extinction, and no-dwelling is the fundamental absence of production and extinction, of right and wrong.

No-thought, no-mark, and no-dwelling are the same as no right and no wrong, no good and no evil, no male and no female. Without deviant thought, how could there be male and female? This is truly marvelous. If you master this dharma there is no mark. Without the mark of self, who has sexual desire? Sexual desire is just a thought; without thought there is no sexual desire and no mark of a self and no attachment. Is this anything but true freedom and true liberation?

No-thought, no-mark, and no-dwelling; no movement, no stillness; no right, no wrong; no male, no female; no good, no evil: this is extremely miraculous. You need only use no-thought, no-mark, and no-dwelling. Without a body, where do you dwell? Right? This is wonderful. You should investigate it in detail.

Sutra:

"Good Knowing Advisors, 'No' means no what? 'Thought' means thought of what? 'No' means no two marks, no thought of defilement. 'Thought' means thought of the original nature of True Suchness. True Suchness is the substance of thought and thought is the function of True Suchness.

"The True Suchness self-nature gives rise to thought. It is not the eye, ear, nose, or tongue which can think. The True Suchness possesses a nature and therefore gives rise to thought. Without True Suchness, the eye, ear, forms, and sounds immediately go bad.

"Good Knowing Advisors, the True Suchness self-nature gives rise to thought, and the six faculties, although they see, hear, feel, and know, are not defiled by the ten thousand states. Your true nature is eternally independent. Therefore, the *Vimalakirti Sutra* says, 'If one is well able to discriminate all dharma marks, then, in the primary meaning, one does not move.'"

Commentary:

The Patriarch addressed the assembly saying, "Good Knowing Advisors, all of you with wisdom, when I say 'no,' what is not? When I say 'thought,' what is the thought of? 'No' means no two marks; further, not even one mark. 'No thought' means no thoughts of defilement; no defiled, improper, deviant thoughts of sexual desire.

"'Thought' means the thought of the True Suchness inherent in each of us. This is the Tathagata Store nature, the Buddha nature."

You ask, "Then if there is no thought, is there no True Suchness?"

'No' means no two marks; 'thought' means thought of the Truly Such original nature.

Thought arising from the Truly Such self-nature is true thought. The eye, ear, nose, and tongue cannot think. True Suchness is the kind spoken of in Chapter III: "When your nature is present, the king is present; when your nature goes, there is no king."

Although thought does arise and seeing, hearing, feeling and knowing do occur at the gates of the six organs, there is no attachment when you use your True Suchness nature because there are no deviant thoughts. The true nature is eternally independent. Because of the function of True Suchness, you are well able to discriminate all dharma marks. Even so, you are not attached to any state and so in the final analysis you do not move.

CHAPTER V

SITTING IN CH'AN

Sutra:

The Master instructed the assembly: "The door of sitting in Ch'an consists fundamentally of attaching oneself neither to the mind nor to purity; it is not non-movement. One might speak of becoming attached to the mind, and yet the mind is fundamentally false. You should know that the mind is like an illusion, and therefore there is nothing to which you can become attached."

Commentary:

Ch'an is not necessarily just sitting in meditation. One may practice Ch'an while walking, standing, sitting, and lying down. In his "Song of Enlightenment," the Great Master Yung Chia wrote:

In Ch'an while walking and while sitting,
Speaking, silent, moving, still,
His body is at peace.

If you know how, you can practice Ch'an at all times, not just while sitting in meditation. But do not become attached to the mind or to purity. Becoming attached to the mind, you have two minds, and becoming attached to purity, you have two purities. Do not think, "I will sit here and not move."

Becoming attached to the mind, you have two false minds, neither of which is the true mind. The mind is an illusion. Why attach yourself to it?

Sutra:

"One might say that to practice Ch'an is to attach oneself to purity, yet the nature of people is basically pure. It is because of false thinking that the True Suchness is obscured. Simply have no false thinking, and the nature will be pure of itself.

"If an attachment to purity arises in your mind, a deluded idea of purity will result. What is delusory does not exist, and the attachment is false. Purity has no form or mark and yet there are those who set up the mark of purity as an achievement. Those with this view obstruct their own original nature and become bound by purity.

Commentary:

Everyone's self-nature is basically pure of itself, but when you cling to purity, you add a head on top of a head and create two purities, a true purity and a false purity. And so you stray from the original pure substance.

Though purity has no form or mark, you postulate a mark to it and in so doing add a head on top of a head. When you consider that to be skill, you obstruct your original mind and nature. Cultivation is for the purpose of breaking attachments. You should not be attached.

Sutra:

"Good Knowing Advisors, one who cultivates non-movement does not notice whether other people are right

or wrong, good or bad, or whether they have other faults. That is the non-movement of the self-nature.

"Good Knowing Advisors, although the body of the confused person may not move, as soon as he opens his mouth he speaks of what is right and wrong about others, of their good points and shortcomings, and so he turns his back on the Way. Attachment to the mind and attachment to purity are obstructions to the Way."

Commentary:

You cultivate non-movement? Non-movement of what? You shouldn't just sit there and not move. You should cultivate non-movement in the midst of movement; in the midst of your daily activities, do not move. Do not insist on criticizing others and pointing out their faults. If you do nothing but censure and browbeat others, it is not non-movement.

Sutra:

The Master instructed the assembly, "Good Knowing Advisors, what is meant by 'sitting in Ch'an?' In this unobstructed and unimpeded Dharma-door, the mind's thoughts do not arise with respect to any good or evil external state. That is what 'sitting' is. To see the unmoving self-nature inwardly is Ch'an.

"Good Knowing Advisors, what is meant by 'Ch'an concentration?' Being separate from external marks is 'Ch'an.' Not being confused inwardly is 'concentration.'

"If you become attached to external marks, your mind will be confused inwardly. If you are separate from external marks, inwardly your mind will be unconfused. The original nature is naturally pure, in a natural state of

concentration. Confusion arises merely because states are seen and attended to. If the mind remains unconfused when any state is encountered, that is true concentration."

Commentary:

Sitting in one place is not necessarily "sitting." You are said to be "sitting" when your mind is no longer disturbed by external conditions, be they good or bad. When you view the unmoving self-nature inwardly, you are practicing Ch'an.

When you are not attached to external marks, you have attained Ch'an. When inwardly you have no illusions or scattered thoughts, you have attained concentration.

Detach yourself from external marks, and your efficacious, bright, enlightened nature will be pure of itself. In that way you will attain concentration.

Sutra:

"Good Knowing Advisors, being separate from all external marks is Ch'an and being inwardly unconfused is concentration. External Ch'an and inward concentration are Ch'an concentration. The *Vimalakirti Sutra* says, 'Just then, suddenly return and regain the original mind.' The *Bodhisattva-shila Sutra* says, 'Our basic nature is pure of itself.' Good Knowing Advisors, in every thought, see your own clear and pure original nature. Cultivate, practice, realize the Buddha Way!"

CHAPTER VI

REPENTANCE AND REFORM

Sutra:

Seeing the scholars and common people of Kuang Chou and Shao Kuan and the four directions assembled on the mountain to hear the Dharma, the Great Master took his seat and spoke to the assembly, saying:

"Come, each of you Good Knowing Advisors! This work must begin within your self-nature. At all times, in every thought, purify your own mind, cultivate your own conduct, see your own Dharma-body and the Buddha of your own mind. Take yourself across; discipline yourself. Only then will your coming here have not been in vain. You have come from afar to attend this gathering because we have karmic affinities in common. Now all of you kneel and I will first transmit to you the five-fold Dharma-body refuge of the self-nature, and then the markless repentance and reform."

Commentary:

Shao Kuan is the present day Ch'ü Chiang. Students and common people from north, east, south, and west went to Nan Hua Temple on Pao Lin Mountain to hear the Great Master explain the Dharma.

The Master said, "The work of sitting in Ch'an meditation, the mind-ground Dharma-door, must arise from within your self-nature. Every thought must be correct, not deviant. Proper thoughts purify the mind; improper thoughts defile it. You personally must cultivate this dharma-door; no one else can do it for you. Your own Dharma body is simply your self-nature, and the Buddha is within your own mind. If you take yourself across by receiving and keeping moral precepts, you will not have wasted your life. We meet here because conditions from former lives have ripened. Now, put your right knee on the ground and I will transmit to you the five-fold Dharma-body refuge and the markless repentance and reform."

Sutra:

The assembly knelt and the Master said, "The first is the morality-refuge, which is simply your own mind when free from error, evil, jealousy, greed, hatred and hostility.

"The second is the concentration-refuge, which is just your own mind which does not become confused when seeing the marks of all good and evil conditions.

"The third is the wisdom-refuge, which is simply your own mind when it is unobstructed and when it constantly uses wisdom to contemplate and illuminate the self-nature, when it does no evil, does good without becoming attached, and is respectful of superiors, considerate of inferiors, and sympathetic towards orphans and widows."

Commentary:

Pay attention! The morality-refuge is simply to have no thoughts of right and wrong, good and evil. In order to keep the precepts you absolutely must not be jealous: neither should you be aggressive, like a bandit.

If the mind remains unperturbed in all states, good and bad, that is the concentration-refuge.

Do not obstruct yourself with feelings of inferiority, but use wisdom to destroy ignorance so that you may view the self-nature. Refrain from evil and practice good, but do not become attached to the idea of merit as the Emperor Wu of Liang did.

If you do good, forget about it. Don't run up to the Heaven of the Thirty-Three and shout, "I gave $500.00! I gave $1,000.00! My merit is higher than the heavens!" This is to be stupid like Emperor Wu; it is not wisdom.

Respect your father, mother, teacher, and elders and never speak of their faults. Do not be like the boy who testified against his own father. The police asked the father if he had stolen a sheep:

"No," said the father.

"What do you mean 'no?'" cried his son. "I saw you kill the sheep, eat it, and sell its wool. How can you deny that you stole it?"

This is wrong. If you know that your father is guilty, when the police come you should run. Refuse to testify! This is called "respecting your superiors."

Be considerate to those beneath you. Don't be mean to little children and unsympathetic to widows. Mencius said, "A child without a father is an orphan and an old woman without a husband is a widow." Orphans and widows deserve pity and support.

Sutra:

"The fourth is the liberation-refuge, which is simply your own mind independent of conditions, not thinking of good or evil, and free and unobstructed.

"The fifth is the refuge of knowledge and views, which is simply your own mind when it is independent of good and evil conditions and when it does not dwell in emptiness or cling to stillness. You should then study this in detail, listen a great deal, recognize your original mind, and penetrate the true principle of all the Buddhas. You should welcome and be in harmony with living creatures; and, without the idea of self or other, arrive directly at Bodhi, the unchanging true nature."

Commentary:

Is this clear? The absence of self-seeking is liberation. If you are self-seeking, you can't put everything down and so continually scheme and plot. To be liberated, do not grasp at good or evil.

If you say, "I will sit here and not study anything. I am empty!" your state is useless like the emptiness inside a rubber ball. It is not the emptiness of the void. These people sit all day thinking of nothing and doing nothing. At mealtime they eat, and at bedtime they sleep and do not even dream. This is a pitiful waste of time.

What should you do then?

You should study the Sutras in detail and listen to Sutra lectures. Those who dwell in emptiness and cling to stillness claim to study Buddhism. They do not listen to lectures or study the Dharma, but if you ask them about it, they say they know it all.

You should welcome living creatures and be in harmony with them. In the Chinese "to be in harmony with" is expressed by the phrase "to unite the light." What does that mean? All lamps give off light, but have you ever known lamplight to fight with lamplight? Has a lamplight ever said, "You are brighter than I am! That is no good. I am going to put out your light!", upon which it hits the other lamplight? Or the other lamp says, "Your light is too small. Either make it bigger or move out!" None of that goes on between lights. Do you understand? It applies to everyone in the world. You practice your way and I will practice mine, "without hindering one another." You cannot decide that someone's reputation is too dazzling and try to ruin him so that your own name will shine.

It is permissible for others to be jealous of me, but I am not jealous of anyone. The better you are, the better I like it. The more success you have, the happier I am. Not to be jealous is to unite the light.

You might say, "I am uniting the light with him, but he is not uniting the light with me." If you were truly uniting the light with him, you wouldn't know that he wasn't uniting the light with you. Do you understand? If you unite the light with him, how can you know that he is not uniting the light with you? He won't unite the light? That's no problem. Just continue to unite the light with him.

Welcome living creatures. If you like Great Vehicle Buddhism, I will explain the Great Vehicle. If you like the Small Vehicle, I will explain the Four Noble Truths of suffering, origination, stopping, and the Way. If you like the Bodhisattva Way, I will explain the Six Paramitas: giving, morality, patience, vigor, concentration, and wisdom, and the Ten Thousand Conducts which lead to realization of the Bodhisattva Way. If you like the dharmas of the Pratyeka Buddhas, I will explain the Twelve Conditioned Causes: ignorance conditions activity; activity conditions consciousness; consciousness conditions name and form; name and form conditions the six senses; the six senses condition contact; contact conditions feeling; feeling conditions love; love conditions grasping; grasping conditions becoming; becoming conditions birth; birth conditions old age and death.

This is called uniting the light and welcoming living creatures, responding to the needs of the individual. One of my disciples looked in the dictionary and found that in Chinese to "welcome living creatures" means to help other people. However, it is not just to help them, it is to induce them to leave suffering and obtain bliss.

"Lacking the idea of self or other, arrive directly at Bodhi, the unchanging true nature." Having helped one person, you cannot say, "I have taken a bhikshu across! How great is my merit?" If one thinks like that, he hasn't a dust mote of merit. Once you have done something, it should be forgotten. If you lead people to Buddhahood you should not be attached to the merit gained from it. Therefore the *Diamond Sutra* says "I must take all beings across to Nirvana... and yet not a single living being has been taken to Nirvana."

You recite the *Diamond Sutra* from morning to night, but do not understand its meaning in the least. "Look at ME!" you say. There is still "me," and "me" comes before everything else. What *Diamond Sutra* do you recite anyway? The *Diamond Sutra* speaks of having no mark of self, no mark of people, of others, of living beings or a life, because all dharmas are empty appearances. Is there anything more wonderful? If you truly understand, you arrive directly at Bodhi, the unchanging true nature. This is called the refuge of proper knowledge and views. You have been liberated from knowledge, views, and attachments.

No self, no other–
Contemplate independence,

No emptiness, no form–
View the One Come Thus.

Without the mark of self: just that is the Bodhisattva Avalokiteshvara. If you do not fall either into emptiness or existence, you can see the Buddha.

Sutra:

"Good Knowing Advisors, the incense of these refuges perfumes each of you within. Do not seek outside. I will now transmit to you the markless repentance and reform to destroy the offensive actions done within the three periods of time and to purify the three karmas."

Commentary:

Repentance is to repent of past misdeeds and reform is to refrain from error in the future. If you receive it with a sincere mind, this repentance and reform can wipe away the offenses of the past and prevent them from being committed in the future. Purify your mind, and the transmission will purify the karma of your body, mouth and mind.

Sutra:

"Good Knowing Advisors, repeat after me: 'May this disciple be, in past, present, and future thought, in every thought, unstained by stupidity and confusion. May it be wiped away at once and never arise again.'"

Commentary:

Defiled by stupidity, turned by stupidity, you soon become quite stupid. It is most important, in every thought, not to go down the road of stupidity but bring forth wisdom instead.

Bad karma is created out of ignorance. Completely repent and reform of all offenses: killing, stealing, sexual misconduct, greed, hatred, stupidity, filthy language, lying, harsh speech, and slander, and in an instant they will be wiped away. Do not commit offenses out of stupidity and confusion.

Sutra:

"'May this disciple be, in past, present, and future thought, in every thought, unstained by arrogance and deceit. Now I completely repent of and reform all bad actions done in the past out of arrogance and deceit and other such offenses. May their effects be wiped away at once and may they never be perpetrated again!'"

Commentary:

Arrogance:

Only knowing there is you;
Unaware that there are others.

Looking down on everything: "In the heavens and below, I alone am honored." "Deceit" is lying; it is also the self-deceit of thinking that you are indispensable number one in the entire world. "I am the highest. The President, the King, and the Chairman cannot compare with me." Do not be stained by arrogance or turned by deceit.

Sutra:

"'May this disciple be in past, present, and future thought, in every thought unstained by jealousy. Now I completely repent of and reform all bad actions done in the past out of jealousy and other such offenses. May they be wiped away at once and never arise again.'"

Commentary:

Jealousy is the very worst thing! Cultivators see someone who is more intelligent than they are and become jealous; they see someone who learns faster and become jealous; they see someone sitting "thus, thus unmoving" and become jealous; they see someone eating more food and become jealous; they see someone sleeping more and become jealous; they see someone drinking more tea and become jealous; even to the point that when someone has been sick for a long time they think, "Why can't *I* get sick, too?" Do not be defiled or turned by jealousy.

Sutra:

"Good Knowing Advisors, the above has been the markless repentance and reform. What is repentance and what is reform? Repentance is to repent of past errors, to repent so completely of all bad actions done in the past out of stupidity, confusion, arrogance, deceit, jealousy, and other such offenses, that they never arise again. Reform is to refrain from such transgressions in the future. Awakening and cutting off such offenses completely and never committing them again is called repentance and reform.

"Common people, stupid and confused, know only how to repent of former errors and do not know how to

reform and refrain from transgressions in the future. Because they do not reform, their former errors are not wiped away, and they will occur in the future. If former errors are not wiped away and transgressions are again committed, how can that be called repentance and reform?

"Good Knowing Advisors, as you have repented and reformed, I will now teach you to make the four all-encompassing vows.

> ***I vow to take across the limitless living beings***
> ***of my own mind.***
> ***I vow to cut off the inexhaustible afflictions***
> ***of my own mind.***
> ***I vow to study the immeasurable Dharma-doors***
> ***of my own nature.***
> ***I vow to realize the supreme Buddha Way***
> ***of my own nature.***

"Good Knowing Advisors, did all of you not just say, 'I vow to take across the limitless living beings'? What does it mean? You should remember that it is not Hui Neng who takes them across. Good Knowing Advisors, the 'living beings' within your mind are deviant and confused thoughts, deceitful and false thoughts, unwholesome thoughts, jealous thoughts, vicious thoughts: all these thoughts are 'living beings.' The self-nature of each one of them must take itself across. That is true crossing over."

Commentary:

You must vow to take across the beings within your own heart, to cut off the afflictions, and to study the Dharma-doors. There is nothing higher than Buddhahood: vow to realize it.

Living beings are incalculably numerous, but you yourself must vow to save them, for it is not the Sixth Patriarch who takes them across. These good and bad living beings exist within your own mind. The good ones seek unsurpassed Bodhi and produce the Bodhi mind, while the bad ones must still be saved. Think it over and ask yourself, "Have I saved the living beings within my own mind? Am I proper in attitude and honorable in conduct or am I jealous, obstructive, and otherwise ignorant?"

The living beings within the mind are limitless, but our first concerns are the deviant and confused living beings, which should be taken across by means of proper wisdom; the deceitful and false living beings, which should be taken across by means of humility, and the unwholesome living beings, which should be taken across by means of goodness. If you find that you have these faults, vow to correct them, for if you do not they will drag you into the inescapable and endless misery of hell.

Respect takes jealous living beings across. Although Bodhiruci was a Dharma Master, he envied other Dharma Masters and viciously tried to poison Bodhidharma. Such thoughts are living beings and you are making a serious mistake if you do not take them across.

Sutra:

"What is meant by 'the self nature taking itself across'? It is to take across by means of right views the living beings of deviant views, affliction, and delusion within your own mind. Once you have right views, use

Prajna Wisdom to destroy the living beings of delusion, confusion, and falsehood. Each one takes itself across. Enlightenment takes confusion across, wisdom takes delusion across, goodness takes evil across. Such crossing over is a true crossing.

"Further, 'I vow to cut off the inexhaustible afflictions.' That is to use the Prajna Wisdom of your own self-nature to cast out the vain and false thoughts in your mind.

"Further, 'I vow to study the immeasurable Dharma-doors.' You must see your own nature and always practice the right Dharma. That is true study.

"Further, 'I vow to realize the supreme Buddha way,' and with humble mind to always practice the true and the proper. Separate yourself from both confusion and enlightenment, and always give rise to Prajna. When you cast out the true and the false, you see your nature and realize the Buddha-way at the very moment it is spoken of. Always be mindful; cultivate the Dharma that possesses the power of this vow."

Commentary:

Use Prajna wisdom to destroy the living beings of delusion, confusion, and falsehood. Beat them to death! You ask, "But isn't that a violation of the precept against killing?" Here you may violate the precept, just a bit. You are indeed hard to teach! When you break precepts, you don't worry about breaking them, but when you do not break precepts you worry about breaking them.

Transform the bad beings within your nature so that the good ones may dwell undisturbed and at peace. You may kill them;

you may beat them to death. Such crossing over is true crossing over.

Afflictions never end, but you must cut them off. Actually, "cut off" means "change." Change your afflictions into Bodhi. Afflictions are actually Bodhi, and if you cut off all afflictions you cut off Bodhi. If you cut off all afflictions you would become a Buddha, and you don't want to do that just yet, do you? So leave just a hair's worth of afflictions and transform the rest into Bodhi. Use genuine Prajna wisdom to get rid of affliction and cast out all vain, false, deviant, and ignorant thoughts.

Recognize your mind, see your original nature, and always practice the right Dharma, not the wrong. You may study the Buddhadharma in detail, but if you do not practice it, it is not true study. True Buddhist studies includes both study and practice. For example, people who used to smoke, drink, and take drugs no longer do so once they have studied the Buddhadharma. They do not even eat meat! Those who were lazy and did nothing but sleep from morning to night and from night to morning, now read and translate Sutras, listen to lectures, and meditate vigorously without a thought of sleeping. If this were not true study, why would they choose to work so hard?

All living beings can cross themselves over. No one needs to take them across.

The four vows in the text above are the basic vows which all Bodhisattvas should make.

As to the humble mind, the *Earth Store Sutra* says,

> *"The Buddha told Earth Store Bodhisattva, 'Perhaps there are kings of countries in Jambudvipa, or noblemen, great ministers, great elders, great Kshatriyas, great Brahmans, and the rest who encounter the tired, the poor, and those who are*

hunchbacked, crippled, dumb, mute, deaf, retarded, eyeless, as well as all others who are handicapped. Perhaps these kings and great men will wish to give and will be able to do so with great compassion, a humble heart, and a smile. Perhaps they will give personally with their own hands or arrange for others to give, speaking gentle and sympathetic words. Such kings and others will obtain blessings comparable to the meritorious virtue they would gain by giving to Buddhas as numerous as the sand-grains in one hundred Ganges Rivers.'"

Vow to realize the unsurpassed path!

A ten-thousand-story building
Is built from the ground up:

Once a person told an illogical tale. "In New York," he said, "the skyscrapers are not built from the ground up. They are built in empty space. They build the roof first." Everyone racked their brains and grew very upset, but no one could figure out how a building could be built in empty space. When I was in New York, I saw that the buildings were, in fact, built from the ground up. His story was nothing but a false rumor.

Another person said, "America is indeed beautiful! The American clouds are not like clouds in other countries. They are multicolored and entwined like garlands! The American moon is triangular and the American sun is square!" Do you believe this?

To realize Buddhahood, one must begin from the ground up, with a humble mind. Do not brag, "Look at me!" Practice the true and proper Dharma with a contrite heart and modest manner.

"Separate yourself from confusion and enlightenment." You say, "Separating oneself from confusion is all right, but how can one possibly separate oneself from enlightenment?" This refers to deviant enlightenment, not right enlightenment. Those with deviant enlightenment are slow to understand the Buddhadharma, but they don't need to be taught how to gamble or take drugs. They can do that on their own. You should keep away from such evil enlightenment. The text here does not say that you should avoid right enlightenment.

"You always give rise to Prajna." When you separate from deviant enlightenment, you give rise to wisdom, understanding, and right enlightenment and constantly generate Prajna.

"When you cast out the true and the false, you see the Buddha-nature and realize the Buddha-way at the very moment of speaking of it." The truth that you cast aside is relative, not actual. Once rid of the true and the false, the original True Suchness-nature is manifest. You cannot say that this nature is either true or false. Truth exists because there is falsehood and falsehood because there is truth. The true nature, however, is neither true nor false. *The Shurangama Sutra* says,

> *Falseness itself manifests all truth;*
> *The false and true are both false.*

The Great Master Yung Chia in his "Song of Enlightenment," said:

> *When truth is not postulated,*
> *falseness is basically empty.*
> *Existence and non-existence both rejected:*
> *what is not empty, make empty.*

Real truth has no opposite.

"Always be mindful; cultivate the Dharma that possesses the power of this vow." Having made these vows, you may practice. Cultivate them in every thought.

Sutra:

> **"Good Knowing Advisors, now that you have made the four all-encompassing vows, I will transmit the precepts of the triple refuge that has no mark. Good Knowing Advisors, take refuge with the enlightened, the honored, the doubly complete. Take refuge with the right, the honored that is apart from desire. Take refuge with the pure, the honored among the multitudes."**

Commentary:

Take refuge with the Buddha; the Buddha is enlightened. Enlightenment is simply the Buddha. The Buddha is nothing but enlightenment. The Buddha is "doubly complete" because he has perfected both blessings and wisdom.

Take refuge with the Dharma which is "right" and proper. Do not take refuge with deviant teachings, heavenly demons, or heterodox religions. Take refuge with the genuine Buddhadharma which is the "honored that is apart from desire."

Everyone has sexual desire and it actually kills people. Why don't we realize Buddhahood? It is because of desire, and the greed, hate, and stupidity which accompany it. We study the Buddhadharma in order to get rid of desire and cut off love. The absence of lust is the honored that is apart from desire.

Take refuge with the Sangha; the Sangha is pure and its members are called "pure fields of merit." True, genuine cultivators should maintain the precept against handling money. Without money, you are pure; with money you are dirty.

Members of the Sangha who truly wish to cultivate should stay away from money.

On the other hand, without money you cannot nourish the Way, you cannot cultivate. Although you need money, you should not be attached to it and depend on its source, thinking all day, "Who has several million in the bank? I'll go and beg from him. Then I can build a temple or a school or perhaps print an edition of the Tripitaka as a meritorious activity." That's just profit seeking.

While in Manchuria there was a short period during which money and I parted company. I never touched money and for a good reason. Living in the temple where I lived when I left home were forty or fifty bhikshus, but sometimes as few as ten. When I first arrived at the temple, the abbot was out begging and none of the bhikshus knew me. "I know the abbot," I said, and they welcomed me.

After leaving home, I practiced austerities, but not the ones you practice. You type, translate Sutras, and meditate, but in the big rural temple where I lived, there was a lot of outside work to be done. Sweeping the courtyard alone took an hour. My first job was to clean the toilets, which weren't flush toilets, but pit toilets, and every day the waste had to be removed because the cultivators did not want to smell the odor. They gave this work to me because I had just left home and had not yet cut off my attachment to smells. I did it every day and didn't mind too much.

I got up at two in the morning to prepare the hall for services. When it snowed I swept the walkways so that they were clear at four when everyone else got up. When the abbot returned and saw me he said, "So you have come!"

"Yes," I said, "I have."

After I had formally left home, he called a meeting, wishing to elect me as manager, a position second only to the abbot. When the abbot retires, the manager becomes the new abbot. Everyone objected. "He has just left home," they said. "How can he possibly be manager!"

"Very well," said the abbot. "Let's go before the image of Wei T'ou Bodhisattva and draw names." Oddly enough, they drew three times and my name came up each time. No one said a word because I had been elected by Wei T'ou Bodhisattva himself. Later, when the abbot wanted to make me an administrator, I said, "All right, but I will not touch money. Other people must handle and count it. That is my condition."

Unusual things happened while I held this precept. Whenever I went to the train station I would sit and wait for someone who knew me to come and offer to buy me a ticket. If no one came I just waited, but strangely enough whenever I went to the station someone came to buy me a ticket.

If you don't handle money, you are pure. If you keep even one cent, you are unclean. Take refuge with the Sangha, which occupies the purest, highest, and most venerable position–"the honored among the multitudes."

Sutra:

"'From this day forward, we call enlightenment our master and will never again take refuge with deviant demons or outside religions. We constantly enlighten ourselves by means of the Triple Jewel of our own self-nature.'

"Good Knowing Advisors, I exhort you all to take refuge with the Triple Jewel of your own nature: the Buddha, which is enlightenment, the Dharma, which is right, and the Sangha, which is pure.

"When your mind takes refuge with enlightenment, deviant confusion does not arise. Desire decreases, so that you know contentment and are able to keep away from wealth and from the opposite sex. That is called the honored, the doubly complete.

"When your own mind takes refuge with what is right, there are no deviant views in any of your thoughts. Because there are no deviant views, there is no self, other, arrogance, greed, love, or attachment. That is called the honored that is apart from desire.

"When your own mind takes refuge with the pure, your self-nature is not stained by attachment to any state of defilement, desire or love. That is called the honored among the multitudes."

Commentary:

To lessen desire, it is not enough to be a vegetarian and to read Sutras. You must cut off all sexual desire:

If one does not cast out thoughts of lust,
One never will escape the dust.

Unless you rid yourself of sexual desire you will never get out of the Triple World: the world of desire, the world of form, and the formless world. "Contentment" means not being greedy. Dying of poverty, dying of starvation, no matter what the difficulty, you are never greedy.

"Separate from wealth and beauty." Do you see how clearly it says that you should not covet wealth, or the opposite sex, or fame? That is to be doubly complete, perfect in blessings and wisdom.

"States of defilement" here refers to all social and political situations. You should not be molded by the society, but rather transform it. Teach living beings; do not be taught by them. Once, when I noticed that one of my students had been talking on the phone for over an hour, I asked her what she was doing. "I'm trying to convert my boyfriend to Buddhism," she said.

"Really?" I said. "What is he now?"

"He's a Catholic," she said.

"Be careful he doesn't convert you." I said. "His belief in Catholicism is firm. Take care that he doesn't take you across!"

Sure enough, not long afterward she ran off. Now what she believes, whether she saved others or was saved by them, is unknown.

The non-defilement of the self-nature is called "the honored among the multitudes." Living beings are all defiled. If you wish to be an exceptional individual, you must leave desire behind. To separate yourself from desire is to be a great hero and true student of the Buddhadharma. Unless you correct your faults, what little Buddhadharma you do know is useless.

Sutra:

"If you cultivate this practice, you take refuge with yourself.

"Common people do not understand that, and so, from morning to night, they take the triple-refuge precepts. They say they take refuge with the Buddha, but where is the Buddha? If they cannot see the Buddha, how can they return to him? Their talk is absurd.

"Good Knowing Advisors, each of you examine yourselves. Do not make wrong use of the mind. *The Avatamsaka Sutra* clearly states that you should take refuge with your own Buddha, not with some other

Buddha. If you do not take refuge with the Buddha in yourself, there is no one you can rely on.

"Now that you are self-awakened, you should each take refuge with the Triple Jewel of your own mind.

"Within yourself, regulate your mind and nature; outside yourself, respect others. That is to take refuge with yourself."

Commentary:

Ordinary people do not understand the principle of taking refuge. If you constantly say, "I take refuge with the Buddha," just where is the Buddha? If you have never seen the Buddha, then how can you take refuge with him? If you say, "I have seen him!" you are lying.

The Sutra tells you to take refuge with your own Buddha, not with some other Buddha. The Buddha of your self-nature is always present, but you didn't know this because until now you never had the instruction of a Good Knowing Advisor. Now that you have taken refuge, you should be clear about the Buddha of your self-nature.

Take refuge with enlightenment.
Take refuge with what is right.
Take refuge with the pure.
Take refuge with enlightenment
and don't do stupid things.
Take refuge with what is right
and don't do what is wrong.
Take refuge with the pure
and don't do unclean things.

Take refuge with the Triple Jewel
within your own mind.

If you really understand the Buddhadharma, you will respect not just your relatives and friends, but everyone, even people you don't know. Instead of slapping someone when you see him and then throwing mud in his face, you must be the most respectful toward those who act the worst toward you. This is a fundamental responsibility of students of Buddhism. You say, "You haven't really been bad to me, so how could I be bad to you?" Isn't this extraordinary? It's just to take refuge with the Triple Jewel of your self-nature.

Sutra:

"Good Knowing Advisors, now that you have taken refuge with the Triple Jewel, you should listen carefully while I explain to you the three bodies of a single substance, the self-nature of the Buddha, so that you may see the three bodies and become completely enlightened to your own self-nature.

"Repeat after me,

I take refuge with the clear, pure Dharma-body
of the Buddha within my own body.
I take refuge with the hundred thousand myriad
Transformation-bodies of the Buddha
within my own body.
I take refuge with the complete and full Reward body
of the Buddha within my own body.

"Good Knowing Advisors, the form-body is an inn; it cannot be returned to. The three bodies of the Buddha

exist within the self-nature of worldly people, but because they are confused, they do not see the nature within them and so seek the three bodies of the Tathagata outside themselves. They do not see that the three bodies of the Buddha are within their own bodies.

"Listen to what I say, for it can cause you to see the three bodies of your own self-nature within your own body. The three bodies of the Buddha arise from your own self-nature and are not obtained from outside.

"What is the clear, pure Dharma-body Buddha? The worldly person's nature is basically clear and pure, and the ten thousand dharmas are produced from it. The thought of evil produces evil actions and the thought of good produces good actions. Thus all dharmas exist within the self-nature. This is like the sky which is always clear, and the sun and moon which are always bright, so that if they are obscured by floating clouds it is bright above the clouds and dark below them. But if the wind suddenly blows and scatters the clouds, there is brightness above and below, and the myriad forms appear. The worldly person's nature constantly drifts like those clouds in the sky.

"Good Knowing Advisors, intelligence is like the sun and wisdom is like the moon. Intelligence and wisdom are constantly bright, but if you are attached to external states, the floating clouds of false thought cover the self-nature so that it cannot shine.

"If you meet a Good Knowing Advisor, if you listen to the true and right Dharma and cast out your own confusion and falseness, then inside and out there will be penetrating brightness, and within the self-nature all the ten thousand dharmas will appear. That is how it is with

those who see their own nature. It is called the clear, pure Dharma-body of the Buddha."

Commentary:

Your physical body is like a house. You must not take refuge in it, but rather take refuge with your own self-nature. Everyone has the three Buddha-bodies within themselves, but because of their delusion they don't know it.

Break through the clouds of illusion! It is just because you have not broken through them that you are deluded and have no wisdom. But if you do away with troubles and ignorance and listen to a Clear-eyed Advisor's explanation of the orthodox Teaching, your own nature will reflect all the dharmas, like a luminous crystal.

Those who see their nature and know their original mind are like a clear sky:

The heart calm–
All worries go away;
The mind still–
Heaven has no clouds.

When your heart is upset there is chaos, but when your mind is calm and resolved, everything is auspicious.

The pure heart
like the moon in water;
The quiet mind
like a cloudless sky;
True wealth: the mind stopped,
thought cut off;

True field of blessing: all passions
put to an end.

You must end your delusion and greed, still the mind and cut off thought. That is true wealth. Truly wealthy people are not greedy. Those who are greedy are thereby poor. They may have a little money, but they are never satisfied.

The passions are just selfish desires and without them you are a true field of merit.

Sutra:

"Good Knowing Advisors, when your own mind takes refuge with your self-nature, it takes refuge with the true Buddha. To take refuge is to rid your self-nature of egotism and unwholesome thoughts as well as of jealousy, obsequiousness, deceitfulness, contempt, pride, conceit, and deviant views, and all other unwholesome tendencies whenever they arise.

"To take refuge is to be always aware of your own transgressions and never to speak of other people's good or bad traits. Always to be humble and polite is to have penetrated to the self-nature without any obstacle. That is taking refuge.

Commentary:

If you turn the light around and reverse the illumination, you take refuge with the true Buddha. Be careful not to envy others. Would you like to know why you are so deluded? It is because in past lives, life after life, you envied others. You envied their intelligence and so now you are stupid; you envied their talent and so now you have none. You were jealous then and now you are inferior.

You should not be devious and indirect. Get rid of egotism: "I, I, me, myself, everything revolves around me!" You should not be deceitful, full of self-importance, and contemptuous of others.

To have deviant views is to misjudge every situation you encounter and then go off in the wrong direction. Deviant views are easy to come by. If you wish to take refuge, see your own faults and quit talking about other people. Criticism is *yin* and praise is *yang*. You should find the Middle Way.

Sutra:

"What is the perfect, full Reward-body of the Buddha? Just as one lamp can disperse the darkness of a thousand years, one thought of wisdom can destroy ten thousand years of delusion.

"Do not think of the past; it is gone and can never be recovered. Instead think always of the future and in every thought, perfect and clear, see your own original nature. Although good and evil differ, the original nature is non-dual. That non-dual nature is the real nature. Undefiled by either good or evil, it is the perfect, full Reward-body of the Buddha.

"One evil thought arising from the self-nature destroys ten thousand eons' worth of good karma. One good thought arising from the self-nature ends evils as numerous as the sand-grains in the Ganges River. To reach the unsurpassed Bodhi directly, see it for yourself in every thought and do not lose the original thought. That is the Reward-body of the Buddha."

Commentary:

When you bring forth wisdom, not just ten thousand years, but ten thousand eons of delusion are wiped away.

Do not regret the past or be anxious about the future. "What am I going to do next?" you ask. If you plant good causes, you will reap good results; if you plant bad causes, you will reap bad results. So do good things and good things will happen; do bad and bad things will happen. Your thoughts should be proper, perfectly lucid, and full of light, not deviant, selfish, and self-seeking, obstructive or jealous. If you are not afraid that others will be better than you, it may be that you are a little better than they are. But if you fear that they will surpass you, then they are all better than you.

The good and evil natures within the self-nature differ, but the self-nature is not dual. The non-dual suchness self-nature is the real nature. Yung Chia wrote in his "Song of Enlightenment":

> *Ignorance and the real nature*
> *are just the Buddha nature;*
> *The illusory empty body*
> *is just the Dharma body.*

In the original, real nature, there is no good or evil. It is entirely perfect and wonderful in itself, far reaching in its penetration, and broad in understanding.

One vicious thought, such as Bodhiruci's desire to poison Bodhidharma, destroys ten thousand eons of good karma, whereas one good thought melts away evil karma as immense as the number of sandgrains in the Ganges. One good thought can cause the realization of Buddhahood, and one bad thought is cause enough for going to hell. If you would like to know whether you are going to become a Buddha or go to hell, take a look at what kind of thoughts you have.

To arrive at Buddhahood directly, see it for yourself in every thought. Understand your own mind and see your own original nature. Do not lose the original thought, the true thought, the true nature.

Sutra:

"What are the hundred thousand myriad Transformation bodies of the Buddha? If you are free of any thought of the ten thousand dharmas, then your nature is basically like emptiness, but in one thought of calculation, transformation occurs. Evil thoughts are transformed into hell-beings and good thoughts into heavenly beings. Viciousness is transformed into dragons and snakes, and compassion into Bodhisattvas. Wisdom is transformed into the upper realms, and delusion into the lower realms. The transformations of the self-nature are extremely many, and yet the confused person, unawakened to that truth, continually gives rise to evil and walks evil paths. Turn a single thought back to goodness, and wisdom is produced. That is the Transformation-body of the Buddha within your self-nature."

Commentary:

Having discussed the perfect full Reward-body which lacks nothing and has nothing in excess, which obtains nothing and loses nothing and is neither defiled nor immaculate, increasing nor decreasing, male nor female, good nor evil–but which is perfect Bodhi that returns to non-attainment–the Sixth Patriarch asks, “What are the hundred-thousand myriad Transformation bodies?”

“Wc havc onc body,” you say. “IIow can wc have a hundred thousand myriad bodies? What do the Buddha’s transformation-bodies have to do with me?”

These transformation-bodies are simply a hundred thousand myriad thoughts and calculations. Shakyamuni Buddha can transform himself to appear in any one of the ten Dharma Realms. That is, he can become a Buddha, a Bodhisattva, a Pratyekabuddha, an Arhat, a god, asura, human, hell-being, hungry ghost, or animal.

You might also say that you and I have a hundred thousand myriad transformation-bodies. I have taken a hundred thousand myriad disciples and all of them imitate their teacher in cultivation. They see their teacher eating only one meal a day, before noon, and say, “I’m going to do that too.” I tell them, “I never stick out my hand and beg. I don’t depend on external situations and neither should you. If no one makes offerings to me and I die, that’s just fine. Those who leave the home life under me must follow my Three Conditions, as I do:

Freezing, I don’t beg,
Starving, I don’t scheme, and
Dying of poverty, I ask for nothing.

The disciples say, “All right! Even if we starve to death, we won’t beg or scheme.”

Because they copy me, they are my transformation bodies. In the future you will have transformation bodies, too. If you have a good way of doing things, you will have a hundred thousand myriad good transformation bodies. If you have an evil, ghostly way, you will have that many ghostly transformation bodies.

"If you are free of any thought of the ten thousand Dharmas, then your nature is basically like emptiness..."

One thought not produced,
The entire substance manifests.

If you do not give rise to a single thought, your original Buddha nature appears. But aren't you producing a thought? Are you without false thinking? Are you not thinking, "What will I eat tomorrow? What time will I get to bed tonight?" or, "I'm thirsty. I think I'll have a cup of tea?"

Without false thinking, you are a Buddha. But if you can't cut off your false thinking, you must not claim to be a Buddha; you must cultivate the Way. If you haven't cultivated and say, "Hey! I'm a Buddha!" you are just a dog of a Buddha. You can't simply say that everyone is Buddha, you have to cultivate and realize Buddhahood. Without cultivation, people are people, animals are animals, and dogs are dogs. But do not be offended. Dogs also have the Buddha nature. They have to cultivate, that's all.

Six roots suddenly move:
A covering of clouds.

When you see something and think it beautiful or hear something and think, "Music!" you are being influenced by externals. Using the six sense organs, the six sense objects and the six consciousnesses in this way, you cover yourself with clouds.

"Evil thoughts are transformed into hell-beings..." Suppose you think, "How can I get famous? How can I succeed? I'll start a riot, murder people, set fires, and loot the streets."

"...and good thoughts into heavenly beings." "Oh," you say, "I want to help people. You have no money? Here is a million to help you get by." Or you think, "No one makes offerings to the Americans who have left home. I'll make an offering." Don't wait for America, such an affluent nation, to allow its new Buddhist Sangha to starve to death: transform into the heavens.

"Wisdom is transformed into the upper realms, and delusion into the lower realms." With intelligence, you go up, but if you are deluded, you fall.

The Superior one mounts on high.
The petty person travels a lower road.

"The transformations of the self-nature are extremely many, and yet the confused person, unawakened to that truth, continually gives rise to evil, and walks evil paths." The confused person's every thought is evil: "That person mistreats me! I'm going to ruin him." The Great Master Shen Hsiu was one who walked evil paths by repeatedly sending hired killers after the Sixth Patriarch.

"Turn a single thought back to goodness, and wisdom is produced. That is the Transformation-body of the Buddha within your self-nature." Do you understand? If you do, you are a Good Knowing Advisor; if you don't, you're an evil knowing advisor. Wouldn't you rather be a Good Knowing Advisor?

Sutra:

"Good Knowing Advisors, the Dharma body of the Buddha is basically complete. To see your own nature in every thought is the Reward body of the Buddha. When the Reward body thinks and calculates, it is the Transformation body of the Buddha. Awaken and

cultivate by your own efforts the merit and virtue of your self-nature. That is truly taking refuge.

"The skin and flesh of the physical body are like an inn to which you cannot return. Simply awaken to the three bodies of your self-nature and you will understand the self-nature Buddha."

Commentary:

You yourself must wake up and cultivate on your own. Do not babble intellectual zen all day, "Yak, yak, yak!" talking but never practicing. Talking a yard is not as good as practicing an inch. If you do nothing but talk, you are cheating people. So pay no attention to whether my lectures are good or bad. Look instead to see if I have ever cheated you.

The Sixth Patriarch tells you to awaken to the three bodies of your self-nature, so you say, "Then taking refuge with myself is to take refuge with my body." No. If you take refuge with your body you are just adding a head on top of a head, like Yajnadatta in the *Shurangama Sutra* who ran everywhere looking for his head. Your physical body is an inn where your self-nature temporarily dwells. Therefore you cannot say, "My body is me." Your body is not you. Then is it someone else's? No your body is yours, it is not mine or his. It is yours, but it is not you. Don't I always say that if you live in a house, you can say the house is yours but you certainly cannot say the house is you? If you say that it is you, everyone will say, "He doesn't even know who he is! He thinks his house is him, but it's just a thing." Your body is like a house; don't mistake it for being you. Understand?

Don't take refuge with the physical body, take refuge with your self-nature. Awaken to the clear, pure Dharma-body Buddha, the perfect, full Reward-body Buddha, and the hundred thousand myriad Transformation-body Buddhas within your own nature. By understanding the Buddha of your self-nature you may perfect the three bodies.

Sutra:

"I have a verse without marks. If you can recite and memorize it, it will wipe away-accumulated eons of confusion and offenses as soon as the words are spoken. The verse runs:

A confused person will foster blessings,
but not cultivate the Way;
And say, "To practice for the blessings
is practice of the Way."

While giving and making offerings
brings blessings without limit,
It is in the mind that the three evils
have their origin.

By seeking blessings you may wish
to obliterate offenses;
But in the future, though you are blessed,
offenses still remain.

You ought to simply strike the evil
conditions from your mind;
By true repentance and reform
within your own self-nature.

A sudden awakening: the true repentance and
reform of the Great Vehicle;

You must cast out the deviant, and practice
the right, to be without offense.

To study the Way, always look
within your own self-nature;
You are then the same in kind
and lineage as all Buddhas.

Our Patriarch passed along only
this Sudden Teaching;
Wishing that all might see the nature
and be of one substance.

In the future if you wish
to find the Dharma body;
Detach yourself from Dharma marks
and inwardly wash the mind.

Strive to see it for yourself
and do not waste your time,
For when the final thought has stopped
your life comes to an end.

Enlightened to the Great Vehicle
you can see your nature;
So reverently join your palms
and seek it with all your heart.

Commentary:

"Don't be nervous," continued the Great Master, "I have some good news! Don't you know? I have a verse without marks. Do you want to hear it? If you do, I'll recite; if not, I'll just put it away."

"Yes!" everyone exclaimed, "we definitely do want to hear it. Please be compassionate and recite it."

"If you can learn this verse by heart," the Master said, "it will cause the confusions and crimes accumulated from beginningless time, passing through limitless ages, life after life, to be eradicated immediately. Where will they go? Do you mean you still want to look for them? What a waste of effort!"

A confused person will foster blessing, but if you tell him to cultivate with vigor, he won't do it. Although there are not many students here, those present are extremely sincere. They do not fear leg-pain, back-pain, any pain whatever. "I will endure this pain and cultivate the Way, even if it means giving up my life!" they say. Such rare determination makes me happy, but I don't show my happiness by joking with you all day. It's not that kind of happiness; it's true happiness.

Deluded people say, "To practice for the blessings is practice of the Way." This is like the Emperor Wu of Liang who said, "I have taken Bhikshus across and have built many temples. I have made offerings and practiced charity and arranged vegetarian banquets. What great merit I must have! It's probably even greater than Shakyamuni Buddha's!"

Giving and making offerings brings limitless blessings, but the origin of the three evils is within the mind. What are the three evils? Greed, hate, and delusion.

Greed: "I think I'll eat a few more peanuts and then I won't be hungry today." Hate: "Hey! Who ate all the peanuts?" Delusion: Hating the one who ate the peanuts which makes you unreasonable and stupid. Cultivating blessings while neglecting wisdom has made you so stupid that you can't quit over-eating and even have the gall to speak of it as a bitter practice.

You cannot get rid of offenses by cultivating blessings, because although you obtain the blessings, the offenses still remain. What you should do is rid the mind of all evil conditions, i.e. thoughts of greed, hate, delusion, jealousy, obstructiveness, conceit, obsequiousness, viciousness and deceitfulness.

"But they're my old friends," you say. "We've been together for millions of years. How can I part with them?" Fine. If you can't part with them, then there's nothing to do but follow them down to hell.

To practice true repentance and reform is to understand the Great Vehicle and immediately get rid of all evil thoughts. It is very clear; no analogies are needed. You truly repent when you "get rid of the deviant and practice the right," as the Sixth Patriarch's verse says. Then you may walk down the straight, great bright road and be without offense.

"To study the Way, always look within the self-nature." Ask yourself, "What am I doing? Am I acting like a person or a ghost, an animal, a horse or a cow?" You are what you do. If you act like a Buddha, you are a Buddha. The Buddha practices friendliness, compassion, sympathetic joy, and giving. His compassion is genuine, not false and greedy. He never thinks, "If I am a little compassionate to you, you will be greatly compassionate to me."

There are no ulterior motives in the compassion I have for you. I would not give you a brick and expect a piece of jade in return.

Cultivators, turn the light around, reverse its illumination, and ask yourself, "Am I thinking like a demon or a Buddha? Am I selfish or generous, self-seeking or charitable?" If you are charitable you are the "same in kind as all the Buddhas." If you act like a Buddha, you are a Buddha, but if you act like a ghost, how can you be a Buddha?

By "our Patriarch" the Sixth Patriarch means Bodhidharma, who transmitted only the Sudden Teaching Dharma-door because he wanted everyone to see the Buddha nature and realize the Buddha Way together.

"If you wish to find the Dharma-body," then separate yourself from all marks. Do not be attached, jealous, obstructive, ignorant, afflicted, or snobbish. You cannot think, as the Buddha did, "In the heavens and below, I alone am honored." *The Diamond Sutra* says, "One who has left all marks is called a Buddha." Apart from marks and unattached to self and to dharmas, the mind-ground is cleansed.

"Strive to see it for yourself" and go forward with heroic vigor. You'll never succeed if you're lazy and waste your time, saying "Wait, I'll cultivate tomorrow. Wait, I'll translate tomorrow." Even at lunchtime you say, "Wait, I'll eat later." Wait, wait, until it's time to die and King Yama won't listen to you when you say, "Wait! I'll die later." If you are truly free, you come and go in birth and death and yet are not subject to birth and death. King Yama has no control over you. This is like the Third Patriarch, Seng Ts'an, who said, "You see others sit in lotus posture to die and think it special. Watch this!" and grabbed a tree branch with one hand and went to Nirvana, just hanging there. Wasn't he free?

If you wait until your dying breath to cultivate, it will be too late, "for when the final thought has stopped, your life comes to an end. Earlier, in Chapter IV, didn't the Sutra say that you should not cut off your thought, because when the last thought is cut off you die and then undergo rebirth in some other place? At the time of death there is nothing–no fame, no riches. Both your hands will be empty and you'll be forced to put down what you can't put down. No matter how dear your loved ones are, you'll have to part with them.

Enlightened to the Great Vehicle
you can see the nature;
So reverently join your palms and
seek it with all your heart.

See the nature and humbly seek to follow the unsurpassed Way.

Sutra:

The Master said, "Good Knowing Advisors, all of you should take up this verse and cultivate according to it. If you see your nature at the moment these words are spoken, even if we are a thousand miles apart you will always be by my side. If you do not awaken at the moment of speaking, then, face to face we are a thousand miles apart, so why did you bother to come from so far? Take care of yourselves and go well."

The united assembly heard this Dharma and there were none who did not awaken. They received it with delight and practiced in accord with it.

Commentary:

I think the Sixth Patriarch liked to talk and so he delivered this *Platform Sutra*. If he hadn't liked to speak, he wouldn't have taught any Sutra at all.

Now I am teaching it to all of you:

"You are quite intelligent," the Master said, "and you have good roots. We have an affinity which goes back for many lifetimes and many ages, and therefore we have met here today." Of course, there were no foreigners in the Master's Dharma-assembly; they were all Chinese. That I have met with so many Americans must be a case of even greater affinity.

CHAPTER VII

OPPORTUNITIES AND CONDITIONS

Sutra:

The Master obtained the Dharma at Huang Mei and returned to Ts'ao Hou Village in Shao Chou where no one knew him. But Liu Chih Liao, a scholar, received him with great courtesy. Chih Liao's aunt, Bhikshuni Wu Chin Tsang, constantly recited the *Mahaparinirvana Sutra*. When the Master heard it, he instantly grasped its wonderful principle and explained it to her. The Bhikshuni then held out a scroll and asked about some characters.

The Master said, "I cannot read; please ask about the meaning."

"If you cannot even read, how can you understand the meaning?" asked the Bhikshuni.

The Master replied, "The subtle meaning of all Buddhas is not based on language."

The Bhikshuni was startled and she announced to all the elders and virtuous ones in the village: "Here is a gentleman who possesses the Way. We should ask him to stay and receive our offerings." Ts'ao Shu Liang, great-grandson of the Marquis Wu of the Wei dynasty, came rushing to pay homage, along with the people of the village.

At that time the pure dwellings of the ancient Pao Lin Temple, which had been destroyed by war and fire at the end of the Sui dynasty, were rebuilt on their old foundation. The Master was invited to stay and soon the temple became a revered place. He dwelt there a little over nine months when he was once again pursued by evil men. The Master hid in the mountain in the front of the temple, and when they set fire to the brush and trees, he escaped by crawling into a rock to hide. The rock still bears the imprints of the Master's knees and of his robe where he sat in lotus posture. Because of this it is called "The Rock of Refuge." Remembering the Fifth Patriarch's instructions to stop at Huai and hide at Hui, he went to conceal himself in those two cities.

Commentary:

After receiving the mind-seal Dharma from the Fifth Patriarch Hung Jen, the Sixth Patriarch returned to Shao Chou. He thereupon went to Ts'ao Hou Village, the present day Shao Kuan in Chü Chiang District. When he arrived in the vicinity of Nan Hua Temple, which before had been Pao Lin Temple, no one knew that he was the one who held the robe and bowl.

Liu Chih Liao was a wealthy retired official who enjoyed studying the Buddhadharma. He welcomed the Master reverently and made offerings to him. Chih Liao and his aunt, Bhikshuni Wu Chin Tsang, "limitless treasury," were the Sixth Patriarch's great Dharma protectors. Wu Chin Tsang liked to recite the *Mahaparinirvana Sutra*. This Sutra, in ten volumes, was spoken by the Buddha just before he went to Nirvana. Hearing the recitation, the Sixth Patriarch understood the subtle principle and explained it to the Bhikshuni. Probably she couldn't read very well, because she asked the Master, "What is this word?"

"Do you mean you can't read it?" said the Master.

"No, I can't," she said.

"Well, I can't either!" said the Master, "But if you ask about the meaning I can explain it for you."

"If you can't even read it, how can you know what it means?" she asked.

The Master said, "The Buddha's heart, the mind-Dharma, the wonderful principle of Sudden Enlightenment, has nothing to do with words. Instead, it points directly to the mind so that we can see our own nature and become Buddhas. Since it is not based on language it doesn't matter whether you can read."

Bhikshuni Wu Chin Tsang thought that was very strange indeed. She told everyone in the village, "Here is a gentleman who has the Way! He is a virtuous Dharma Master. He may not be able to read, but he's enlightened, so we should make offerings to him."

Although she didn't know a lot of characters, Wu Chin Tsang was nevertheless an incredible Bhikshuni. She ate one meal a day and never lay down to sleep, because she knew that the Fourth Patriarch recommended these practices. Although her family was wealthy, she kept the precept of never holding money. She studied and recited Sutras industriously, and when the time came, she died sitting up in meditation. Many days, many years have passed and her body still has not decayed. Because she was vigorous and worked hard at cultivation and had no sexual desire, her flesh transformed into indestructible vajra. I saw the body in a temple in Chü Chiang. It is truly awesome.

Among the villagers who paid homage to the Great Master was the great-grandson of Marquis Wu. Marquis Wu was very intelligent. He was, in fact, as clever as a fox. He was a genius, but he had a tendency to be jealous.

Bhikshuni Wu Chin Tsang promoted the Sixth Patriarch: "Do you know who he is?" she would say, "He's the rightful successor to the Fifth Patriarch! He holds the robe and bowl."

One flower may be beautiful, but it looks much better surrounded by greenery. If no one had protected him, the Sixth Patriarch would surely have been murdered by Shen Hsiu's gang, or those of other religions. His Dharma assembly flourished because his disciples and laypeople such as Bhikshuni Wu Chin Tsang and her nephew, Liu Chih Liao, the scholar, guarded and protected him. Vinaya Master T'ung Ying also brought several hundred of his students to study with the Master, and each student told his friends to come. So every day for lunch there were between 1,500 and 2,000 people, seven or eight hundred of whom were members of the Sangha.

Everyone made heartfelt offerings to help rebuild Nan Hua Temple. Some gave ten thousand ounces of silver, some gave a million. They asked the Master to live there and before long it was a great Bodhimanda, big enough for several thousand people.

A little over nine months later, several hundred of Shen Hsiu's men left Huang Mei, passing through the Ta Yü mountain range on their way to Nan Hua Temple. They traveled for over two months. If they hadn't been intent on killing the Master and stealing the robe and bowl, they would have given up after a couple of days. Think it over: Sixteen or seventeen years had passed since the transmission, and the Master had only been staying at Nan Hua for nine months when the evil men returned. It's not easy to be a Patriarch, unless you are a phony. Real Patriarchs live in great danger.

"If you understand the verse I have recited," said the Master, "you will 'get rid of the deviant, practice the right, and be without offense,' and although we are a thousand miles apart, you will be right beside me."

If my disciples understand and remember the Sutras I have explained, they will be right beside me. But if instead they take advantage of external circumstances or get jealous and angry, they will have studied the Way in vain. If they don't understand this verse, then even if we should stand face to face, we would still be a thousand miles apart.

If they believe in me, although we are a thousand miles apart, we are face to face. "Are you trying to make people believe in you?" you ask. No! Why should I want you to believe in me? You're better off believing in yourself, because if you cultivate, you do it for yourself. You don't eat to make me full. All I do is teach you the methods. If you have come all this way just to be a thousand miles from me, why did you bother to come at all?

"Take care of yourselves." Don't look down on yourself and say, "I'm not going to cultivate. I'm nothing but a dog anyway." See yourself as a person, not a dog, and go to a good place, not a bad one.

The Sixth Patriarch had spiritual powers and he knew that not just one or two, but several hundred men were after him. He hid in the "Rock of Refuge" which is just big enough to hold one person sitting in meditation. The evil men mingled in with the large crowd and stealthily set fire to the mountain. They burned off the entire area, but never found the Master. While hiding, the Master probably meditated with great intensity because the texture of his robe and the marks of his knees can still be seen imprinted in the rock. When I was at Nan Hua Temple I sat in the rock for a time, but I wasn't seeking refuge, I was just trying it out. When you sit inside it, no one can see you.

Bhikshu Fa Hai

Sutra:

When Bhikshu Fa Hai of Chü Chiang city in Shao Chou first called on the Patriarch, he asked, "Will you please instruct me on the sentence, 'Mind is Buddha'?"

The Master said, "When one's preceding thoughts are not produced this is mind and when one's subsequent thoughts are not extinguished this is Buddha. The setting up of marks is mind, and separation from them is Buddha. Were I to explain it fully, I would not finish before the end of the present age.

"Listen to my verse:

When the mind is called wisdom,
Then the Buddha is called concentration.
When concentration and wisdom are equal.
The intellect is pure.

Understand this Dharma teaching
By practicing within your own nature.
The function is basically unproduced;
It is right to cultivate both."

At these words, Fa Hai was greatly enlightened and spoke a verse in praise:

This mind is basically Buddha;
By not understanding I disgrace myself.
I know the cause of concentration and wisdom
Is to cultivate both and separate myself
from all things.

Commentary:

Bhikshu Fa Hai, also called Wen Yün, compiled and edited the *Platform Sutra* from the Sixth Patriarch's lectures. Although I dare not say that he liked to be first, when he wrote this chapter he certainly thought, "I am the Master's number one great disciple!" and consequently wrote about himself first.

"Great Master," said Fa Hai, "I don't understand the sentence 'This mind is Buddha.' Please explain it."

"Do not produce the former thought," said the Master, "and just that is mind. Do not extinguish the latter thought and just that is Buddha. With neither production nor extinction, the mind itself is Buddha. All appearances are set up by the mind, and if you can set up all appearances and be separate from them, that is Buddha."

The mind is called wisdom and the Buddha is called concentration. When concentration and wisdom are equal, the mind is Buddha and Buddha is the mind. They are one substance. When thought is pure, then wisdom and concentration, mind and Buddha, are equal. If you understand the Sudden Teaching you know that the Buddha is not separate from the mind and the mind is not separate from the Buddha; concentration is not separate from wisdom and wisdom is not separate from concentration.

You don't understand because you have accumulated bad habits for many ages. The wonderful function of the self-nature is basically unproduced and undestroyed, so when you cultivate the mind, you cultivate the Buddha; when you cultivate the Buddha, you cultivate the mind. The same applies to concentration and wisdom. You should cultivate them equally.

When you don't understand, there are two: mind and Buddha, When you understand you know that they are originally one. In cultivating concentration and wisdom, you should separate yourself from all marks.

Bhikshu Fa Ta

Sutra:

Bhikshu Fa Ta of Hung Chou left home at age seven and constantly recited the *Dharma Flower Sutra*, but when he came to bow before the Patriarch, his head did not touch the ground. The Master scolded him, saying, "If you do not touch the ground, isn't it better not to bow? There must be something on your mind. What do you practice?"

"I have recited the *Dharma Flower Sutra* over three thousand times," he replied.

The Master said, "I don't care if you have recited it ten thousand times. If you understood the Sutra's meaning, you would not be so overbearing, and you could walk along with me. You have failed in your work and do not even recognize your error.

Listen to my verse:

As bowing is basically to cut off arrogance,
Why don't you touch your head to the ground?
When you possess a self, offenses arise,
But forgetting merit brings supreme blessings."

The Master asked further, "What is your name?"

"Fa Ta," he replied.

The Master said, "Your name means 'Dharma Penetration,' but what Dharma have you penetrated?" He then spoke a verse:

Your name means Dharma Penetration,
And you earnestly recite without pause to rest.
Recitation is mere sound,
But one who understands his mind is called
a Bodhisattva.
Now, because of your karmic conditions,
I will explain it to you:
Believe only that the Buddha is without words
And the lotus blossom will bloom from your mouth.

Commentary:

Dharma Masters Fa Hai (Dharma Sea) and Fa Ta (Dharma Penetration) both received the Sixth Patriarch's Dharma. Fa Ta left home at age seven and constantly recited the *Lotus Sutra*, but when he met the Patriarch he didn't bow properly, he just pretended. He had to make some sort of show of it since everybody knew that the Great Master held Huang Mei's robe and bowl. But the most respect he could muster was to throw himself hastily on the ground, without even touching his head to the floor, and in his heart he felt that his own merit certainly was greater than the Master's. "After all," he thought, "I've recited the Sutra over three thousand times." When Fa Ta saw ordinary people, he couldn't even manage a half bow. He was like a rich snob who only sees other rich snobs and looks down on everyone else. The Sixth Patriarch took one look and knew that Fa Ta had something on his mind.

The Lotus Sutra is seven volumes long and, reciting quickly, you could read through it once in a day, or three hundred and sixty-five times a year. Therefore Fa Ta had been reciting it for over ten years.

"I don't care if you've recited it ten thousand times!" said the Master. "If you really understood it you wouldn't revel in your own merit and could study with me. Not everyone can study with a Patriarch, you know. If you have obstructions and afflictions, he may not want you."

Therefore, if you come to study here but break the rules, you are not welcome. In order to cultivate with me you must offer up your conduct in accord with the teaching.

"So many recitations," said the Master, "and you still don't know how conceited you are! No doubt you think your merit is even greater than mine. Such pride is an offense. But if you could forget your merit and consider your three thousand recitations as no recitations, then your merit would be limitless and boundless."

"Speak up, Dharma Penetration!" the Master continued, "What Dharma have you penetrated?"

Fa Ta was speechless.

"Not bad," the Master said, "You work hard. However, your recitation is of no benefit because you don't understand what the Sutra means. If you could only understand your mind and see your nature, you would be a Bodhisattva. You have come all this way from Hung Chou because we have an affinity from circumstances in former lives. Now just believe that the Buddha is without words, and the lotus blossom will bloom from your mouth. Believe! The Buddha never said a thing, and if you recite without understanding the principle, you are wasting your time."

The Diamond Sutra says,

One who sees me by form
Or seeks me in sound,
Walks a deviant path
Not seeing the Tathagata.

The Buddha taught for forty-nine years in over three hundred Dharma assemblies, but when he was about to enter Nirvana and his disciples asked him about the Sutras, he said, "I never said a word." Was he lying?

The Sixth Patriarch also taught that the Buddha said nothing, and if you believe this the Lotus will bloom from your mouth. But how does one obtain such rare faith?

The Sutra's principles exist in the minds of people; they can be spoken by you; they can be spoken by me. Everyone has this wisdom and everyone can speak the Sutras. The Buddha spoke the Sutras for living beings and the Sutras flow from the minds of living beings. Therefore the Buddha spoke without speaking. This means that you should not be attached to Dharma or to emptiness. Nevertheless, you cannot say, "I don't know any Dharma. I'm empty!"

To understand that the Buddha spoke and yet did not speak is the most difficult and yet the easiest thing one can do. Can you do it? If you can, the Buddha has not spoken. If you cannot, then the Buddha has said too much.

Sutra:

Hearing the verse, Fa Ta was remorseful and he said, "From now on I will respect everyone. Your disciple recites the *Dharma Flower Sutra* but has not yet understood its meaning. His mind often has doubts. High Master, your wisdom is vast and great. Will you please explain the general meaning of the Sutra for me?"

The Master said, "Dharma Penetration, the Dharma is extremely penetrating, but your mind does not penetrate it. There is basically nothing doubtful in the Sutra. The doubts are in your own mind. You recite this Sutra, but what do you think its teaching is?"

Fa Ta said, "This student's faculties are dull and dim. Since I have only recited it by rote, how could I understand its doctrine?"

The Master said, "I cannot read, but if you take the Sutra and read it once, I will explain it to you."

Fa Ta recited loudly until he came to the "Analogies Chapter." The Master said, "Stop! This Sutra fundamentally is based on the principles underlying the causes and conditions of the Buddha's appearance in the world. None of the analogies spoken go beyond that. What are the causes and conditions? The Sutra says, 'All Buddhas, the World-Honored Ones, appear in the world for the causes and conditions of the One Important Matter.' The One Important Matter is the knowledge and vision of the Buddha. Worldly people, deluded by the external world, attach themselves to marks, and deluded by the inner world, they attach themselves to emptiness. If you can live among marks and yet be separate from it, then you will be confused by neither the internal nor the external. If you awaken to this Dharma, in one moment your mind will open to enlightenment. The knowledge and vision of the Buddha is simply that.

The Buddha is enlightenment. There are four divisions:

1. Opening to the enlightened knowledge and vision;
2. Demonstrating the enlightened knowledge and vision;

3. **Awakening to the enlightened knowledge and vision; and**
4. **Entering the enlightened knowledge and vision.**

If you listen to the opening and demonstrating (of the Dharma), you can easily awaken and enter. That is the enlightened knowledge and vision, the original true nature becoming manifest. Be careful not to misinterpret the Sutra by thinking that the opening, demonstrating, awakening, and entering of which it speaks is the Buddha's knowledge and vision and that we have no share in it. To explain it that way would be to slander the Sutra and defame the Buddha. Since he is already a Buddha, perfect in knowledge and vision, what is the use of his opening to it again? You should now believe that the Buddha's knowledge and vision is simply your own mind, for there is no other Buddha.

"But, because living beings cover their brilliance with greed and with the love of states of defilement, external conditions and inner disturbance make slaves of them. That troubles the World-Honored One to rise from Samadhi, and with various reproaches and expedients, he exhorts living beings to stop and rest, not to seek outside themselves, and to make themselves the same as he is. That is called 'opening the knowledge and vision of the Buddha.' I, too, am always exhorting all people to open to the knowledge and vision of the Buddha within their own minds.

"The minds of worldly people are deviant. Confused and deluded, they commit offenses. Their speech may be good, but their minds are evil. They are greedy, hateful, envious, given over to flattery, deceit, and arrogance. They oppress one another and harm living creatures,

thus they open not the knowledge and vision of Buddhas but that of living beings. If you can with an upright mind constantly bring forth wisdom, contemplating and illumining your own mind, and if you can practice the good and refrain from evil, you, yourself will open to the knowledge and vision of the Buddha. In every thought you should open up to the knowledge and vision of the Buddha; do not open up to the knowledge and vision of living beings. To be open to the knowledge and vision of the Buddha is transcendental; to be open to the knowledge and vision of living beings is mundane. If you exert yourself in recitation, clinging to it as a meritorious exercise, how does that make you different from a yak who loves his own tail?"

Commentary:

To be unconfused, be unattached. Do not get attached to emptiness or fall into existence. If you suddenly awaken to this dharma your heart will open to the knowledge and vision of the Buddha.

If you listen to opening and demonstrating, that is, to instruction on the principles of the Sutras, you can easily wake up and understand the enlightened knowledge and vision. The Buddha's knowledge and vision is simply that of your own mind, because your mind fundamentally *is* the Buddha.

What darkens your light?

Thoughts of greed
Create thoughts of love.
Greed is dirt,
And love defiled.
The impurities

Of greed and love
Cause self-seeking
And make you a slave.
By now you should
Have become enlightened.
Stop depending on
Outer conditions
Which only make trouble within.
Without them there is
No trouble: there is
Peace and purity.

There are many varieties of external conditions: eyes, ears, noses, tongues, bodies, and minds; forms, sounds, smells, tastes, tangible objects, and objects of the mind; and the six consciousnesses where sense-organs and sense-objects meet. When you seek outside yourself, your mind is not at peace; you are upset and anxious, and your mind, originally the master, becomes the body's slave. The Buddhas trouble themselves to arise from Samadhi just to tell you not to seek outside yourself. When you quit seeking outside, you are one with the Buddhas; you open up to their knowledge and vision and become just like them.

The deviant views and delusion of ordinary people causes them to perform offensive acts. While their speech may be as compassionate as the Buddha, their minds are as poisonous as a snake. Of the offenses they commit, greed, hate, and jealousy are the worst. But when they shine the light within and straighten out their own minds, they naturally are open to the knowledge and vision of the Buddha.

Sutra:

Fa Ta said, "If this is so, then I need only understand the meaning and need not exert myself in reciting the Sutra. Isn't that correct?"

The Master replied, "What fault does the Sutra have that would stop you from reciting it? Confusion and enlightenment are in you. Loss or gain comes from yourself. If your mouth recites and your mind practices, you 'turn' the Sutra, but if your mouth recites and your mind does not practice, the Sutra 'turns' you. Listen to my verse:

When the mind is confused,
the Dharma Flower turns it.
The enlightened mind
will turn the Dharma Flower.

Reciting the Sutra so long
without understanding
Has made you an enemy
of its meaning.

Without a thought
your recitation is right.
With thought,
your recitation is wrong.

With no "with"
and no "without"
You may ride forever
in the White Ox Cart.

Fa Ta heard this verse and wept without knowing it. At the moment the words were spoken, he achieved a great enlightenment and said to the Master, "Until today I have never actually turned the Dharma Flower; instead it has turned me."

Commentary:

If you are confused, your recitation is of no benefit, but if you are enlightened, there is merit. What does this have to do with the Sutra? If you recite the Sutra and put it into practice as well, you are truly reciting the Sutra and turning the Dharma wheel. You set the Dharma Flower spinning. But if you recite the Sutra with a confused mind, the reciting turns you around so that, the more recitation you do, the less you understand. After more than ten years of work, Fa Ta was still unclear; he was a stranger to the Sutra. Without false thoughts, recitation is a correct thing, but with arrogant thoughts and conceit about your merit and virtue, your recitation becomes deviant. You should pay no attention to having or not having merit, and recite as if not reciting. Do not be attached, and you will always ride in the White Ox Cart. The White Ox Cart is an analogy for The One Buddha Vehicle.

You ask, "If I recite as if not reciting, then may I not recite as if reciting?" If you don't recite it, you cannot understand the Sutra's principles, and it is not as if you were reciting it. The phrase:

Reciting as if not reciting,
Not reciting as if reciting,

is to instruct you to be unattached. But you cannot say, "I'll be unattached and forget about reciting the Sutra."

After listening to the Master, Fa Ta wept without even knowing it, but it wasn't because he had been bullied or tricked. Before, he had stupidly wasted his time reciting the Sutra without obtaining the slightest benefit. Now, at the Master's explanation, he was so overcome with joy that he burst into tears, just like friends or relatives do when they meet after a long separation. He cried because of his great enlightenment.

Sutra:

Fa Ta asked further, "The *Lotus Sutra* says, 'If everyone from Shravakas up to the Bodhisattvas were to exhaust all their thought in order to measure the Buddha's wisdom, they still could not fathom it.' Now, you cause common people merely to understand their own minds, and you call that the knowledge and vision of the Buddha. Because of this, I am afraid that those without superior faculties will not be able to avoid doubting and slandering the Sutra. The Sutra also speaks of three carts. How do the sheep, deer, and ox carts differ from the White Ox Cart? I pray the High Master will once again instruct me."

The Master said, "The Sutra's meaning is clear. You yourself are confused. Disciples of all three vehicles are unable to fathom the Buddha's wisdom; the fault is in their thinking and measuring. The more they think, the further away they go. From the start the Buddha speaks for the sake of common people, not for the sake of other Buddhas. Those who chose not to believe were free to leave the assembly. Not knowing that they were sitting in the White Ox Cart, they sought three vehicles outside the gate. What is more, the Sutra text clearly tells you 'There is only the One Buddha Vehicle, no other vehicle,

whether two or three, and the same is true for countless expedients, for various causes and conditions, and for analogies and rhetoric. All these Dharmas are for the sake of the One Buddha Vehicle.'"

Commentary:

The *Lotus Sutra* says,

If the world were filled
With those like Shariputra
Exhausting their thought to measure the
Buddha's wisdom,
They couldn't fathom it.

Fa Ta questioned the Master: "Shariputra was the wisest of the Buddha's disciples. Now, if you filled the entire universe with Shariputras, and they all tried to fathom the Buddha's wisdom, they wouldn't be able to do it. Great Master, how can you say that when common people merely understand their own minds, they are open to the knowledge and vision of the Buddhas? I am afraid that unless one had supreme wisdom and good roots, one couldn't avoid slandering the Sutra. Please be compassionate and tell me how the sheep and deer carts differ from the White Ox Cart."

The Master said, "The Sutra is perfectly clear on this point. The Shravakas, Pratyekabuddhas and Bodhisattvas cannot know the Buddha's wisdom simply because they do try to measure it. If their minds did not have such calculating thoughts, they could understand it. The Buddha spoke Sutras for common people, not for other Buddhas. If you don't believe the Sutras, you can get up and walk out as you please. What is more, there is only One Buddha Vehicle; there are no other vehicles, whether two

(Shravakas and Pratyeka Buddhas) or three (Shravakas, Pratyeka Buddhas, and Bodhisattvas) or any number of parables, causes and conditions, and uncountable expedient devices: all are spoken for the sake of the One Buddha Vehicle."

Sutra:

"Why don't you wake up? The three carts are false, because they are preliminary. The one vehicle is real because it is the immediate present. You are merely taught to go from the false and return to the real. Once you have returned to reality, the real is also nameless. You should know that all the treasure and wealth is ultimately your own, for your own use. Do not think further of the father, nor of the son, nor of the use. That is called maintaining the *Dharma Flower Sutra.* Then from eon to eon your hands will never let go of the scrolls; from morning to night you will recite it unceasingly."

Fa Ta received this instruction and, overwhelmed with joy, he spoke a verse:

Three thousand Sutra recitations:
At Ts'ao Hsi not one single word.
Before I knew why he appeared in the world,
How could I stop the madness of
accumulated births?
Sheep, deer, and ox provisionally set up;
Beginning, middle, end, well set forth.
Who would have thought that within the
burning house
Originally the king of Dharma dwelt?

The Master said, "From now on you may be called the monk mindful of the Sutra." From then on, although he understood the profound meaning, Fa Ta continued to recite the Sutra unceasingly.

Commentary:

Once you have returned to the real vehicle, even the real is nameless; you should discard the notion of reality. All the treasure and wealth of the Buddhadharma is yours, originally. It is the wind and light of your homeland; use it as you wish. But do not think, "These were given to me by my father. I have received them as an inheritance." You shouldn't think of the father, the son, or the use: just use them, that's all. That is genuine recitation of the Sutra. From the first to the last eon, your hands won't set the text down and you will recite it from morning to night.

"Before I knew why the Buddha appeared in the world," said Fa Ta, "I had no way to stop the karmic process of this mad mind. But now I know that the beginning Shravaka vehicle, the middle Pratyekabuddha Vehicle, and the Mahayana Bodhisattva vehicle are nothing but expedient devices. They are not real. Who would have guessed? Who would have guessed! Nobody! Why, it's just right here in the flaming house of the triple world, the realm of desire, the realm of form, and the formless realm, that one can cultivate, realize Buddhahood and be a Great Dharma King!"

"Yes," said the Master, "I see that you understand, and so now you have the right to be called a Sutra-reciting monk."

Fa Ta understood the doctrine, but he did not make the mistake some people might have and think, "I understand it, so I don't have to recite it. I have reached the level where I:

Recite and yet do not recite;
Do not recite and yet recite.

If this is the case, then can you:

Eat as if not eating, and
Not eat as if eating;

or

Steal as if not stealing, and
Not steal as if stealing;

or even

Kill as if not killing, and
Not kill as if killing?

Can you get away with this? Of course not! If you truly understand and are unattached to what you do, you will not babble intellectual zen and say that you recite without reciting. Before you can make that claim, you must first have reached that level of accomplishment.

Bhikshu Chih T'ung

Sutra:

Bhikshu Chih T'ung, a native of An Feng in Shao Chou, had read the *Lankavatara Sutra* over a thousand times but still did not understand the three bodies and the four wisdoms. He made obeisance to the Master, seeking an explanation of the meaning. The Master said, "The three bodies are: the clear, pure Dharma-body, which is your nature; the perfect, full Reward-body, which is your wisdom; and the hundred thousand myriad Transformation bodies, which are your conduct. To speak of the three bodies as separate from your original nature is to have the bodies but not the wisdoms. To remember that the three bodies have no self-nature is to understand the four wisdoms of Bodhi. Listen to my verse:

Three bodies complete in your own self-nature
When understood become four wisdoms.
While not apart from seeing and hearing
Transcend them and ascend to the Buddha realm.

I will now explain it for you.
If you are attentive and faithful, you will never be deluded.

Don't run outside in search of them,
By saying 'Bodhi' to the end of your days.

Chih T'ung asked further, "May I hear about the meaning of the four wisdoms?"

The Master said, "Since you understand the three bodies, you should also understand the four wisdoms. Why do you ask again? To speak of the four wisdoms as separate from the three bodies is to have the wisdoms but not the bodies, in which case the wisdoms become non-wisdoms." He then spoke this verse:

The wisdom of the great, perfect mirror
Is your clear, pure nature.
The wisdom of equal nature
Is the mind without disease.
Wonderfully observing wisdom
Is seeing without effort.
Perfecting wisdom is
The same as the perfect mirror.

Five, eight, six, seven–
Effect and cause both turn;
Merely useful names:
They are without real nature.
If, in the place of turning,
Emotion is not kept,
You always and forever dwell
In Naga concentration.

Commentary:

Bhikshu Chih T'ung studied the *Lankavatara Sutra* because Bodhidharma recommended it above all other texts for the Ch'an School. Although he had read it over a thousand times, he still had to ask the Master about the three bodies and the four wisdoms. The Master always teaches Dharma of and from self-nature. "The clear, pure Dharma-body is your own original nature," he said, "and the Reward-body is your wisdom. The transformation-bodies are your conduct, because you are what you do; you are transformed according to what you practice. If you try to explain the three bodies as something apart from your self-nature, you have the bodies, but not the wisdoms. But when you understand that the three bodies are devoid of self-nature, you possess the four wisdoms of Bodhi.

"When you understand that the three bodies are immanent in the self-nature, you realize the four wisdoms. Without being separated from the conditions of sight and hearing, you ascend directly to the Buddha-realm. Now, I have spoken this verse," the Sixth Patriarch said, "and you must truly believe it. Then you will never again be confused like those people who go around saying 'Bodhi, Bodhi, Bodhi' all day long, but who never practice or understand Bodhi. Don't chatter 'head-mouth' zen! You must truly understand the three bodies for it to count.

The Master continued, "Since you understand the three bodies, you should understand the four wisdoms as well. If you try to explain the four wisdoms as something apart from the three bodies, then although you know the name 'four wisdoms' you do not possess their actual substance or know their function. Your wisdoms are non-wisdoms."

The Buddha has four wisdoms. The wisdom of the great, perfect mirror is the eighth consciousness (alayavijnana) when it has been transformed from consciousness into wisdom. The eighth consciousness is also called the "store" consciousness, because it stores up all the good and bad seeds you have planted in the past, all the good and bad things you have done in this and past lives. If you have planted good causes, you reap good effects; if you have planted bad causes, you reap bad effects. As the potential of all good and bad karma is stored in the eighth consciousness, it also comes to be called the "field of the eighth-consciousness," because whatever you plant in it eventually sprouts.

When you are unable to use it, it is merely consciousness, but when you return to the root and go back to the source, the eighth consciousness is transmuted into the great perfect mirror wisdom, which in its essence is pure and undefiled.

The wisdom of equal nature is the seventh consciousness when it has been transformed from consciousness into wisdom. Before you understand, it is the seventh consciousness, but once you are enlightened, it is the wisdom of equal nature. The seventh consciousness is also called the "transmitting consciousness" because it acts as a transmitter between the sixth and eighth consciousness. It is called "the wisdom of equal nature" because the minds of all Buddhas and living beings are equal when the latter's consciousness have been transformed into wisdom. "The mind without disease" means that there is no obstruction, no jealousy, no greed, hate, or stupidity. Without these defilements the seventh consciousness is transmuted into the wisdom of equal nature.

The wonderful observing wisdom is the sixth consciousness when it has been transformed into wisdom. It is the wisdom of subtle observation. The sixth consciousness, what we think of as the ordinary mind, is the consciousness of discrimination; it discriminates good and evil, right and wrong, male and female. Such discrimination is not actually the work of intelligence, as it seems to be, but is merely a kind of consciousness. When you turn it into wisdom, it becomes wonderfully observing wisdom, which sees all realms without having to go through the process of discrimination. This wonderful observation is quite different from mere discriminative thoughts.

When certified Arhats wish to use the wonderful observing wisdom to know something, they must first sit quietly in meditation and intentionally observe, for unless they intentionally observe, their minds are no different from those of ordinary people. By intentionally observing, they can know the events of the past eighty thousand eons.

Perfecting wisdom comes from the transformation of the first five consciousnesses–eye, ear, nose, tongue, and body–into wisdom.

"Five, eight, six, seven–effect and cause both turn." The five consciousnesses and the eighth consciousness are transformed in the period of reaping effects and the sixth and seventh are transformed in the period of planting causes. In transforming the consciousnesses into the four wisdoms, first turn the sixth and seventh in the period of planting causes, and next the eighth and five in the period of reaping effects.

"Merely useful names: they are without real nature." Although they are said to be changed in the realms of causes and effects, there is nothing in reality which corresponds to them; they are merely names and nothing more.

"If, in the place of 'turning,' emotion isn't kept;" if, in the place where your emotional feelings are being 'turned' you do not use your common mind and become caught up in the 'turning...'

"You always and forever dwell in Naga concentration." At all times you are in Naga samadhi. Naga means "dragon." Dragons can magically appear in big or small bodies because they have a great deal of concentration. As Fa Hai tells us in his introduction to the Sutra, the Sixth Patriarch defeated a dragon by saying, "If you are really a magic dragon, you should be able to appear in a small body as well as a large one." Then, when the dragon turned up in a small body the Master dared him to climb into his bowl. As the little dragon had a big temper and much ignorance, he jumped at the dare; but when he tried to jump out again, he couldn't do it. The Master explained the Dharma to the dragon and the dragon then went to rebirth.

The dragon may have been constantly in samadhi, but he had not destroyed his ignorance and therefore lost his temper. "I'll show you!" he said, "I'll change my body into a little one right now!" If he had really been in samadhi he would have said, "You say I can't appear in a small body? O.K. So what? I'll just appear in this large one." But he lost his concentration and was 'turned,' caught, and defeated by the Great Master.

Still, Naga samadhi is an inconceivable state. How do dragons get to be dragons? They study the Buddhadharma with mighty effort, morning to night, but they do not keep the precepts. "Precepts are for common people," they say. "I'm extraordinary. I'm not in the same category as they are, and I do not have to keep precepts!" That's how they turn into dragons.

Sutra:

Note: The transformation of consciousness into wisdom has been described. The teaching says, "The first five consciousnesses turned become the perfecting wisdom; the sixth consciousness turned becomes the wonderfully observing wisdom; the seventh consciousness turned becomes the wisdom of equal nature, the eighth consciousness turned becomes the wisdom of the great perfect mirror."

Although the sixth and seventh are turned in the cause and the first five and the eighth in the effect, it is merely the names which turn. Their substance does not turn.

Commentary:

The above passage was not part of the original text, but was added later.

Sutra:

Instantly enlightened to the nature of wisdom, Chih T'ung submitted the following verse:

Three bodies are my basic substance,
Four wisdoms my original bright mind.
Body and wisdom in unobstructed fusion:
In response to beings I accordingly take form.
Arising to cultivate them is false movement.
Holding to or pondering over them a waste of effort.
Through the Master I know the wonderful principle,
And in the end I lose the stain of names.

Commentary:

Chih T'ung understood the function of the three bodies and the four wisdoms. "The three bodies are not to be found outside of my own body," he said, "and the four wisdoms, too, are produced from my own bright, understanding mind. When the bodies and wisdoms interpenetrate, then I may dispense the Dharma in accord with the needs of living beings–in accord with external conditions and yet not changing; unchanging, and yet in accord with conditions. If you wonder, "How can I cultivate the three bodies and four wisdoms?" that is nothing but false thinking, false movement. The same is true of holding to them and being attached to them.

From beginning to end there is no stain of names. What is unstained by names is the original self-nature, which is untouched by worldly emotion. Unless you have no defilement, you cannot return to the root and go back to the source, which is undefiled.

Bhikshu Chih Ch'ang

Sutra:

Bhikshu Chih Ch'ang, a native of Kuei Hsi in Hsin Chou, left home when he was a child and resolutely sought to see his own nature. One day he called on the Master, who asked him, "Where are you from and what do you want?"

Chih Ch'ang replied, "Your student has recently been to Pai Feng Mountain in Hung Chou to call on the High Master Ta T'ung and receive his instruction on the principle of seeing one's nature and realizing Buddhahood. As I have not yet resolved my doubts, I have come from a great distance to bow reverently and request the Master's compassionate instruction."

The Master said, "What instruction did he give you? Try to repeat it to me."

Chih Ch'ang said, "After arriving there, three months passed and still I had received no instruction. Being eager for the Dharma, one evening I went alone into the Abbot's room and asked him, 'What is my original mind and original substance?'"

"Ta T'ung then said to me, 'Do you see empty space?'

"'Yes,' I said, 'I see it.'

"Ta T'ung said, 'Do you know what appearance it has?'

"I replied, 'Empty space has no form. How could it have an appearance?'

"Ta T'ung said, 'Your original mind is just like empty space. To understand that nothing can be seen is called right seeing; to know that nothing can be known is called true knowing. There is nothing blue or yellow, long or short. Simply seeing the clear, pure original source, the perfect, bright enlightened substance, this is what is called 'seeing one's nature and realizing Buddhahood.' It is also called 'the knowledge and vision of the Tathagata.'

"Although I heard his instruction, I still do not understand and beg you, O Master to instruct me."

The Master said, "Your former master's explanation still retains the concepts of knowing and seeing; and that is why you have not understood. Now, I will teach you with a verse:

Not to see a single dharma
still retains no-seeing,
Greatly resembling floating clouds
covering the sun.
Not to know a single dharma
holds to empty knowing,
Even as a lightning flash
comes out of empty space.
This knowing and seeing
arise in an instant.
When seen wrongly,
can expedients be understood?
If, in the space of a thought,
you can know your own error,

Your own spiritual light
will always be manifest.

Commentary:

Bhikshu Chih Ch'ang left home at the early age of seven or eight. When he called on the Sixth Patriarch, the Master remembered his first meeting with the Fifth Patriarch, who had asked him, "Where are you from and what do you seek?"

"I'm from Hsin Chou," the Master had said, "and I seek nothing but Buddhahood."

"Hsin Chou people are barbarians," the Fifth Patriarch had said. "How can you become a Buddha?"

"The Barbarian's body and the High Master's body are not the same," countered the Sixth Patriarch, "but in the Buddha nature where is the distinction?"

Remembering this, the Sixth Patriarch asked Chih Ch'ang, "Where are you from? Just what do you think you're doing?"

Chih Ch'ang had received instruction on seeing the nature and realizing Buddhahood, but he still had doubts. The Chinese word for doubts is literally "fox doubt" because foxes are wary of everything. When a fox walks across the ice, he takes a step, cocks his head, and listens: if the ice crackles he runs back to shore; if it does not, he keeps on walking and listening, walking and listening. Although foxes are extremely intelligent, they are full of doubts.

In his verse the Sixth Patriarch explains, "If you do not see a single dharma and the ten thousand dharmas all are empty, you still have the view of not seeing any dharmas; you still hold that view. This is just like floating clouds covering the sun, because if you truly do not see anything, you are free of the idea of not seeing.

"In the same way, if you don't establish a single dharma and don't know a single dharma, but still have the knowledge that you neither establish nor know dharmas, you still hold on to an empty, false kind of knowing. Your principles seem coherent, but knowing and seeing still remain. This is like the great void: originally there is nothing there, but suddenly there is a flash of lightning. Now, do you see, or not?

"This 'knowing and seeing' arise in an instant." Your seeing nothing and your empty knowing, your view of not seeing and your knowledge of knowing nothing, are there before your eyes.

You should understand right this instant that you are wrong in holding to the idea of seeing nothing and knowing emptiness. Then your original wisdom, your original intelligence, your inherent Buddha nature which is the Tathagata's Treasury will always be manifest.

Sutra:

Hearing the verse, Chih Ch'ang understood it with his heart and mind, and he composed this verse:

Without beginning,
knowing and seeing arise.
When one is attached to marks
bodhi is sought out.
Clinging to a
thought of enlightenment,
Do I rise above my former confusion?
The inherently enlightened
substance of my nature
Illuminates the turning
twisting flow.

But had I not entered
the Patriarch's room,
I'd still be running, lost
between the two extremes.

Commentary:

When Chih Ch'ang heard this verse, he put it all down. Having put it all down he didn't say, "I put it all down!" If you put it down, put it down; don't keep saying, "I put it down!" If you keep on saying that you've put it down, you haven't really done it. If you truly have no knowledge or view and have returned to the root and gone back to the source, why do you keep a 'knowing' and a 'viewing'?

Chih Ch'ang understood and spoke a wonderful verse: "Without beginning, knowing and seeing arise." Without a head, without a tail, the idea of seeing nothing and the knowledge of emptiness arise from no beginning, without a causal basis or foundation. Though one is attached to marks, Bodhi is sought out. You should not be attached to marks, but now you have become attached to seeing nothing and knowing emptiness. Previously, when I explained "no-thought," I said that if you think, "I have no thought," just that is a thought. Isn't it?

If you really are without thought, you are also without no-thought. The concept of no-thought is just another thought.

In Ch'an (Dhyana) meditation, when we reflect on the question, "Who is reciting the Buddha's name?" we search for the "who" but don't find it, because basically there is no "who." But people can't understand, and keep looking for a "self," saying "Who?" In your search, do not be attached to marks; do not be attached to the mark of self when you seek Bodhi.

When you think, "I'm seeing emptiness and there is nothing at all!" you still have the thought of knowing; you still have the thought of seeing, and you don't overcome your confusion. This is certainly not enlightenment.

"The inherently enlightened substance of my nature illuminates the turning, twisting flow." The basic substance of the self-nature, which is enlightened from the beginning, is in accord with the shift and flow of external conditions, and yet it does not change. Understanding this, Chih Ch'ang finds the middle way between the "two extremes" of 'seeing' nothing and 'knowing' emptiness.

Sutra:

One day Chih Ch'ang asked the Master, "The Buddha taught the dharma of the three vehicles and also the Supreme Vehicle. Your disciple has not yet understood that and would like to be instructed."

The Master said, "Contemplate only your own original mind and do not be attached to the marks of external dharmas. The Dharma doesn't have four vehicles; it is people's minds that differ. Seeing, hearing, and reciting is the small vehicle. Awakening to the Dharma and understanding the meaning is the middle vehicle. Cultivating in accord with Dharma is the great vehicle. To penetrate the ten thousand dharmas entirely and completely while remaining without defilement, and to sever attachment to the marks of all the dharmas with nothing whatsoever gained in return: that is the Supreme Vehicle. Vehicles are methods of practice, not subjects for debate. Cultivate on your own and do not ask me, for at all times your own self-nature is itself 'thus.'"

Chih Ch'ang bowed and thanked the Master and served him to the end of the Master's life.

Commentary:

The Master said, "Chih Ch'ang, the Dharma doesn't even have one vehicle, much less four! People's minds are what differ. If you see, hear, and recite, you belong to the small vehicle; if you understand and awaken, you belong to the middle vehicle; if you practice in accord with the Dharma, you belong to the great vehicle. When you understand all dharmas, when they are perfected in your own mind without any obstruction, and when you know that the ten thousand dharmas are the mind and the mind is the ten thousand dharmas, and further when you are not defiled by any state, then you belong to the Supreme Vehicle. But you must cultivate on your own; I can't do it for you.

Eat your own food and fill yourself;
End your own birth and death.

From that time on, Chih Ch'ang served the Master. When he wanted a cup of tea, Chih Ch'ang brought it for him; when he was hungry, Chih Ch'ang brought him food. He served the Master right up until the Master's death, at which time he left Nan Hua Temple.

Bhikshu Chih Tao

Sutra:

Bhikshu Chih Tao, a native of Nan Hai in Kuang Chou, asked a favor: "Since leaving home, your student has studied the *Nirvana Sutra* for over ten years and has still not understood its great purport. I hope that the High Master will bestow his instruction."

The Master said, "What point haven't you understood?"

Chih Tao replied,

"All activities are impermanent,
Characterized by production and extinction;
When production and extinction are extinguished,
That still extinction is bliss.

My doubts are with respect to this passage."

Commentary:

Once in the past, during the period when Shakyamuni Buddha was cultivating to plant causes for the attainment of Buddhahood, he was a Brahman. Deep in the mountains he cultivated many Dharma doors so heroically that the god Shakra was moved and said, "He works so hard! I wonder if I can break him?" and he transformed himself into a rakshasa ghost to test the Brahman. He told him, "The Buddha known as 'Free from Fear' said, 'All activities are impermanent, characterized by production and extinction.'"

"Who said that?" said the Brahman.

The rakshasa ghost, who was hideously ugly, appeared and said, "I was just quoting a verse spoken by the Buddha who is free from fear."

"But you didn't recite the entire verse, only the first half. Please complete it," said the Brahman.

"I don't have the energy because I haven't eaten for several days. Find me something to eat and I will speak it for you," the ghost said.

"What would you like?" asked the Brahman.

"I don't eat anything but fresh, warm, human meat," said the ghost.

"In that case," replied the Brahman, "you may speak the verse and then I will give you my own body to eat."

The ghost stared at him. "Can you really do such an awesome deed? Can you really give up your body for half a verse?"

"I speak the truth; I do not lie," said the Brahman, "and if you don't believe me I can ask the Buddhas of the ten directions to bear testimony to the fact. Now, recite the verse and then I will feed you."

The ghost quickly recited, "'All activities are impermanent, characterized by production and extinction; When production and extinction are extinguished, that still extinction is bliss.' Now give me your body!"

"Wait a minute," said the Brahman. "Once you have eaten me there will be nothing left of the verse unless I write it down. Let me carve it on this tree so that future generations may cultivate according to it." Then he stripped the bark from a tree and carved the verse on its trunk.

The ghost said, "Can I eat you now?"

"Just a minute..." said the Brahman.

"So you're backing out, are you?" the ghost said.

"No, I'm not," said the Brahman, "but what I have written on the tree will eventually be worn away by the wind and rain. I want to carve the verse in stone so that it will last forever. I'll gladly give you my body, but I must also leave the Buddhadharma for those of the future."

"Not a bad idea," said the ghost.

The Brahman carved the words in stone and said, "All right, I've done what I had to do. I give my body to you as an offering. You may eat me now," and he shut his eyes and waited for the ghost to devour him. But just then the ghost flew up into empty space, transformed himself back into Shakra and said, "Very good! Very good! You are a true cultivator, one who gives up his own body for the sake of the Buddha Way. In the future you are sure to become a Buddha!"

This is an event in a former life of Shakyamuni Buddha, when, as a Brahman, he offered his life for half a verse.

Sutra:

The Master said, "What are your doubts?"

"All living beings have two bodies," Chih Tao replied, "the physical body and the Dharma-body. The physical body is impermanent and is produced and destroyed. The Dharma-body is permanent and is without knowing or awareness. The Sutra says that the extinction of production and extinction is bliss, but I do not know which body is in tranquil extinction and which receives the bliss.

"How could it be the physical body which receives the bliss? When this physical body is extinguished, the four

elements scatter. That is total suffering and suffering cannot be called bliss. If the Dharma-body were extinguished it would become like grass, trees, tiles, or stones; then what would receive the bliss?

"Moreover, the Dharma-nature is the substance of production and extinction and the five heaps are the function of production and extinction. With one body having five functions, production and extinction are permanent; at the time of production, the functions arise from the substance, and at the time of extinction, the functions return to the substance. If there were rebirth then sentient beings would not cease to exist or be extinguished. If there were not rebirth, they would return to tranquil extinction and be just like insentient objects. Thus all dharmas would be suppressed by Nirvana and there would not even be production. How could there be bliss?"

The Master said, "You are a son of Shakya! How can you hold the deviant views of annihilationism and permanence which belongs to other religions and criticise the Supreme Vehicle Dharma! According to what you say, there is a Dharma-body that exists apart from physical form and a tranquil extinction to be sought apart from production and extinction. Moreover you propose that there is a body which enjoys the permanence and bliss of Nirvana. But that is to grasp tightly onto birth and death and indulge in worldly bliss."

Commentary:

"Is it the physical body which is extinct and the Dharma body which receives the bliss?" Chih Tao wanted to know, "or is it the

Dharma body which is extinct and the physical body which receives the bliss?

"How could it be the physical body which receives the bliss? The body is composed of the elements earth, air, fire, and water. At death, the elements scatter and that is a state of unspeakable suffering. You can't call suffering happiness."

"Hey!" said the Great Master, "you are a disciple of Shakyamuni Buddha. You have left home and are a member of the Sangha. How can you harbor the deviant views and deviant knowledge of non-Buddhist religions? You say that there is a Dharma-body apart from the physical body and its extinction and that there is a tranquil extinction apart from the process of production and extinction. Isn't this what you're saying? You also say that there is a body which enjoys the four virtues of Nirvana: permanence, bliss, true self, and purity. In fact, your theories are nothing but niggardly attachment to birth and death and worldly pleasure. Stuck in the mundane world, you cannot possibly know transcendental bliss."

Sutra:

"You should now know that deluded people mistook the union of five heaps for their own bodies and discriminated dharmas as external to themselves. They loved life, dreaded death, and drifted from thought to thought, not knowing that this illusory dream is empty and false. They turned vainly around on the wheel of birth and death and mistook the permanence and bliss of Nirvana for a form of suffering. All day long they sought after something else. Taking pity on them, the Buddha made manifest in the space of an instant the true bliss of Nirvana, which has no mark of production or extinction; it has no production or extinction to be extinguished.

That, then, is the manifestation of tranquil extinction. Its manifestation cannot be reckoned; it is permanent and blissful. The bliss has neither an enjoyer nor a non-enjoyer. How can you call it 'one substance with five functions?' Worse, how can you say that Nirvana suppresses all dharmas, causing them to be forever unproduced? That is to slander the Buddha and defame the Dharma."

Commentary:

The Buddha spoke for those who thought that their bodies were actually made up of a union of the five heaps, and who thought dharmas were something external to themselves. They were attached to life and death because they didn't know that everything is like a dream, a bubble, a lightning flash, or a dew drop–illusory. They underwent birth and death over and over again, uselessly and pitifully spinning on the wheel of the six paths of rebirth.

Some people thought that the wonderful virtues of Nirvana were a kind of suffering, but the Buddha mercifully revealed to them the true happiness of Nirvana, where there is no mark of production and no mark of extinction. Further, there is absolutely no extinction of production and extinction, because right within production and extinction there appears the state of non-production and non-extinction. That is the manifestation of tranquil extinction.

You can't say that the manifestation of tranquil extinction is so long or so short, so high or so wide. It's a kind of permanent happiness which is without an enjoyer or a non-enjoyer. If you would like to have this kind of happiness, you should know that there is no one who enjoys it or does not enjoy it. Why? It is the manifestation of the original self-nature.

Sutra:

"Listen to my verse:

Supreme, great Nirvana is bright
Perfect, permanent, still and shining.
Deluded common people call it death,
Other teachings hold it to be annihilation.
All those who seek two vehicles
Regard it as non-action.
Ultimately these notions arise from feeling,
And form the basis for sixty-two views,
Wrongly establishing unreal names.
What is the true, real principle?
Only one who has gone beyond measuring
Penetrates without grasping or rejecting,
And knows that the dharma of the five heaps
And the self within the heaps,
The outward appearances–a mass of images–
The mark of every sound,
Are equally like the illusion of dreams,
For him, views of common and holy do not arise
Nor are explanations of Nirvana made.
The two boundaries, the three limits are cut off.
All organs have their function,
But there never arises the thought of the function.
All dharmas are discriminated
Without a thought of discrimination arising.
When the fire at the eon's end

burns the bottom of the sea
And the winds blow the mountains
against each other,
The true, permanent, still extinct bliss,
The mark of Nirvana is 'thus.'
I have struggled to explain it,
To cause you to reject your false views.
Don't understand it by words alone
And maybe you'll understand a bit of this."

After hearing this verse, Chih Tao was greatly enlightened. Overwhelmed with joy, he made obeisance and withdrew.

Commentary:

The Sixth Patriarch said, "Listen. Great Nirvana is full, complete and bright. It's permanent, unchanging, and constantly illuminating. Ordinary people say that it is death, and those of non-Buddhist religions say that it is annihilation. The two vehicles of the Shravakas and Pratyeka Buddhas think that it is non-action; that it is uncreated and arises spontaneously. But these are all discriminations which arise from emotion, and they form the basis of sixty-two wrong views. What are the sixty-two wrong views?

1. The heap (skandha) is big and I am contained in the heap.
2. I am big and the heap is contained in me.
3. The heap itself is me.
4. I am separate from the heap.

When each of the four above are applied to the five heaps–form, feelings, perceptions, impulses, and consciousness–they make twenty. The twenty multiplied by the three periods of time–past, present, and future–make sixty. Adding the two extremes of permanence and annihilation makes sixty-two. None of them are real; they are all empty and false."

Then "what is the true real principle?" Only one who has gone beyond measuring penetrates without grasping at or rejecting them. Therefore he truly understands that the dharma of the five heaps and the self within those heaps, the marks of form and sound, are all like dreams, illusions, bubbles and shadows.

"For him, views of common and holy do not arise." He doesn't have the views of a common person, he doesn't have the understanding of the sage, and he doesn't try to explain the bliss of Nirvana. "The two boundaries, the three limits are cut off." He is attached neither to the boundary of emptiness, nor to the boundary of existence. Therefore the three limits of the past, present, and future are cut off and he is not attached to them.

"All organs have their function, but there never arises the thought of the function." The true suchness self-nature has the ability to function in accord with external conditions and yet not change. It's responsiveness is inexhaustible and yet there is no thought of "Ah! I am functioning!" All "Dharmas are discriminated without a thought of discrimination arising." You don't think, "I am not making discriminations." If you do think that, you have the mark of discrimination. To be truly without discrimination is to be without the mark of non-discrimination as well.

"When the fire at the end of the eon burns the bottom of the sea and the wind blows the mountains against each other:" At the end of an eon, there are three disasters: flood, fire, and wind.

"The true permanent, still, extinct bliss, the mark of Nirvana is 'thus.'" If you have attained true permanence and the bliss of tranquil extinction, then the mark of Nirvana is just as it was explained above, and the three disasters cannot affect you.

The Great Master concludes by saying that he has spoken the verse to encourage his listeners to cast aside their present knowledge and views. "When you no longer rely on the text in order to explain the Sutras," he said, "I will grant that you understand just a little bit of what I've said."

Bhikshu Hsing Szu

Sutra:

Dhyana Master Hsing Szu was born into the Liu family, which lived in An Ch'eng district in Chi Chou. Hearing of the flourishing influence of the Ts'ao Hsi Dharma Assembly, Hsing Szu went directly there to pay homage and asked, "What is required to avoid falling into successive stages?"

The Master said, "What did you do before coming here?"

He replied, "I did not even practice the Holy Truths."

The Master said, "Then into what successive states could you fall?"

He replied, "If one isn't practicing the Four Holy Truths, what successive stages are there?"

The Master greatly admired his capacity and made him the leader of the assembly.

One day the Master said, "You should go elsewhere to teach. Do not allow the teaching to be cut off."

Having obtained the Dharma, Hsing Szu returned to Ch'ing Yüan Mountain in Chi Chou, to propagate the Dharma and transform living beings. After his death he was given the posthumous title "Dhyana Master Hung Chi."

Commentary:

Dhyana Master Hsing Szu walked and thought about things at the same time. What did he think about? Do you know? I know. He walked and thought, "Who is mindful of the Buddha? Who is mindful of the Buddha?" and so he was called Hsing Szu, "walking thinker."

At that time the reputation of the Dharma Assembly at Ts'ao Hsi had spread all over China. Everyone knew that the person to whom the Fifth Patriarch had transmitted the robe and bowl was spreading the Dharma there. People "drift away from the empty and gather with the flourishing." If there are only a few people in your place, it will soon be empty. For instance, here there are thirty people, but if there were only three or four people, soon they would all run away. The more people there are, the more will come from the outside. "There are a lot of people at the Buddhist Lecture Hall!" "Hippies who go there cut their hair and shave their beards. It's inconceivable. There must be something happening there. Let's go and see!"

The Dharma Assembly at Ts'ao Hsi flourished. "Gather with the flourishing" can also be explained as "gather with the sages," because in Chinese the words "flourishing" and "sage" sound the same. Many sages and common people came to support the Patriarch.

Hsing Szu asked the Patriarch which Dharma door he should cultivate in order to avoid the successive stages of the gradual teaching. The sudden teaching does not have successive stages. Therefore, what he actually asked was, "How do I cultivate the sudden dharma?" He must have heard someone say, "The Sixth Patriarch is truly inconceivable. He has the five eyes and the six spiritual penetrations. I went there and didn't say a thing and he knew what I was thinking and asked me about, it!"

The Master regarded Hsing Szu highly. "What this man says makes sense," he thought. "He surely must have good roots." He appointed Hsing Szu head of the assembly and thereafter Hsing Szu always walked in front, leading the others during the ceremonies.

The Sixth Patriarch saw Hsing Szu as a vessel of the Dharma, a Dharma-door "elephant and dragon." This means that he had the capability of a patriarch, not a self-made patriarch, but one who had received the Sixth Patriarch's certification and permission to teach. "Go and teach elsewhere," said the Master. "You should not stay here with me but should go in such and such a direction to be a teaching master. Do not let the Dharma become extinct!"

Hsing Szu received the robe and bowl and carried the transmission of the lamp of the wonderful Dharma.

The posthumous title was conferred by the Emperor. Hsing Szu was given the name Hung Chi, "extensive crossing," just as the Sixth Patriarch received the name Ta Chien, "great mirror."

Dhyana Master Huai Jang

Sutra:

Dhyana Master Huai Jang was the son of the Tu family in Chin Chou. He first visited National Master An of Sung Mountain, who told him to go to Ts'ao Hsi to pay homage. When he arrived, he bowed, and the Master asked him, "What has come?"

He replied, "Sung Shan."

The Master said, "What thing is it and how does it come?"

He replied, "To say that it is like a thing is to miss the point."

The Master said, "Then can there still be that which is cultivated and certified?"

He replied, "Cultivation and certification are not absent, but there can be no defilement."

The Master said, "It is just the lack of defilement of which all Buddhas are mindful and protective. You are like that, and I am like that, too. In the West, Prajnatara predicted that a colt would run from under your feet, trampling and killing people under heaven. You should keep that in mind, but do not speak of it too soon."

Huai Jang suddenly understood. Accordingly he waited upon the Master for fifteen years, daily penetrating more deeply into the profound and

mysterious. He later went to Nan Yao where he spread the Dhyana School. The title "Dhyana Master Ta Hui" was bestowed upon him posthumously.

Commentary:

Huai Jang received the Dharma-transmission from the Great Master and became the Seventh Patriarch. Huai means "to cherish." What did he cherish? Jang, which means "to yield." He was never arrogant toward anyone, but kept his mind humble and modest, respecting everyone above and below him. In his mind he always cherished politeness. What this Dhyana Master had, he appeared to be without; what was real appeared false. Although he had the Way, it seemed as though he didn't. He was actually highly educated, but if anyone brought it up, he politely insisted that he was really just a beginner.

He first went to study the Buddhadharma with National Master An. National Master An sent him to study at Ts'ao Hsi, because at that time everyone knew that Ts'ao Hsi was the place of the true orthodox Buddhadharma. If you really wanted to study and cultivate faith in the Buddhadharma you went to Ts'ao Hsi. Now, in America, if you really want to study the Buddhadharma, you should come and study the Sutras here. Don't fear difficulty! Don't fear suffering! Don't be lazy! Study the Buddhadharma.

At that time at Nan Hua Temple, the site of the platform of the Sixth Patriarch, there was Dhyana meditation and work on the mountain slopes every day. Everyone got up at three-thirty in the morning. At four o'clock they went to morning recitation, which was very vigorous and lasted until five-thirty. Then they sat in meditation until sunrise. After they had eaten some rice gruel, there was another hour of meditation. At eight o'clock they went out on the mountain slopes for two hours until ten o'clock. Because there were about two thousand people, in two hours they were able to do a lot of work. It was not like one or two people doing the work and not being able to finish it.

At ten they returned from the slopes and rested until eleven, at which time they ate. From twelve to two they sat in meditation, and at two o'clock they went back out on the mountain slopes to work for two more hours. Then they returned and sat in meditation for six hours until ten o'clock. Afterwards, some did their own work, bowing in homage to the Sutras, or performing repentance ceremonies, until midnight. Every day it was this way.

The "wind of the Way" blew severely at Nan Hua Temple. Everyone had to follow the rules. There were several thousand people and you never heard a person speak. No one spoke because they feared that they might strike up false thinking and then their work would not succeed. If you single-mindedly apply effort, you never pursue any train of random thought whatsoever. The Sixth Patriarch therefore established work in common which was very rigorous.

When Dhyana Master Huai Jang arrived at Nan Hua Temple he bowed, and the Master said, "What has come?" This is Ch'an. In the Ch'an School, one never speaks of the principle outright. He merely said, "What has come?" Ostensibly it was a Bhikshu, but he said, "What comes?" At least he didn't ask if it was a ghost.

Huai Jang replied, "Sung Shan." He meant, "I am from Sung Mountain."

The two were using the language of the Ch'an School–repartee.

"Cultivation and certification are not absent, but there can be no defilement." Cultivation has that which is cultivated and certification has that which is certified. Therefore cultivation and certification are not non-existent. So cultivation and certification can exist, but defilement cannot; that is, you cannot be stained. The self-nature must be bright and light.

When Huai Jang said this, the Master replied that there was no defilement, no filth in the self-nature. The defilements are self-seeking, jealousy, greed, hate, and delusion. "Without these defilements," he said, "you are 'thus', just as I am. We two are the same–equal."

The Twenty-seventh Indian Patriarch, Prajnatara, the predecessor of Bodhidharma, had said that a colt would run from under Huai Jang's feet. Who was the colt? He was Huai Jang's Dharma successor, Great Master Ma Tsu "horse patriarch" Tao I.

"Under your feet" means that the colt would be Huai Jang's disciple, because a disciple behaves as if he were under his teacher's foot. "In the future," Prajnatara had said, "a colt will run out of your gate, trampling people all over the world. No other Dharma Master will match his superb eloquence and vast wisdom. None will defeat him. Under heaven, he will be supreme."

Master Huai Jang became the Sixth Patriarch's personal attendant. Later he went to Heng Mountain in Nan Yao, which is in Hu Nan Province in south-central China, to propagate the Dhyana School. After Huai Jang died, the Emperor gave him the title "Great Master Ta Hui," "Great Wisdom."

Dhyana Master Hsüan Chiao

Sutra:

Dhyana Master Hsüan Chiao of Yung Chia was the son of a family called Tai in Wen Chou. When he was young he studied the Sutras and commentaries and was skilled in the T'ien T'ai Dharma-door of "Stop and Look." Upon reading the *Vimalakirti Sutra*, he understood the mind-ground. One day he happened to meet the Master's disciple Hsüan Ch'e and they had a pleasant talk. As Hsüan Chiao's words were consonant with the words of all the Patriarchs, Hsüan Ch'e asked him, "Kind Sir, from whom did you obtain the Dharma?"

He replied, "I have heard the Vaipulya Sutras and Shastras, receiving each from a master. Later, upon reading the *Vimalakirti Sutra*, I awakened to the doctrine of the Buddha-mind, but as yet no one has certified me."

Hsüan Ch'e said, "That was acceptable before the time of the Buddha called the Awesome-Voiced King. But since the coming of that Buddha, all those who 'self-enlighten' without a master belong to other religions which hold to the tenet of spontaneity."

"Then will you please certify me, Kind Sir?" said Hsüan Chiao.

Hsüan Ch'e said, "My words are of little worth, but the Great Master, the Sixth Patriarch, is at Ts'ao Hsi,

where people gather like clouds from the four directions. He is one who has received the Dharma. If you wish to go, I will accompany you."

Commentary:

Yung Chia is the name of a place. Because everyone greatly respected this Dharma Master, they addressed him after the name of his birthplace, according to Chinese custom. When he was young Yung Chia investigated the Buddhist Sutras and the commentaries written by the Patriarchs. When he read the *Vimalakirti Sutra*, he understood the Dharma-door of his own mind-ground. One day he had a chat with the Sixth Patriarch's disciple Hsüan Ch'e, and Hsüan Ch'e found that their views were in agreement and that they both agreed with the principles of the Patriarchs. Supposing him to be a member of his own school, Hsüan Ch'e asked, "Who transmitted our Dharma to you, Great Master Hsüan Chiao? Who certified you?"

When he learned Hsüan Chiao had enlightened himself by reading *Vimalakirti Sutra*, he said, "Before the time of Awesome-Voiced King Buddha, that would have been all right. But he was the first Buddha, and now, since his advent, anyone who claims to be enlightened without a master's certification is simply not a Buddhist."

"Not a Buddhist? Oh no!" said Hsüan Chiao. "Then please certify me!"

I don't know what certain people in America who certify themselves and then lecture on *The Sixth Patriarch's Sutra* do when they come to this passage of text. How do they explain it?

Awesome-Voiced King Buddha's name means that the sound of his voice penetrates to the most remote places, through the wind and light to the original ground.

"I can't certify you," said Hsüan Ch'e, "because I don't have the authority. Besides, it's not certain that I myself am enlightened. However the Sixth Patriarch is at Nan Hua Temple. The Fifth Patriarch has transmitted both the Dharma and Bodhidharma's robe and bowl to him."

Sutra:

Thereupon Hsüan Chiao went with Hsüan Ch'e to call upon the Master. On arriving, he circumambulated the Master three times, shook his staff, and stood in front of him. The Master said, "Inasmuch as a Shramana has perfected the three thousand awesome deportments and the eighty thousand fine practices, where does this Virtuous One come from and what makes him so arrogant?"

Hsüan Chiao said, "The affair of birth and death is great and impermanence comes quickly."

The Master said, "Why not embody non-production and understand that which is not quick?"

He replied, "The body itself is not produced and fundamentally there is no quickness."

The Master said, "So it is; so it is."

Commentary:

When the two arrived at Ts'ao Hsi, Hsüan Chiao marched around the Sixth Patriarch three times, pounded his tin staff into the ground, and stood there as if angry.

The Sixth Patriarch politely asked, "How did you get here and why are you so obnoxious? One who has left home has perfected the three thousand awesome deportments and the eighty thousand fine practices, and yet you didn't even bow to me."

There are two hundred and fifty deportments for each of the four body postures: standing, sitting, walking, and lying down. These thousand comportments multiplied by the past, present, and future make three thousand. There are actually eighty four thousand fine practices, although the text here gives the number as eighty thousand.

Hsüan Chiao said, "I act this way because birth and death is a serious problem and one never knows when the Ghost of Impermanence will pay his inevitable call. It all happens very fast, you know." What Hsüan Chiao actually meant was, "I am trying to end birth and death and I have no time for good manners. Besides, I've put that sort of thing down."

"Then why don't you think of a way to embody and comprehend that which is not produced and to understand what is not quick?" said the Master. "You should be clear about the principles of non-production and quickness."

"The body itself is not produced," said Hsüan Chiao, "and, fundamentally the understanding is without quickness. That is, if I clearly understand birth and death, then there is no birth and death, and if I maintain that clear understanding, then in fact there is no quickness. Why then should I fear the Ghost of Impermanence?"

Seeing that he understood, the Sixth Patriarch certified him saying, "Right! Good work! It's just as you say."

Sutra:

Hsüan Chiao then made obeisance with perfect awesome deportment. A short while later he announced that he was leaving and the Master said, "Aren't you leaving too quickly?"

He replied, "Fundamentally I don't move; how can I be quick?"

The Master said, "Who knows you don't move?"

He replied, "Kind Sir, you yourself make this discrimination."

The Master said, "You have truly got the idea of non-production."

"But does non-production possess an 'idea'?" asked Hsüan Chiao.

"If it is without ideas, then who discriminates it?" said the Master.

"What discriminates is not an idea either," he replied.

The Master exclaimed, "Good indeed! Please stay for a night."

During his time he was called "The One Enlightened Overnight" and later he wrote the "Song of Certifying to the Way," which circulated widely in the world. His posthumous title is "Great Master Wu Hsiang," and during his lifetime he was called "Chen Chiao."

Commentary:

The Master and Hsüan Chiao carried on some repartee: "Your eloquence indicates that you have truly understood the idea of non-production," said the Master.

"How can non-production have an idea?" Hsüan Chiao replied.

"Without ideas, who could discriminate it?" said the Master.

Hsüan Chiao said, "Although there is discrimination, it is not done on the basis of the mind's ideas; it is not the intellect engaging in intellection which discriminates. Rather, it is the Buddha's wonderful observing wisdom which has no need to resort to the process of reasoning and which yet knows everything. Therefore, what discriminates is not an idea either."

"You're absolutely right," said the Master.

Hsüan Chiao stayed one night at Nan Hua Temple and became enlightened, so everyone called him "The One Enlightened Overnight." Later on, he wrote the "Song of Certifying to the Way" which I am sure you all know. It begins:

Have you not seen the man of the Way
Who has cut off learning and, in leisure,
does nothing
Who does not reject false thinking or seek
reality?
For him, the real nature of ignorance is the
Buddha nature
And the empty body of illusion is the
Dharma-body.

After he died, the Emperor gave him the title, "Wu Hsiang" which means, "without marks," and his contemporaries called him "Chen Chiao," "true enlightenment."

Dhyana Master Chih Huang

Sutra:

Dhyana cultivator Chih Huang had formerly studied under the Fifth Patriarch and said of himself that he had attained to the "right reception." He lived in a hut, constantly sitting, for twenty years.

In his travels, the Master's disciple Hsüan Ch'e reached Ho Shuo, where he heard of Chih Huang's reputation. He paid a visit to his hut and asked him, "What are you doing here?"

"Entering concentration," replied Chih Huang.

Hsüan Ch'e said, "You say you are entering concentration. Do you enter with thought or without thought? If you enter without thought, then all insentient things, such as grass, trees, tiles, and stones, should likewise attain concentration. If you enter with thought, then all sentient things which have consciousness should also attain concentration."

Chih Huang said, "When I properly enter concentration I do not notice whether I have thought or not."

Hsüan Ch'e said, "Not to notice whether or not you have thought is eternal concentration. How can you enter it or come out of it? If you come out of it or enter it, it is not the great concentration."

Chih Huang was speechless. After a long while, he finally asked, "Who is your teacher?"

Hsüan Ch'e said, "My master is the Sixth Patriarch at Ts'ao Hsi."

Chih Huang said, "What does your master take to be Dhyana Concentration?"

Commentary:

Chih Huang practiced Dhyana meditation; his first teacher was the Fifth Patriarch, Hung Jen. Formerly, when cultivators left the home-life they would travel everywhere in search of a "bright-eyed knowing one."

Hsüan Ch'e did public relations work for the Sixth Patriarch. He traveled all over China saying, "My teacher is the Sixth Patriarch, the genuine recipient of the robe and bowl!" When he heard about Chih Huang's cultivation he went to visit him and said, "Hey! What are you doing here, huh?"

Chih Huang just said, "I am entering concentration."

"You say you are entering concentration," said Hsüan Ch'e. "Tell me, do you do it with the thought in mind that you want to enter concentration, or don't you have such a thought? If you do not enter it with such a thought in mind, then all inanimate objects could also enter concentration, because they don't have thought either. But if you do, then all living, conscious creatures could enter as well."

Chih Huang said, "When I enter concentration I don't notice whether I have thought or not. At that time I'm empty."

Hsüan Ch'e said, "If you don't notice whether or not you have thought, then that is permanent concentration. How can you come out of it or enter it? How do you go in? How do you come out? If you can enter or leave it, it's not the great concentration of the Buddha."

Chih Huang was dumbfounded. "What am I going to do?" he thought. "I do go into concentration and come out of it." He couldn't open his mouth for a long time. He knew that his own words had no principle, that Hsüan Ch'e's wisdom was higher than his own, and that he had no means to debate with him. Finally he asked, "Who is your teacher? Your eloquence is superb. Surely your master is even more clever than you. Who transmitted the Dharma to you?"

"My teacher is the Sixth Patriarch, the Abbot of Nan Hua Temple in Ts'ao Hsi," said Hsüan Ch'e.

"What does he take to be Dhyana concentration?" Chih Huang asked.

Sutra:

Hsüan Ch'e said, "My teacher speaks of the wonderful, clear, perfect stillness, the suchness of the substance and function, the fundamental emptiness of the five skandhas, and the non-existence of the six organs. There is neither emerging nor entering, neither concentration nor confusion. The nature of Dhyana is non-dwelling and is beyond the act of dwelling in Dhyana stillness. The nature of Dhyana is unproduced and beyond the production of the thought of Dhyana. The mind is like empty space and is without the measure of empty space."

Commentary:

The Sixth Patriarch says that the original nature is wonderful, clear, perfectly still and unmoving. Its substance and function both are "thus, thus unmoving, clear, clear, and illuminating." The five shadows, i.e. the five skandhic heaps of form, feeling, perception, impulses, and consciousness are fundamentally void and the six sense objects of form, sound, smell, taste, tangible objects, and objects of the mind are also non-existent.

When you understand the wonderful function of the original substance, there is no question of either dwelling or not dwelling in Dhyana. The Dhyana nature transcends that kind of "dead Dhyana" which is attached to stillness.

The nature of Dhyana itself is unproduced and transcends such thoughts as, "Here I sit in Dhyana meditation."

Sutra:

Hearing this explanation, Chih Huang went directly to visit the Master. The Master asked him, "Kind Sir, where are you from?" Chih Huang related the above incident in detail. The Master then said, "It is truly just as he said. Simply let your mind be like empty space without being attached to the idea of emptiness and the correct function of the self-nature will no longer be obstructed. Have no thought, whether in motion or stillness; forget any feeling of being common or holy, put an end to both subject and object. The nature and mark will be 'thus, thus,' and at no time will you be out of the state of concentration."

Commentary:

"What Hsüan Ch'e told you was correct," said the Master. "Just make your mind like empty space, but do not hold onto the idea of empty space. You will then function in an unhindered way. When something presents itself, you will respond and when it passes, you will be still. This is to be unobstructed.

Whether moving or still, whether walking, standing, sitting, or lying down, have no thought. Do not think, "I'm a sage!" and do not think, "I'm just a common person." Forget about feeling holy or common; get rid of emotional feelings altogether. Be without subject or object: do not have something which sees and something which is seen, something which makes empty and something which is made empty. You should know that when you see brightness, your seeing is not bright; when you see darkness, your seeing is not dark; when you see emptiness, your seeing is not empty; when you see form, your seeing has no form; when you see existence, your seeing is not existent; and when you see non-existence, your seeing is not non-existent. *The Shurangama Sutra* says, "When your seeing sees the seeing (nature), that seeing is no (longer) seeing. Your seeing nature is beyond your seeing and your seeing cannot reach it." Your seeing nature should be separate from and unattached to your false discriminating seeing and you should not hold onto the thought of seeing. If you adhere to the idea of subject and object, maintaining that there is someone who sees as well as an emptiness which is seen, you are left with just that knowledge and vision. You should put an end to both subject and object.

Sutra:

Just then Chih Huang attained the great enlightenment. What he had gained in twenty years vanished from his mind without a trace. That night the people of Hopei heard a voice in space announcing, "Today, Dhyana Master Chih Huang has attained the Way." Later, he made obeisance and left, returning to Hopei to teach and convert the four assemblies there.

Commentary:

All of a sudden, Chih Huang had a great, not a small, enlightenment and the skill he had acquired in twenty years of diligent cultivation completely left him. There was not a trace, not an echo. Before he had entered samadhi thinking, "I am entering samadhi," but now he had nothing at all. Everything was empty. He had returned to the root and source of all dharmas.

Although Chih Huang himself was in Ho Shuo, that night in his native village on the outskirts of Peking, his neighbors, disciples, and Dharma protectors all heard a voice in space saying, "You should all know that today Dhyana Master Chih Huang reached enlightenment."

Later, Chih Huang bowed to the Sixth Patriarch, took leave and returned to Hopei to teach the Bhikshus, Bhikshunis, laymen, and laywomen there.

Hopei is about fifteen hundred miles from Ho Shuo. That's a long walk.

One Member Of The Sangha

Sutra:

One of the Sangha asked the Master, "Who got the principle of Huang Mei?"

The Master replied, "The one who understands the Buddhadharma."

The Sangha member said, "High Master, have you obtained it?"

"I do not understand the Buddhadharma," the Master replied.

Commentary:

This member of the Sangha was truly a barbarian, an uneducated savage. He rudely confronted the Master and asked, "Who got the robe and bowl of the Fifth Patriarch Hung Jen of Huang Mei?" He knew very well that the Sixth Patriarch had it, but he asked anyway. From this we know that among those who came to the Master for instruction there were rude country peasants as well as good disciples. He knew that his question was insulting to the Master and what he meant by it was, "You can't even read. How can you be worthy of the robe and bowl?"

The Master said, "One who thoroughly comprehends the Buddhadharma obtains that principle and the Fifth Patriarch's robe and bowl."

"But High Master," the Bhikshu said, "have you got it or not?" He didn't believe that the Master had received the transmission.

The Sixth Patriarch didn't say yes and he didn't say no, he simply said, "I don't understand the Buddhadharma." What do you think? Was he telling the truth?

Bhikshu Fang Pien

Sutra:

One day the Master wanted to wash the robe which he had inherited, but there was no clear stream nearby. He walked about two miles behind the temple where he saw good energies revolving in a dense grove of trees. He shook his staff, stuck it in the ground, and a spring bubbled up and formed a pool.

Commentary:

The Master walked about two miles behind the temple, where he found a luxuriant grove filled with tall trees and good vibrations. People who have opened their five eyes and obtained the six spiritual powers can tell at a glance the geomantic properties of any particular piece of land. So when the Master planted his tin staff in the ground, the nine metal rings which hung from the head of his staff echoed through the wood, and a spring gushed forth to form a clear, pure pool.

The public washing stream is about a third of a mile behind Nan Hua Temple. Whether this present stream is the same source that was used during the Sixth Patriarch's time is uncertain.

Sutra:

As he knelt to wash his robe on a rock, suddenly a monk came up and bowed before him saying, "I am Fang

Pien, a native of Hsi Shu. A while ago I was in India, where I visited the Great Master Bodhidharma. He told me to return to China immediately, saying, 'The orthodox Dharma Eye Treasury and the samghati robe which I inherited from Mahakashyapa has been transmitted to the sixth generation at Ts'ao Hsi, Shao Chou. Go there and pay reverence.' Fang Pien has come from afar, hoping to see the robe and bowl that his Master transmitted."

The Master showed them to him and asked, "Superior One, what work do you do?"

"I am good at sculpting," he replied.

Keeping a straight face, the Master said, "Then sculpt something for me to see."

Fang Pien was bewildered, but after several days he completed a lifelike image of the Patriarch, seven inches high and wonderful in every detail. The Master laughed and said, "You only understand the nature of sculpture; you do not understand the nature of the Buddha." Then the Master stretched out his hand and rubbed the crown of Fang Pien's head, saying, "You will forever be a field of blessing for gods and humans."

The Master rewarded him with a robe, which Fang Pien divided into three parts: one he used to wrap the sculpture, one he kept for himself, and the third he wrapped in palm leaves and buried in the ground, vowing, "In the future, when this robe is found again, I will appear in the world to be abbot here and restore these buildings."

Note: During the Sung Dynasty in the eighth year of the Chia Yu reign period (1063 A.D.), while Bhikshu Wei Hsien was repairing the hall, he excavated the earth and

found the robe which was like new. The image is at Kao Ch'üan Temple and those who pray before it obtain a quick response.

Commentary:

Think about it: Bodhidharma had long since died in China, but Bhikshu Fang Pien met him in India. That is not surprising, however, because to this day no one knows exactly what happened to Bodhidharma.

I will now tell you a true story. While I was living in Manchuria I decided, for various reasons, to leave the home-life and cultivate the Way. The man I most respected was Wang Hsiao Tzu, 'Filial-Son Wang.' When he was twenty-eight years old his mother died and he practiced filial piety by sitting beside her grave. He built a small hut out of scrap lumber to protect himself from the bitter Manchurian cold and lived there for three years, according to the Confucian custom. When the first three years were up he decided to stay for another three years, so in all he practiced for six years.

During the second three-year period he did not speak, no matter who came. Every day he sat in his hut, meditating and reciting the *Diamond Sutra*. Toward the end of the sixth year he had a daydream. "In Ch'ien and Kuang Ling Mountains," he thought, "there are cultivators who live for over a thousand years. When I fulfill my filial obligations I'll go there to cultivate." The following morning, during meditation, he heard a Dharma Protector say, "Today an important guest will visit you." He thought perhaps a great official was coming and he waited until ten o'clock when he saw a monk approaching wearing rag robes and carrying a bumble stick. Filial Son Wang did not speak out loud, but in his mind he wondered, "Where is he from?"

The monk replied, "I'm from Kuang Ling Mountain."

Filial Son Wang then thought, "What is his name?" The monk told him his name and added, "In the Ming dynasty I was a general and later I left home to cultivate. We two have a karmic affinity for one another, and so when I heard that you wanted to go to Kuang Ling Mountain, I felt I should advise you that the monks there cultivate solely for their own benefit. You, on the other hand, should cultivate for the good of all. After you have finished your act of filial piety, build a temple right here and spread the Buddhadharma."

Now, 'Filial-Son Wang' hadn't spoken to the monk, and yet the monk read the questions in his mind. That shows that the monk had the spiritual power of knowing others' thoughts and had obtained the five eyes and six spiritual penetrations. He said he was from the Ming dynasty. 'Filial-Son Wang' lived during the first years of the Republic, some three hundred years later. So you see that Bodhidharma could easily have been seen in southern India several hundred years after his disappearance from China. That he met Fang Pien there and told him about the robe and bowl is a very ordinary matter–nothing strange at all.

Bhikshu Fang Pien knew how to make Buddha images. He carved them in wood and molded them in clay. The Master very solemnly said to him, "Please sculpt an image for me to see"

Caught off guard, Fang Pien just stood there in silence, but a few days later he had finished making a true image of the Patriarch. It looked just like the Master. The nose, ears, eyes, all the features were exactly right. It was a perfect likeness right down to the finest detail.

When the Master saw the little statue of himself he couldn't help but smile. "Fang Pien," he said, "you may know how to model clay, but you don't know the Buddha nature. In any case, you should leave home in every life, become a Bhikshu, and act as a field of blessing for humans and gods."

Master Wo Lun's Verse

Sutra:

One Bhikshu was reciting Dhyana Master Wo Lun's verse:

Wo Lun has the talent
To stop the hundred thoughts:
Facing situations his mind won't move;
Bodhi grows day by day.

When the Master heard it he said, "This verse shows no understanding of the mind-ground, and to cultivate according to it will increase one's bondage. Then he spoke this verse:

Hui Neng has no talent
To stop the hundred thoughts.
Facing situations his mind often moves;
How can Bodhi grow?

Commentary:

The name of the reciter of Wo Lun's verse is not given. Perhaps he had no name or perhaps he didn't want to be famous.

Dhyana Master Wo Lun could cut off his thoughts, but Wo Lun himself, the cutter-off of thoughts, still remained. Thus he had fallen into the second or third position. He was not in the first position.

Upon hearing Wo Lun's verse, the Great Master replied,

I haven't a single talent,
Nor even the thought of cutting off thought.
My mind responds in a natural way:
Who cares whether Bodhi grows or not?

Here he expresses the same principle as in the verse he wrote while still a layman at Huang Mei: "Originally there is not one thing. Where can the dust alight?" The absolute is pure; what need is there to dust it off?

Chapter VIII

Sudden and Gradual

Commentary:

"Sudden" refers to the immediate understanding of a principle. You may be suddenly enlightened to a principle, but until you have been certified as one who is fully enlightened, you still must cultivate that principle gradually by putting it into practice in everyday life.

Sutra:

While the Patriarch was staying at Pao Lin Temple in Ts'ao Hsi, the Great Master Shen Hsiu was at Yü Ch'üan Temple in Ching Nan. At that time the two schools flourished and everyone called them, "Southern Neng and Northern Hsiu." So it was that the two schools, northern and southern, were divided into "sudden" and "gradual." As the students did not understand the doctrine, the Master said to them, "The Dharma is originally of one school. It is people who think of North and South. The Dharma is of one kind, but people understand it slowly or quickly. Dharma is not sudden or gradual. Rather it is people who are sharp or dull. Hence the terms sudden and gradual."

Nonetheless, Shen Hsiu's followers continually ridiculed the southern Patriarch, saying that he couldn't read a single word and had nothing in his favor. But Shen Hsiu said, "He has obtained wisdom without the aid of a

teacher and understands the Supreme Vehicle deeply. I am inferior to him. Furthermore, my Master, the Fifth Patriarch, personally transmitted the robe and Dharma to him, and not without good reason. I regret that I am unable to make the long journey to visit him, as I unworthily receive state patronage here. But do not let me stop you. Go to Ts'ao Hsi and call on him."

Commentary:

You all remember Shen Hsiu, the Great Master who was obsessed with the deadly ambition to be a patriarch. He was an intelligent man, and yet he couldn't cut off his desire for the Patriarchate.

In the south, the Sixth Patriarch taught the "sudden" Dharma to a flourishing assembly of over a thousand people. Shen Hsiu, in Ching Nan, was busy teaching "gradual" Dharma to an even larger crowd of over ten thousand people. Originally, Shen Hsiu had about two hundred followers, but every day more and more people came. However, everyone knew that the Fifth Patriarch had transmitted the robe and bowl to Hui Neng in the south. In spite of the fact that Shen Hsiu had been teaching master under the Fifth Patriarch and was extremely well-educated, he did not have the transmission. Still, Shen Hsiu's disciples advertised him as the Sixth Patriarch and finally even sent an assassin to try to kill the Master and seize the robe and bowl.

Because of the division into Northern and Southern schools, students of the Way did not know where to turn. Should they study with the Sixth Patriarch? He was illiterate and sometimes his teachings seemed to contradict the scriptures. On the other hand, Shen Hsiu didn't have the robe and bowl.

Seeing their dilemma, the Master said, "There is only one Dharma. People may come from the north or south but there is actually only one non-dual Dharma door. Intelligent people understand it all of a sudden and stupid people come to understand it gradually, but the Dharma itself is neither sudden nor gradual."

Still, Shen Hsiu's men constantly made fun of the Sixth Patriarch. "Hey, look at him!" they said. "He can't even read. The Southern School disciples are following an illiterate. That is perfectly ridiculous. What could they possibly learn from him?" Thus they slighted the Patriarch and his disciples, saying that they were ignorant, not having even one doctorate among them.

Shen Hsiu said, "Don't talk like that! He's an enlightened man. He has obtained wisdom through his own effort, without the aid of a teacher, and has a thorough grasp of the Supreme Vehicle. Frankly, I'm not as good as he is; I do not possess his enlightened wisdom. Our teacher, the Fifth Patriarch, passed the wonderful mind-seal Dharma on to him, and for a good reason. It was no accident."

Shen Hsiu was a National Master. He and Masters Lao An, Chih Hsien, and Fa Ju were among the Fifth Patriarch's ten great disciples. As they had received invitations to the Imperial Palace from Empress Wu Tsai T'ien, they received state patronage. Shen Hsiu told his disciples, "I can't get away, as I receive state aid here. But don't let me stop you. You may go to Ts'ao Hsi to call on the Great Master."

Actually, Shen Hsiu was just testing his disciples to see whether or not they would go. He said that the Sixth Patriarch had more virtue than he, but what he really meant was, "If you believe in me you won't leave, even though he has more virtue. But if you don't believe, you'll go as soon as I tell you to leave. Go!"

No one went.

Sutra:

One day Shen Hsiu told his disciple Chih Ch'eng, "You are intelligent and very wise. You may go to Ts'ao Hsi on my behalf and listen to the Dharma. Remember it all and take careful notes to read to me when you return."

As ordered, Chih Ch'eng proceeded to Ts'ao Hsi and joined the assembly without saying where he had come from. The Patriarch told the assembly, "Today there is a Dharma thief hidden in this assembly!"

Chih Ch'eng immediately stepped forward, bowed, and explained his mission. The Master said, "You are from Yü Ch'üan; you must be a spy."

"No," he replied, "I am not."

The Master said, "What do you mean?"

He replied, "Before I confessed, I was; but now that I have confessed, I am not."

The Master said, "How does your Master instruct his followers?"

Chih Ch'eng replied, "He always instructs us to dwell with the mind contemplating stillness and to sit up all the time without lying down."

The Master said, "To dwell with the mind contemplating stillness is sickness, not Dhyana. Constant sitting restrains the body. How can it be beneficial? Listen to my verse:

> ***When living, sit, don't lie.***
> ***When dead, lie down, don't sit.***
> ***How can a set of stinking bones***
> ***Be used for training?***

Chih Ch'eng bowed again and said, "Your disciple studied the Way for nine years at the place of Great Master Hsiu but obtained no enlightenment. Now, hearing one speech from the High Master, I am united with my original mind. Your disciple's birth and death is a serious matter. Will the High Master be compassionate enough to instruct me further?"

Commentary:

Chih Ch'eng was a good disciple to Shen Hsiu, one of his favorites. "You may represent me at Ts'ao Hsi," Shen Hsiu said. "I cannot go. If I were to go personally, Hui Neng would surely recognize me and not speak the Dharma. Write down everything he says without getting one word wrong. Then bring back your notes and read them to me."

When Chih Ch'eng asked for instruction at Ts'ao Hsi, he didn't say where he was from. "I've been here and there," he said, beating around the bush.

That day there were several thousand people gathered to hear the Dharma. The Sixth Patriarch announced: "Everyone should be careful! There is a Dharma thief hidden in the assembly!"

Chih Ch'eng pushed his way through the crowd, bowed at the Master's feet and said, "I confess! I'm a spy. Shen Hsiu sent me here."

The Master explained the Dharma to Chih Cheng. "Contemplating stillness is a kind of occupational disease," he said, "It is not Dhyana. As to constant sitting in meditation, this is a mere constraint on the body. What is the principle behind it? When you eat, just eat; when you sleep, just sleep. Don't lock yourself up."

Shen Hsiu was just working on his stinking skin-bag. He didn't know how to work in the self-nature. That is sickness. The

Sixth Patriarch worked naturally in the self-nature, and he spoke this verse to say,

> *You sit up when you're alive,*
> *You lie down when you're dead.*
> *Your body's a bone-bag composed of four elements:*
> *Why not work on the self-nature instead?*

To dwell with the mind contemplating stillness contradicts the principle of the *Diamond Sutra*, which tells us to "produce that thought which is nowhere supported." The Sixth Patriarch spoke this verse to break Chih Ch'eng's attachment to marks.

Shen Hsiu taught people to dwell with the mind contemplating stillness and the Sixth Patriarch said that that was wrong. Nonetheless, if you can do it, bit by bit, you will gain benefit. If you always sit and do not lie down, although it is not very natural, it will assist your body and mind in cultivation. Then why did the Sixth Patriarch object to these practices? It was because Chih Ch'eng had just come from Shen Hsiu and it was necessary to break his attachments before he could properly receive the genuine Buddhadharma. In cultivation you should not be attached to your work and think, "Look at me! I really work hard, constantly sitting and never lying down!" Such thoughts will obstruct your progress.

If the mind "dwells," it is attached. In order to be united with the original wisdom of the self-nature, you must "produce that thought which is nowhere supported," as the *Diamond Sutra* says. The Sixth Patriarch gave Chih Ch'eng this teaching in order to break his attachments. If you can constantly sit and feel natural and unforced doing so, then go ahead, but do not force yourself. Force is not the way. You should work naturally.

"Good!" you say. "Then I don't have to follow the rules."

This does not mean that you can ignore the rules. If you lie down when people sit, and sit when they lie down, you are not in accord with Dharma and are just trying to show that you think you are special. In general, you must follow the rules and be natural with yourself as well. But "being natural" does not mean that you can break the rules. Is this clear?

Chih Ch'eng had studied nine years with Shen Hsiu. How many years have you studied here? One year. And you think that is a very long time. Cultivators may study for ten, twenty, or thirty years with great effort. You can't graduate in just a few months.

As soon as the Sixth Patriarch spoke, his principles entered Chih Ch'eng's heart like water flowing into water: "thus, thus," like milk mixing with milk. There was not the slightest difference between them. "The Patriarch's heart is my heart," said Chih Ch'eng, "and my heart is the Patriarch's heart. I am suddenly united with the original mind because our minds are fundamentally one and the same."

"But I do not know when I will die," Chih Ch'eng continued, "and I do not know when I will be born again. This matter of birth and death is most pressing. Please be compassionate and help me understand."

Sutra:

The Master said, "I have heard that your Master instructs his students in the dharmas of morality, concentration, and wisdom. Please tell me how he defines the terms."

Chih Ch'eng said, "Great Master Shen Hsiu says that morality is abstaining from doing evil, wisdom is offering up all good conduct, and concentration is purifying one's own mind. This is how he explains them, but I do not

know, High Master, what dharma of instruction you use."

The Master said, "If I said that I had a dharma to give to others, I would be lying to you. I merely use expedients to untie bonds and falsely call that samadhi. Your master's explanation of morality, concentration, and wisdom is truly inconceivably good but my conception of morality, concentration, and wisdom is different from his."

Commentary:

"I don't have any dharmas at all," said the Sixth Patriarch. "I'd be cheating you if I said that I did. I have no special dharma to give to people. For each individual I use an appropriate teaching to untie his bonds. To 'untie bonds' means to break attachments. The attachments of living beings bind them up. I just untie their bonds and set them free of their attachments. Fundamentally this teaching has no name whatsoever, but it is hypothetically called 'samadhi.' Thus, my view of morality, concentration, and wisdom is special; it is not the same as Shen Hsiu's."

Sutra:

Chih Ch'eng said, "There can only be one kind of morality, concentration, and wisdom. How can there be a difference?"

The Master said, "Your master's morality, concentration, and wisdom guide those of the Great Vehicle, whereas my morality, concentration, and wisdom guide those of the Supreme Vehicle.

Enlightenment is not the same as understanding; seeing may take place slowly or quickly.

Commentary:

When you become enlightened, in that moment of enlightenment you attain your aim. Understanding, on the other hand, is a gradual process. Thus perception may be sudden or gradual, fast or slow.

Sutra:

"Listen to my explanation. Is it the same as Shen Hsiu's? The Dharma which I speak does not depart from the self-nature, for to depart from the self-nature in explaining the Dharma is to speak of marks and continually confuse the self-nature. You should know that the functions of the ten thousand dharmas all arise from the self-nature and that this is the true morality, concentration, and wisdom. Listen to my verse:

Mind-ground without wrong:
Self-nature morality.
Mind-ground without delusion:
Self-nature wisdom.
Mind-ground without confusion:
Self-nature concentration.
Neither increasing nor decreasing:
You are vajra.
Body comes, body goes:
The original samadhi.

Commentary:

"When I speak the Dharma," said the Sixth Patriarch, "I never stray from the self-nature. When you stray from the self-nature you become attached to marks and confuse the self-nature. All dharmas are composed of the substance of the self-nature and respond with unlimited function. Now, listen to this:

Mind-ground without wrong:
Self-nature morality.

"The mind is like a piece of ground. Whatever you plant in it grows there. If you plant a good cause, you reap a good result in the future; if you plant a bad cause, you reap a bad result. When the mind-ground contains no thoughts of greed, malice, envy, or selfishness, it is without wrong thoughts, and that is the morality of the self-nature."

Master Shen Hsiu said that morality is to abstain from evil; that is almost the same as the Sixth Patriarch's instructions to clear the mind-ground of wrong thoughts. But Shen Hsiu gave morality another name, calling it the abstention from evil, while the Sixth Patriarch spoke of the morality of the mind-ground, the morality of the self-nature.

Mind-ground without delusion:
Self-nature wisdom.

When your mind-ground is free of delusion, the conduct you offer can be extremely good, just as Shen Hsiu instructed. But Shen Hsiu merely passed out names. He did not speak of morality, concentration, and wisdom in terms of the self-nature and the mind-ground. Do not plant the causes of stupidity in the mind-ground: that is the self-nature's wisdom.

Mind-ground without confusion:
Self-nature concentration.

When it is without confusion, the mind is purified. Shen Hsiu's instructions to purify the mind did not relate concentration to the self-nature, whereas the Sixth Patriarch always spoke Dharma from the mind-ground. His Dharma arose from the self-nature and did not come from outside. Shen Hsiu spoke about external dharmas and was attached to marks. In other words, Shen Hsiu spoke from outside the mind; the Sixth Patriarch spoke from within.

Neither increasing nor decreasing:
You are vajra.

The brilliant light of the self-nature illuminates everything; it is miraculous, profound, and all-inclusive. The self-nature neither increases nor decreases; it is your very own indestructible vajra.

Body comes, body goes:
The original samadhi.

You go away, you come back, and you're in samadhi all the time: standing, sitting, walking, and lying down.

Sutra:

Hearing this verse, Chih Ch'eng regretted his former mistakes, and he expressed his gratitude by saying this verse:

These five heaps are
A body of illusion.
And what is illusion,

Ultimately?
If you tend toward
True suchness
The Dharma is
Not yet pure.

Commentary:

The five skandhas are not real. The body, too, is false–merely a combination of the four elements. Knowing this, you should not attach so much importance to it by looking for good food, good clothes, a nice place to live, or a good wife or husband.

How do the four elements combine to form your body? The earth is the hard part of your body: the skin, nails, bones, and muscles. Tears, mucus, saliva and excrement are the water and your body heat is the fire. The circulatory and respiratory systems are the wind. After you die, the body decomposes and the earth returns to the earth, the water to the water, the fire to the fire, and the wind to the wind. But where do *you* go? You don't know, do you? We are studying the Buddhadharma just to understand this question.

The body, then, is nothing but a transformation of the five skandhas and the four elements. And what, ultimately, is this illusion?

If you tend toward true suchness, the Dharma is not pure yet, for you have not arrived at the root-substance and you have not returned to purity. Why? Because you still have the thought, "I'd like to go back to true suchness." If you have even one thought, you cannot penetrate the basic substance, because the basic substance functions independently and freely, without obstruction. There is no grasping or rejecting it, no thinking of this or that.

Sutra:

The Master approved, and he said further to Chih Ch'eng, "Your Master's morality, concentration, and wisdom exhort those of lesser faculties and lesser wisdom, while my morality, concentration, and wisdom exhort those of great faculties and great wisdom. If you are enlightened to your self-nature, you do not set up in your mind the notion of Bodhi or of Nirvana or of the liberation of knowledge and vision. When not a single dharma is established in the mind, then the ten thousand dharmas can be established there. To understand this principle is to achieve the Buddha's body which is also called Bodhi, Nirvana, and the liberation of knowledge and vision as well. Those who see their own nature can establish dharmas in their minds or not establish them as they choose. They come and go freely, without impediments or obstacles. They function correctly and speak appropriately, seeing all transformation bodies as integral with the self-nature. That is precisely the way they obtain independence, spiritual powers, and the samadhi of playfulness. This is what is called seeing the nature."

Commentary:

"You're right," said the Master, "and your verse is not bad at all. You should know that my morality, concentration, and wisdom are not the same as Shen Hsiu's. His teaching is for people of lesser wisdom."

Here the Master describes the people of great wisdom for whom his teaching is intended. "They have awakened to the self-nature," he said, "and they don't even entertain the notion of

Bodhi, Nirvana, or the liberation of knowledge and vision." None of these dharmas exist for them. Not a single thing remains.

Not one dharma established,
ten thousand dharmas are empty.

Because such people do not set up the notion of a single dharma, they can set up the ten thousand dharmas. Although not a single dharma exists, the ten thousand dharmas are present all the same.

If you understand this principle, you may become a Buddha on the spot. Then you may call it Bodhi, Nirvana, or the liberation of knowledge and vision. You may call it anything you like. But first you must understand it. If you don't understand it, you can't call it anything at all.

People of genuine enlightenment who have understood the mind and seen the nature can establish dharmas or not establish them. They come and go without obstruction. You say, "I'm this way too. If I want to come to the Buddhist Lecture Hall, I come; if I want to go, I go." You're wrong. The Sixth Patriarch was speaking of freedom over life and death. With this kind of freedom, if you want to live, you live; if you want to die, you can die any place, any time, like the Third Patriarch Seng Ts'an, who died of his own will, hanging by one hand from a tree. That's why I often say to you, "Everything's O.K." If you are master of this, you hold the power of life and death in your hands. Live or die, as you please. No one can stop you. "Freedom to come and go" is not like your coming and going from the Buddhist Lecture Hall.

People who see the nature "function correctly and speak appropriately, seeing all transformation bodies as integral with the self-nature." They don't need to think, they just speak. But they always speak with principle. If someone asks you about the heavens and you reply, "On earth there are mountains and rivers," or if they ask, "What's a horse?" and you say, "Oxen have two horns," you are just confusing the issue and going against common sense.

People who see the nature "obtain independence" just like Avalokiteshvara Bodhisattva. The "spiritual powers" that they obtain are the six spiritual powers: 1) the heavenly eye; 2) the heavenly ear; 3) the knowledge of others' thoughts; 4) the knowledge of former lives; 5) the knowledge of the extinction of outflows; 6) psychic power.

One who has obtained the "samadhi of playfulness" sings, but not like other singers; he eats, but not like other people. For example, he may say, "Lunch time! Let's eat!" and then run to the table and eat every morsel of food in sight. Then he'll say, "The food is still in the kitchen." When everyone looks in the kitchen the food is still there. He didn't really eat it after all. That is a lot of fun.

Sutra:

Chih Ch'eng asked the Master further, "What is meant by 'not establishing?'"

The Master replied, "When your self-nature is free from error, obstruction, and confusion, when Prajna is present in every thought, contemplating and shedding illumination, and when you are constantly apart from the dharma marks and are free and independent, both horizontally and vertically, then what is there to be established?

"In the self-nature, in self-enlightenment, in sudden enlightenment, and in sudden cultivation there are no degrees. Therefore, not a single dharma is established.

All dharmas are still and extinct. How can there be stages?"

Chih Ch'eng made obeisance and attended on the Master day and night without laziness. He was a native of T'ai Ho in Chi Chou.

Commentary:

When there is nothing in your self-nature which is obstructive or confused, what is there to be established? "Confusion" means "upside-down." You should not think that if your hand points to the earth it is upside-down down and if you raise it above your head it is right-side up. There is actually no such thing as upside-down or right-side up.

"Prajna is present in every thought, contemplating and shedding illumination." Similarly, the Master said earlier, "You should know that the self-nature constantly generates wisdom." Further, you should be separate from any attachment to dharma marks, and then you will be free to come and go. Vertically, if you want to jump, jump! Horizontally, if you want to move sideways, go ahead. Ascend into the heavens or plunge into the hells; visit the Western Paradise or the Eastern Crystal Azure World. You can go anywhere and always be in accord with Dharma. So what dharma is there to be established? That is why the Master says that not a single dharma is established.

You should enlighten your self-nature by yourself. If you are enlightened immediately, you will cultivate immediately and there will be no question of sudden and gradual stages of progress. Therefore no dharmas are established: all dharmas are empty–marked with still extinction. How can you arrange them in stages according to number one, number two, and so on?

Hearing the Master's instruction, the former spy defected and was converted to the Master's teaching. He changed his mind and reformed his conduct. That is called "going straight." He did whatever the Patriarch told him to do, no matter how difficult, because he knew that the Sixth Patriarch had become a patriarch by doing bitter work, threshing rice at Huang Mei for over eight months. He thought, "I have an opportunity to serve a Patriarch and I should work diligently."

Bhikshu Chih Ch'e

Sutra:

Bhikshu Chih Ch'e, a native of Chiang Hsi, had the family name Chang and the personal name Hsing Ch'ang. As a youth he was an itinerant warrior. When the schools split into the Northern and Southern, although the two leaders had lost the notion of self and other, the disciples stirred up love and hate. The disciples of the Northern School secretly set up Shen Hsiu as the Sixth Patriarch. Fearing that the country would hear of the transmission of the robe, they hired Hsing Ch'ang to assassinate the Master. But the Master had the power of knowing the thoughts of others. He knew of this matter in advance and set ten ounces of gold on his chair. That night Hsing Ch'ang entered his room intending to kill him. The Master just stretched out his neck. Hsing Ch'ang swung the blade three times but could not harm him.

Commentary:

Neither Shen Hsiu nor the Sixth Patriarch had thoughts of "self" or "others." But their disciples agitated, stirring up thoughts of love and hate in people. More specifically, Shen Hsiu's disciples did the agitating, denouncing the Southern Patriarch as illiterate and incompetent.

The Sixth Patriarch's disciples really believed in him. "You can't talk that way about our teacher!" they said. "He has obtained wisdom without the aid of a master."

It never occurred to the Sixth Patriarch's disciples that they should kill Shen Hsiu, but Shen Hsiu's disciples were jealous and wanted to kill the Sixth Patriarch. They knew that the robe and bowl were in the South. The rumors flew. "That Hui Neng would do anything: homicide, manslaughter. Why, in the old days he was a confidence man and now he's pretending to be a Patriarch. How absurd."

Others said, "He used to be a poor firewood gatherer in the mountains. What talent could he have? The people in the south have made him their leader, but it's only talk." They did everything they could to ruin him. "At Huang Mei everyone knew that he was a barbarian. He doesn't know anything at all."

Shen Hsiu had several thousand men behind him, even though he did not have the robe and bowl. They each wanted to be the Seventh Patriarch, and without a father how can there be a son? With Shen Hsiu as the Sixth Patriarch, the Seventh Patriarch would surely be one of them. But they didn't dare make the news public because it was all too obvious that the position rightly belonged to Hui Neng.

T'ang dynasty Buddhism was extremely complex.

Hsing Ch'ang's family name had been Chang, but after he left home the Master named him Chih Ch'e. As a boy, he robbed from the rich and gave to the poor, always fighting for the underdog. His martial skills were outstanding. Light and limber, he could leap twenty feet in the air in a single bound. They called him "Flying Cat" Chang because he ran so fast and with such agility that he could break into your house without a sound, just like a cat. Not only could this cat walk silently, he could fly. But you won't find this nickname in any of the history books; you would have to have been there.

Having unsuccessfully tried to capture the Master by burning off the mountain behind Nan Hua Temple, Shen Hsiu's men decided to hire an assassin to kill the master and steal the robe and bowl.

The Sixth Patriarch could read minds, and so he was expecting his visitor. He put some gold on his chair and waited until midnight, when the sky was black and Hsing Ch'ang came creeping up the stairs, down the hall, and into his room.

Was this a tense situation or not? What do you think the Master did? He just stretched out his neck, and although he didn't say anything, he thought, "Go ahead and swing your sword. Come on, kill me!" This is called "sticking your neck out."

Hsing Ch'ang was oblivious to the Master. He was determined to carry out orders and had nothing on his mind but murder. "I don't care if you're a Bhikshu, an Arhat, or even a Patriarch, I'm going to kill you!" he said, swinging at the Master's neck. He swung three times and nothing happened. Now, just what do you think this means?

Sutra:

The Master said,

A straight sword is not bent.
A bent sword is not straight.
I merely owe you gold.
I do not owe you life.

Hsing Ch'ang fell to the ground in fright. After a while he came to and begged for mercy, repenting of his

error and vowing to leave home. The Master gave him the gold and said, "Go! I fear that my followers will come to take revenge. Change your appearance and return another day and I will accept you."

Commentary:

The Master said, "A straight sword is not bent," that is, the straight sword of the proper Dharma cannot be harmed by deviant dharma. "The deviant cannot defeat the right; the right always overcomes the deviant. You may have a sword, but you can't harm me with it. I merely owe you the gold which I borrowed in a past life," the Master said, "I don't owe you my life because I never killed you."

It was all too much for Hsing Ch'ang, and he fainted. When he came to, the Master talked with him for a long time, "Why did you want to kill me?" he asked.

"It wasn't my idea," said Hsing Ch'ang. "They told me that you were a scoundrel, a thief, and a hunter. They said that you were nothing but a firewood gatherer who was pretending to be a Patriarch. Hearing this, I felt it was my duty to kill you, but now I know that I was wrong. Why? If you had no virtue, my sharp sword would have sliced your head right off. Having met you, I realized that the affairs of the world are of no great interest. Please let me leave home and bow to you as my teacher."

The Master said, "Here, take this gold and go quickly. My disciples are fond of me and they would kill you if they found out about this. Go somewhere else and leave home. When you return I will teach and transform you."

Sutra:

Hsing Ch'ang received his orders and disappeared into the night. Later he left home under another Bhikshu, received the complete precepts and was vigorous in practice. One day, remembering the Master's words, he made the long journey to have an audience. The Master said, "I have thought of you for a long time. What took you so long?"

He replied, "The High Master once favored me by pardoning my crime. Although I have left home and although I practice austerities, I shall never be able to repay his kindness. May I try to repay you by transmitting the Dharma and taking living beings across?

"Your disciple often studies the *Mahaparinirvana Sutra*, but he has not yet understood the principles of permanence and impermanence. I beg the High Master to be compassionate and explain them for me.

The Master said, "Impermanence is just the Buddha nature and permanence is just the mind discriminating good and evil dharmas."

"High Master, your explanation contradicts the Sutra text!" Hsing Ch'ang replied.

The Master said, "I transmit the Buddha's mind-seal. How could I dare to contradict the Buddhas' Sutras?"

Hsing Ch'ang replied, "The Sutra says that the Buddha nature is permanent and the High Master has just said that it is impermanent; it says that good and evil dharmas, reaching even to the Bodhi Mind, are impermanent and the High Master has just said that they are permanent. This contradiction has merely intensified your student's doubt and delusion."

The Master said, "Formerly, I heard Bhikshuni Wu Chin Tsang recite the *Nirvana Sutra*. When I commented on it, there was not one word or principle which did not accord with the Sutra text. My explanation to you now is not different."

Hsing Ch'ang replied, "Your student's capacity for understanding is superficial. Will the High Master please explain further?"

The Master said, "Don't you understand? If the Buddha nature were permanent, what use would there be in speaking of good and evil dharmas? To the end of an eon not one person would produce the Bodhi Mind. Therefore I explain it as impermanent. That is exactly what the Buddha explained as the meaning of true permanence."

Commentary:

The Buddha explained the Buddha nature as permanent to those attached to impermanence, and he explained it as impermanent to those attached to permanence. If you say that the Buddha nature is permanent, what good and evil dharmas remain for discussion? Living beings would have all become Buddhas long ago. Why should one bother to speak the Dharma to them in order to take them across? If the Buddha nature is permanent, everyone would be a Buddha and there would be no need to cultivate. "So," the Master said, "you see that my explanation of the Buddha nature as impermanent is exactly what the Buddha meant when he spoke of permanence."

Sutra:

"Furthermore, if all dharmas were impermanent, all things would have a self-nature subject to birth and death, and the true permanent nature would not pervade all places. Therefore, I explain it as permanent. That is exactly what the Buddha explained as the meaning of true impermanence."

Commentary:

Basically, the Buddha nature is neither permanent nor impermanent. That is the ultimate principle of the middle way. Then why did the Sixth Patriarch say that it was impermanent? Why did he say that the mind which discriminates good and evil was permanent? He did it to cure Hsing Ch'ang of his attachments. Once you are rid of attachment, you do not need the Buddhadharma. The Sixth Patriarch took advantage of an opportunity to heal Hsing Ch'ang, but he wouldn't necessarily have explained it the same way to every one.

Sutra:

"It was for the sake of common people and those who belong to other religions who cling to deviant views of permanence, and for all those who follow the two-vehicle way, mistaking permanence for impermanence formulating the eight perverted views, that the Buddha in the ultimate Nirvana teaching destroyed their prejudiced views. He explained true permanence, true bliss, true selfhood, and true purity."

Commentary:

Common people and non-Buddhists cling to false permanence; Shravakas and Pratyeka Buddhas mistake permanence for impermanence. These two groups each have four perverted views, making eight in all.

Common people and non-Buddhists turn the four marks of conditioned existence upside-down and say:

1. The suffering of conditioned existence is bliss;
2. Its impermanence is permanent;
3. Its impurity is pure; and
4. Its "no-self" is "self."

The Shravakas and Pratyeka Buddhas turn the four virtues of Nirvana upside-down and say:

5. The bliss of Nirvana is suffering;
6. Its permanence is impermanent;
7. Its purity is impure; and
8. Its "self" is "no-self."

Sutra:

"You now contradict this meaning by relying on the words, taking annihilation to be impermanence and fixing on a lifeless permanence. In this way you misinterpret the last, subtle, complete and wonderful words of the Buddha. Even if you read it a thousand times, what benefit could you derive from it?"

Hsing Ch'ang suddenly achieved the great enlightenment and spoke this verse:

To those who hold impermanence in mind,
The Buddha speaks of the permanent nature;

Not knowing expedients is like
Picking up pebbles from a spring pond.

But now without an effort
The Buddha nature manifests;
The Master did not transmit it,
And I did not obtain a thing.

The Master said, "Now you understand! You should be called 'Chih Ch'e' (breadth of understanding)."

Chih Ch'e thanked the Master, bowed, and withdrew.

Commentary:

Unless you understand that the Buddha's dharmas are expedient devices, you might as well collect rocks from the bottom of a pool: you're useless.

Hearing the Master's instruction, Hsing Ch'ang returned to the source and went back home. Suddenly enlightened, he understood his mind and saw his nature. But his enlightenment was not given to him by the Sixth Patriarch, and his attainment was actually no attainment. He simply opened up to his own inherent wisdom.

The Master gave him certification saying, "Now that you are truly enlightened, I'll give you the name 'Chih Ch'e.'"

Bhikshu Shen Hui

Sutra:

A young boy thirteen years old named Shen Hui, who was from a Kao family in Hsiang Yang, came from Yü Ch'üan to pay homage. The Master said, "The Knowing One's journey must have been difficult. Did you bring the original with you? If you have the original, you should know the owner. Try to explain it to me."

Shen Hui said, "I take non-dwelling as the original and seeing as the owner."

The Master said, "This Shramanera imitates the talk of others."

Shen Hui then asked, "When you sit in Ch'an, High Master, do you see or not?"

The Master hit him three times with his staff and said, "When I hit you, does it hurt or not?"

He replied, "It both hurts and does not hurt."

The Master said, "I both see and do not see."

Shen Hui asked, "How can you both see and not see?"

The Master said, "What I see is the transgression and error of my own mind. I do not see the right, wrong, good, or bad of other people. This is my seeing and not seeing. How can you say it both hurts and does not hurt? If it does not hurt you are like a piece of wood or a stone, but if it does hurt you are just like a common person and will

give rise to hatred. Your 'seeing and not seeing' are two extremes and your 'hurting and not hurting' are production and extinction. You have not even seen your own nature and yet you dare to ridicule others."

Commentary:

Shen Hui was an exceptional child. Precocious and brilliant, he forgot his body for the sake of the Dharma. He could tell at a glance that Shen Hsiu didn't have the genuine Buddhadharma; he set out for the Sixth Patriarch's place, eighteen hundred miles distant. His shoes fell apart and the rocks and slivers of glass on the road cut into his feet, but he continued to walk, tearing up his robe to bandage his bleeding feet and acting as if there were no pain at all. When the Great Master saw him he knew that he had undergone much suffering.

"Good Knowing Advisor," he said, "your journey must have been difficult. Did you bring the original with you? Have you attained your original face or not? Do you recognize your original face? If you have the original, you should know the owner. If you have the original, the Buddha-nature, and if you have understood your mind, seen your nature, you should know the owner. The owner is the Buddha-nature. Tell me about it!"

But this unruly child had a mind of his own. "I take 'not dwelling anywhere' as my original face," he said, "and my seeing nature as the host."

The Sixth Patriarch said, "You're just imitating the talk of other people. You pretend to know what you do not know, to understand what you do not understand, and to see what you do not see. This is nothing but verbal zen. It is not an expression of the self-nature.

Shen Hui had a lot of gall. "When the High Master sits in meditation," he asked, "does he see or not?" This child was wild and difficult to teach. The Patriarch, not being an ordinary person, gave no ordinary answer. He hit Shen Hui with his staff and shouted, "Does that hurt?"

It is not known whether the child was afraid, or whether he cried or not.

Shen Hui said, "It both hurts and does not hurt."

The Master said, "I both see and do not see."

"How can this be?" said Shen Hui.

"I see my own mistakes," said the Master. "I keep an eye on my evil false thinking and immediately put a stop to it. I do not see the faults of others: others' evils, others' obsessions, others' conditions, others' transgressions." Students of the Buddhadharma should take note of this. See your own errors, not those of other people. Don't be like a watchdog watching someone else's door. The dog doesn't have anything of its own and so it watches over other people's things. Don't be critical and don't gossip: see and do not see.

"I see and do not see," said the Master, "but how can you both hurt and not hurt? If you don't hurt, you are just like a rock. If you do hurt, then you'll catch fire and get angry and afflicted, just like an unenlightened common person. Seeing and not seeing are two extremes and hurting and not hurting are dharmas of production and extinction. You haven't even seen your own nature and yet you have the nerve to come here and talk down to me?"

Sutra:

Shen Hui bowed, apologized, and thanked the Master. The Master continued, "If your mind is confused and you do not see, then ask a Good Knowing Advisor to help you find the Way. If your mind is enlightened, then see your own nature and cultivate according to the Dharma. You

yourself are confused and do not see your own mind, and yet you come to ask me whether or not I see. If I see, I know it for myself, but is that of any help to you in your confusion? In the same way your seeing is of no use to me. Why don't you know and see it for yourself, instead of asking me whether or not I see?"

Shen Hui bowed again over one hundred times, seeking forgiveness for his error. He served the Master with diligence, never leaving his side.

Commentary:

The Master said, "Shen Hui, if your mind is unclear and you cannot see the nature, then ask a Good Knowing Advisor to teach you how to work at cultivation. If your mind is enlightened and you have understood the mind and seen the nature, then you should cultivate according to Dharma. You haven't even seen your original mind, and yet you come to ask me whether or not I have seen it. If I've seen it, that's my own business, of no use to you in your deluded condition. If you've seen the nature and obtained the original face, that's of no use to me. Why not turn the light around and reverse the illumination to find out whether you've seen your own mind or not? Isn't that better than asking me? What difference does it make whether I've seen it or not?"

After that, Shen Hui was really sorry. Why had he been so incorrigible? Did he really have no conscience? His questioning of the Patriarch was like trying to sell dime novels to Confucius or going to the home of Lu Pan, China's first engineer and foremost carpenter, to do remodeling. He begged for forgiveness, saying, "I'm just a kid. I don't know how high the heavens are or how deep the earth is. Please don't hold it against me." From then on, Shen Hui waited on the Master, following along everywhere the Master went to give lectures on the Sutras and speak about the Dharma.

Sutra:

One day the Master addressed the assembly as follows: "I have a thing. It has no head or tail, no name or label, no back or front. Do you all know what it is?"

Shen Hui stepped forward and said, "It is the root source of all Buddhas, Shen Hui's Buddha nature!"

The Master said, "I just told you that it had no name or label, and you immediately call it the root-source of all Buddhas. Go and build a thatched hut over your head! You're nothing but a follower who pursues knowledge and interpretation."

After the Master's extinction, Shen Hui went to Ching Lo where he propagated the Ts'ao Hsi Sudden Teaching. He wrote the *Hsien Tsung Chi* which circulated widely throughout the land. He is known as Dhyana Master Ho Che.

Commentary:

Everyone shut their mouths; no one said a word. Some of them didn't speak because they knew and some didn't speak because they did not know. Seeing that no one was going to answer, Shen Hui jumped out from the assembly and said, "I know what it is! It's the origin of all Buddhas: my Buddha nature!"

"In the ranks of the Ch'an School," said the Master, "you're nothing but a scholar. You have no genuine understanding."

In a way the Master's scolding was a compliment. It isn't easy to be a Ch'an scholar of the school of those who know and interpret.

When the Sixth Patriarch died, Shen Hui went to the capital at Loyang to spread the Sudden Teaching of the Ch'an School. He later wrote the *Hsien Tsung Chi*, a treatise on the Northern and Southern Schools, which exposed Shen Hsiu as a false pretender and proclaimed the Southern Patriarch Hui Neng as the real Sixth Patriarch, the recipient of the Buddha's mind-seal. Had Shen Hui not written this book, Shen Hsiu would have stolen the title of the Sixth Patriarch.

Shen Hui came to be known as Ho Che, which is the name of the place where he went to live.

Difficult Questions

Sutra:

The Master saw many disciples of other schools, all with evil intentions, gathered beneath his seat to ask him difficult questions. Pitying them, he said, "Students of the Way, all thoughts of good or evil should be completely cast away. What cannot be named by any name is called the self-nature. This non-dual nature is the real nature, and it is within the real nature that all teaching doors are established. At these words you should see it for yourselves."

Hearing this, they all made obeisance and asked him to be their master.

Commentary:

Not only did Shen Hsiu's party want to murder the Great Master, but those of other sects, such as the Consciousness Only School, came to ask the Master difficult questions. "Which came first," they would ask, "the Buddha or the Dharma? Where does the Buddhadharma begin?" They had many questions.

The Sixth Patriarch said, "If you can speak the Dharma, then it's first the Buddha, then the Dharma. If you can listen to the Dharma, then it's first the Dharma and then the Buddha. The Buddhadharma comes from the minds of living beings."

On this occasion he saw that the crowd was full of spies and would-be assassins. "Cultivators should not hold thoughts of good or evil," he said, "What cannot be named by any name is called the self-nature. The self-nature is non-dual; it is also called the real nature, the real mark. Within it all schools and sects are set up. It's not enough just to talk about it, however. You must understand and immediately give proof to the state of no-mark."

Hearing these words, the assembly realized that all their thoughts had been bound up in good and evil and they were greatly ashamed. They bowed down before him and said, "From now on we'll be different. Please, Great Master, be our teacher."

CHAPTER IX

PROCLAMATIONS

Sutra:

On the fifteenth day of the first month, during the first year of the Shen Lung reign (A.D. 705) Empress Tse T'ien and Emperor Chung Tsung issued the following proclamation:

"We have invited Masters Hui An and Shen Hsiu to the palace to receive offerings so that we may investigate the One Vehicle in the leisure time remaining after our myriad duties. The two Masters have declined, saying that in the South there is Dhyana Master Hui Neng, who was secretly transmitted the robe and Dharma of the Great Master Hung Jen who now transmits the Buddhas' mind-seal.

"We now send Chamberlain Hsieh Chien with this invitation, hoping that the Master will remember us with compassion and come to the capital."

The Master sent back a petition pleading illness saying that he wished to spend his remaining years at the foot of the mountain.

Commentary:

The Ninth Chapter is entitled "Proclamations."

Wu Tse T'ien was an empress during the T'ang dynasty. She believed in the Buddha, but she wasn't very orthodox. In fact, she would do anything. But she believed in Buddhism and so she invited all the high monks to the palace to receive offerings.

Her son, Emperor Chung Tsung, reigned only a short time before the empress had him exiled to Lu Ling to be king there, so that she could take the throne.

A proclamation was a letter from the emperor. When ordinary people received a proclamation, they bowed to it as a gesture of respect to the emperor, but people who have left home don't do this, of course.

Wishing to study the One Buddha Vehicle, the Sudden Teaching Dharma door, the empress invited Masters Hui An and Shen Hsiu to come to the palace to receive offerings. But they refused. "We do not have enough virtue," they said, "You should invite Hui Neng. He has received the Fifth Patriarch's robe and bowl and is a true transmitter of the mind seal."

The empress took the two masters' advice and invited the Sixth Patriarch to the capital, Ch'ang An. The invitation was brought by a chamberlain, that is, by an official of the inner court. The chamberlain, Hsieh Chien, was a eunuch. Eunuchs began serving Chinese emperors during the Han dynasty.

The Sixth Patriarch wrote back "I am very ill." Actually, he wasn't ill at all; this was merely an expedient device, because the Sixth Patriarch did not wish to visit a ruler. More specifically, he did not wish to visit an empress. It would have been against the rules. Wu Tse T'ien knew nothing about moral precepts and she didn't follow any rules. But the Sixth Patriarch couldn't say, "You are an empress and I am a Patriarch and I don't have to visit you," so he said, "I am old and sick."

Sutra:

Hsieh Chien said, "The Virtuous Dhyana Masters at the capital all say that to master the Way one must sit in

Dhyana meditation and practice concentration, for without Dhyana concentration, liberation is impossible. I do not know how the Master explains this dharma.

The Master said, "The Way is awakened to from the mind. How could it be found in sitting? *The Diamond Sutra* states that to say that Tathagata either sits or lies down is to walk a deviant path. Why? The clear pure Dhyana of the Tathagata comes from nowhere and goes nowhere and is neither produced nor extinguished. The Tathagata's clear pure 'sitting' is the state of all dharmas being empty and still. Ultimately there is no certification; even less is there any 'sitting.'"

Commentary:

For an illiterate, the Master was quite intelligent. He answered, "You awaken to the Way from within your mind. You can't just sit there. You have to understand the principles of the Buddhadharma and be enlightened to them. The enlightenment is 'understanding' and the sitting is 'practice.' Practicing without understanding is stupid; understanding without practice is nothing but intellectual zen."

You must understand and practice. Don't just sit, sit, sit for several decades without even understanding the principle of enlightening your mind.

The Master added, "Since ultimately there is nothing to be attained or certified to, why be attached to sitting in meditation?"

Sutra:

Hsieh Chien said, "When your disciple returns to the capital, their majesties will surely question him. Will the High Master please be compassionate and instruct me on

the essentials of the mind so that I can transmit them to the two palaces and to students of the Way at the capital? It will be like one lamp setting a hundred thousand lamps burning, making all the darkness endlessly light."

The Master said, "The Way is without light or darkness. Light and darkness belong to the principle of alternation. 'Endless light' has an end, too, because such terms are relative. Therefore the *Vimalakirti Sutra* says, 'The Dharma is incomparable because it is not relative.'"

Hsieh Chien said, "Light represents wisdom and darkness represents affliction. If cultivators of the Way do not use wisdom to expose and destroy affliction, how can they escape from the birth and death that have no beginning?"

The Master said, "Affliction is Bodhi; they are not two and not different. One who uses wisdom to expose and destroy affliction has the views and understanding of the two vehicles and the potential of the sheep and deer carts. Those of superior wisdom and great roots are completely different."

Hsieh Chien said, "What are the views and understanding of the Great Vehicle?"

The Master said, "The common person sees light and darkness as two, but the wise person comprehends that their nature is non-dual. The non-dual nature is the real nature. The real nature does not decrease in common people nor increase in worthy sages. In afflictions it is not confused and in Dhyana concentration it is not still. It is neither cut off nor permanent. It does not come or go. It is not inside, outside, or in the middle. It is not produced or destroyed. The nature and mark is 'thus, thus.' It

permanently dwells and does not change. It is called the 'Way.'"

Commentary:

Hsieh Chien wished for instruction on the essentials of the principle of using the mind to seal the mind. He said that the Patriarch was like a lamp, setting a hundred thousand lamps burning in the capital: bright, bright limitless light.

The Master said, "You shouldn't see light and darkness as different or affliction and Bodhi as different. Affliction and the enlightenment nature are one. Shravakas and Pratyekabuddhas destroy affliction by means of wisdom, but Buddhas and Bodhisattvas are completely different from them. Ordinary people see understanding and ignorance as two, but wise people know that in essence they are one, not two. That non-dual nature is the real nature. In states of confusion, the real nature is not confused; in Dhyana concentration, it is not still. It is both still and moving; it both moves and is still. The nature and mark are both 'thus'. We call it the 'Way.'"

Sutra:

Hsieh Chien said, "How does your explanation of the self-nature as neither produced nor destroyed differ from that of other religions?"

The Master answered, "As non-production and non-extinction are explained by other religions, extinction ends production and production reveals extinction. Their extinction is not extinction and what they call production is not production. My explanation of non-production and non-extinction is this: originally there was no production

and now there is no extinction. For this reason my explanation differs from that of other religions.

"If you wish to know the essentials of the mind, simply do not think of good or evil. You will then enter naturally the clear, pure substance of the mind, which is deep and permanently still, and whose wonderful abilities are as numerous as the sand grains in the Ganges River."

Commentary:

Other religions see production and extinction as two. They say that extinction puts an end to production and that production reveals extinction. Their explanation is not the ultimate one. As I explain the terms, originally there was no production, and so now there is no extinction.

The Master continued, "If you would like to know about the wonderful mind-transmission Dharma, the essential points of the mind-ground Dharma door, I will tell you: simply do not think of good or evil. Then you will spontaneously understand the true principle and enter into the pure substance of the mind." The mind-substance is deep and constantly pure and still. Although it is always still, within its true emptiness there is wonderful existence, and its wonderful abilities are innumerable.

Sutra:

Hsieh Chien received this instruction and was suddenly greatly enlightened. He bowed, took leave, and returned to the palace to report the Master's speech. That year on the third of the ninth month a proclamation was issued in praise of the Master. It read:

"The Master has declined our invitation because of old age and illness. He cultivates the Way for us and is a

field of blessings for the country. The Master is like Vimalakirti who pleaded illness in Vaishali. He spreads the great fruit widely, transmitting thc Buddha-mind and discoursing on the non-dual Dharma.

"Hsieh Chien has conveyed the Master's instruction, the knowledge and vision of the Tathagata. It must be due to accumulated good acts, abundant blessings, and good roots planted in former lives that we now have met with the Master when he appears in the world and have suddenly been enlightened to the Supreme Vehicle. We are extremely grateful for his kindness which we receive with bowed heads, and now offer in return a Mo Na robe and crystal bowl as gifts. We order the Magistrate of Shao Chou to rebuild the temple buildings and convert the Master's former dwelling place into a temple to be called 'Kuo En,' (Country's Kindness)."

Commentary:

Hsieh Chien returned to the capital and submitted a written report to the empress which set forth the principles the Master had discussed with him. The palace then issued a statement in praise of the Master, saying he was the highest Master in the nation and one of unexcelled cultivation. They said that the Sixth Patriarch was like the layman Vimalakirti, who was sick in Vaishali.

"The Master propagates the 'great fruit,' the Mahayana Buddhadharma, and transmits the 'Buddha-mind,' the mind-seal of all Buddhas. At Nan Hua Temple he expounds the non-dual Dharma door, saying that production and extinction are one and the nature and mark are not two. His knowledge and vision are that of the Buddha. We must have done a lot of good things in past lives in order to meet the Master now and suddenly awaken to the wonderful principle of the Supreme Vehicle. We bow to his teaching every day and hold it respectfully above our heads."

They offered the Master an expensive robe made of Korean cloth which had been sent as tribute to the empress. It was a patchwork robe, with a Buddha image embroidered on each patch. Some say that the empress embroidered them herself, but there is no way to know with certainty.

CHAPTER X

FINAL INSTRUCTIONS

Sutra:

One day the Master summoned his disciples Fa Hai, Chih Ch'eng, Fa Ta, Shen Hui, Chih Ch'ang, Chih T'ung, Chih Ch'e, Chih Tao, Fa Chen and Fa Ju, and said to them, "You are not like other people. After my passage into extinction, you should each be a master in a different direction. I will now teach you how to explain the Dharma without deviating from the tradition of our school.

"First bring up the three classes of Dharma-doors, and then use the thirty-six pairs of opposites, so that, whether coming or going, you remain in the Bodhimandala. While explaining all the dharmas, do not become separated from your self-nature. Should someone suddenly ask you about a dharma, answer him with its opposite. If you always answer with the opposite, both will be eliminated and nothing will be left, since each depends on the other for existence."

Commentary:

One day the Master called his room-entering disciples together for a talk. They are called room-entering disciples because they had received the transmission of the Master's Dharma and were therefore permitted to enter his room.

The first of the ten was Fa Hai. You remember him. He edited *The Sixth Patriarch Sutra* and was a great disciple. He put his name at the head of the list here because, no matter what, he had to be number one.

Chih Ch'eng was the Dharma-thief who later reformed and joined the Master. Fa Ta was the arrogant, Bhikshu who had read *The Lotus Sutra* over three thousand times but couldn't bring himself to put his head on the ground before the Master even once. Shen Hui was the thirteen-year-old child who had talked back to the Master. There was also Chih Ch'ang, Chih T'ung, and Chih Ch'e, also known as Flying Cat Chang; Chih Tao, Fa Chen, and Fa Ju. These were the Master's ten great disciples.

The Master said, "You ten men should each be a master teacher in a certain direction and receive offerings there from humans and gods. I will now teach you how to spread the Dharma without straying from the tradition of our Sudden Enlightenment Dharma Door Teaching.

"In speaking the Dharma," the Master went on, "the most important thing is to base your speech on the self-nature. How does one do this? Suppose someone asks you a question about the Buddhadharma. Whatever his principle may be, it's bound to have an opposite. You should answer him with the opposite dharma. For example, coming and going are relative concepts. Without a coming there is no going; without a going there is no coming. Coming is the prerequisite of going and going can only result from coming. Since opposites depend upon each other for existence, ultimately they both will be cast out, canceling each other out so that nothing is left behind. There will be no coming and no going, for there will be no place left to go.

Sutra:

"The three classes of Dharma doors are the heaps, the realms, and the entrances. The five heaps are: form, feeling, perception, impulses, and consciousness. The twelve entrances are the six sense objects outside: forms, sounds, smells, tastes, tangible objects, and objects of the mind, and the six sense organs within: eye, ear, nose, tongue, body, and mind. The eighteen realms are the six sense objects, the six sense organs and the six consciousnesses.

"The self-nature is able to contain all dharmas; it is the 'store-enveloping consciousness.' If one gives rise to a thought, it turns into consciousness, and the six consciousnesses are produced which go out the six organs and perceive the six sense objects.

"Thus the eighteen realms arise as a function of the self-nature. If the self-nature is wrong, it gives rise to eighteen wrongs; if the self-nature is right it gives rise to eighteen rights. Evil functioning is that of a living being, while good functioning is that of a Buddha. What is the functioning based on? It is based on opposing dharmas within the self-nature."

Commentary:

The self-nature includes all dharma doors, and so it is called the "store-enveloping consciousness." This is the eighth consciousness, which may be transformed into the wisdom of the great perfect mirror. If you give rise to thinking and considering, the store–enveloping consciousness turns to the seventh consciousness which in turn produces the six consciousnesses which go out the six organs and perceive the six sense objects.

If you use the self-nature correctly, it is the Buddha-use, but if you misuse it you are just a living being. How do the different usages arise? They come from the opposites within the self-nature.

Sutra:

"External insentient things have five pairs of opposites: heaven and earth, sun and moon, light and darkness, yin and yang, and water and fire.

"In speaking of the marks of dharmas one should delineate twelve opposites: speech and dharmas, existence and non-existence, form and formlessness, the marked and the unmarked, the presence of outflows and the lack of outflows, form and emptiness, motion and stillness, clarity and turbidity, the common and the holy, membership in the Sangha and membership in the laity, old age and youth, and largeness and smallness.

"From the self-nature nineteen pairs of opposites arise: length and shortness, deviance and orthodoxy, foolishness and wisdom, stupidity and intelligence, confusion and concentration, kindness and cruelty, morality and immorality, straightness and crookedness, reality and unreality, danger and safety, affliction and Bodhi, permanence and impermanence, compassion and harm, joy and anger, generosity and stinginess, advance and retreat, production and extinction, the Dharma-body and the Form-body, the Transformation-body and the Reward-body."

The Master said, "If you can understand and use these thirty-six pairs of opposites you can connect

yourself with the dharmas of all the Sutras and avoid extremes, whether coming or going. When you act from your self-nature in speaking with others, you are separate from external marks while in the midst of them and separate from inward emptiness while in the midst of emptiness. If you are attached to marks, you will add to your wrong views and if you grasp at emptiness, you will increase your ignorance."

Commentary:

"Opposite" means mutually dependent and mutually opposed. Nineteen opposites arise as a function of the true-suchness self-nature. For example, if there was no long, there would be no short. Long is the opposite of short and short is the opposite of long. Long and short are relative terms and between them is the Middle Way.

Kindness bestows happiness and is the opposite of cruelty. Morality and immorality are opposites. Morality is the practice of all good actions and the absence of all evil. Compassion pulls living beings out of suffering and is the opposite of harmfulness. Generosity means giving; if you can give, you are not stingy. The Dharma-body pervades all places and is the opposite of the form-body.

Sutra:

"Those who grasp at emptiness slander the Sutras by maintaining that written words have no use. Since they maintain they have no need of written words, they should not speak either, because written words are merely the marks of spoken language. They also maintain that the direct way cannot be established by written words, and

yet these two words, 'not established' are themselves written.

"When they hear others speaking, they slander them by saying that they are attached to written words. You should know that to be confused as they are may be permissible, but to slander the Buddha's Sutras is not. Do not slander the Sutras for if you do, your offense will create countless obstacles for you.

"One who attaches himself to external marks and practices dharmas in search of truth, or who builds many Bodhimandalas and speaks of the error and evil of existence and non-existence will not see his nature for many eons.

"Listen to the Dharma and cultivate accordingly. Do not think of the hundred things, for that will obstruct the nature of the Way. Listening without cultivating will cause others to form deviant views. Simply cultivate according to the Dharma, and do not dwell in marks when bestowing it."

Commentary:

People who are attached to emptiness say that they don't need anything at all. They say that it isn't necessary to study the Sutras. They say that they don't use written words. "Everything's empty," they say, don't use words. Words are nothing but an attachment to marks! If that is so, then nobody should even speak, because written words are simply the visible manifestation of spoken language.

They also say, "The direct mind is the Bodhimandala. Do not set up written words." But unless you quit speaking altogether, you still have language, and the phrase "do not set up" is itself made up of words.

"Your own confusion is your own business," the Master adds, "but do not slander the Buddha's Sutras. You should not refrain from thinking, for if you do, you fall into a useless, dull kind of emptiness. You should cultivate in the way I have instructed you. Do not become attached to appearances.

Sutra:

"If you understand, then speak accordingly, function accordingly, practice accordingly, and act accordingly, and you will not stray from the basis of our school.

"If someone asks you about a meaning, and the question is about existence, answer with non-existence; if you are asked about non-existence, answer with existence; asked about the common life, answer with the holy life; asked about the holy life, answer with the common life. Since in each case the two principles are interdependent, the meaning of the Middle Way will arise between them. If you answer every question with an opposite, you will not stray from the basic principle.

"Suppose someone asks, 'What is darkness?' You should answer, 'Brightness is the cause and darkness the condition. When there is no brightness, there is darkness. Brightness reveals darkness and darkness reveals brightness.' Since opposites are interdependent, the principle of the Middle Way is established.

"Answer every question that way, and in the future, when you transmit the Dharma, transmit it in the way I am instructing you. Then you will not stray from the tradition of our school."

Commentary:

If you answer every question with an opposite dharma, you will not deviate from the basic principle of the Sudden Enlightenment doctrine.

Sutra:

In the seventh month of the year Jen Tsu, the first year of the T'ai Chi and Yen Ho reigns (ca 712 A.D.), the Master sent his disciples to Hsin Chou to build a pagoda at Kuo En Temple. He ordered them to hurry the work and it was completed by the end of the summer of the following year.

Commentary:

During the cyclical year Jen Tsu, the reign was renamed twice. In the fifth month it was changed from T'ai Chi to Yen Ho. In the seventh month the emperor abdicated in favor of his son and in the eighth month the reign was renamed Hsien T'ien.

Hsin Chou was the Master's homeland. His disciples built a pagoda there so that the Master's body might rest in it after his death.

Sutra:

On the first day of the seventh month he gathered his disciples together and said, "In the eighth month I wish to leave this world. Those of you with doubts should ask about them soon so that I may resolve them for you and put an end to your confusion, because when I am gone there will be no one to teach you."

Hearing this, Fa Hai and the others wept. Only Shen Hui was unmoved and did not cry. The Master said,

"Little Master Shen Hui has attained to the equality of good and evil. He is not moved by blame or praise and does not feel sadness or joy. None of the rest of you have attained that. All these years on the mountain–how have you been cultivating?

"Now you cry. Who are you worrying about? Are you worrying that I don't know where I'm going? I know where I'm going. If I didn't know, I wouldn't have been able to tell you about it in advance. No doubt you are crying because you don't know where I am going, but if you knew you wouldn't need to cry. Originally the Dharma nature is not produced or extinguished; it does not come or go."

Commentary:

The Great Master rang the bell and beat the drum. The sound rang out, summoning all of his disciples to his side. "Pay attention!" he said. "In the eighth month of this year I am going to leave this world."

Then here he is again! Fa Hai–number one! He didn't even list the names of the other disciples; he just said, "Fa Hai and the others."

They all wept. Their eyes ran with tears and their noses ran with snot, just like children who have lost their mother and have no milk to drink. "Waaah! Waaah!" They cried like babies. Some of them cried in secret, some cried openly, and some faked tears, fearing it would be bad manners not to cry along with everyone else. There was both truth and falsehood in the situation; it was exactly like a play.

But the youngest of the babies did not cry. Was it because he was too young to understand or care that he was about to lose his mother, or in this case, his teacher? Was it that?

No. Shen Hui was young in years, but old in wisdom. He understood the principle of not moving in any state. Mencius was forty years old before he reached that level. With an unmoving mind,

They praise: you are not pleased;
They scold: you are not annoyed.
They say you work hard, you are not moved.
They say you are lazy: no matter what
You are not moved.

However, when you are really being lazy and someone scolds you, you can't say, "I have samadhi. He doesn't bother me at all." You must have a true unmoving mind, like that of little Shen Hui.

The Sixth Patriarch called Shen Hui "Little Master." In the first ten years after taking precepts one is called a "little master," or "junior-seated." From ten to twenty years one is "middle-seated" and from twenty to thirty years one is "senior seated."

"Little Master Shen Hui is better than all of you," the Master said, "because he doesn't have a discriminating mind. He has truly turned his consciousness into wisdom."

Shen Hui was not moved by praise or blame. "That Dharma Master does not cultivate! All he does is run after women." Criticism like that didn't bother him. "He really works hard. Not only does he not sleep, he doesn't even lie down. And he only eats once a day. Such austerity!" Praise like that didn't affect him either.

If you don't react, then people can slander you but it's as if nothing happened. "You're a pig," they may say. "Fine," you answer, "I'm a pig. No problem." If you don't react, then they can praise you and it doesn't matter either. "You have both virtue and learning," they may say, but you pay no attention.

If you are pleased when someone praises your learning, then you really have no learning at all. If you get angry when someone scolds you, you have been influenced by an outside state. To be unmoved by any state is to neither grasp nor reject, neither love nor hate.

You can tell Little Master Shen Hui that he is good, but he will not be happy; you can tell him he is bad, but he will not get angry. He has no thoughts of misery or delight. There truly is complete understanding of the Middle Way. Rare indeed!

"You old ones," the Master said, "you middle-aged ones, none of you passes. None of you has out-waited the fire."

When anger sets you ablaze, you should think, "Wait. Wait a minute. Wait a minute and then get angry." Then you wait, and your anger disappears. That is called "out-waiting the fire." If you don't wait, the fire burns, but if you can wait, it will die out.

When steel is red hot, you can shape it into a vessel. But unless you wait for the fire to burn it red hot, you can't mold the metal; you haven't out-waited the fire.

"You have been on the mountain for so many years," said the Master. "What have you been doing all this time? Huh? You hear that I am going to complete the stillness and you cry like babies; you're all worthless. How have you been cultivating? By eating and sleeping! Are you upset because you think I don't know where I'm going? I will tell you something! I do know. Of course I know! There is no reason for you to worry about me. I can take care of myself:

No big, no small,
No within or without;
You cultivate, you understand:
You make the arrangements yourself."

Sutra:

"All of you sit down, and I will recite a verse called 'The True-False Motion-Stillness Verse.' If you take it up and recite it, you will be of the same mind as I am. If you rely on it to cultivate, you will not stray from the true principle of our school."

The assembly bowed and begged the Master to recite the verse.

There is nothing true in anything,
So don't view anything as true.
If you view anything as true,
Your view will be completely false.
You can know what is true by yourself.
Being apart from the false is the truth of the mind.
When your own mind is not apart from the false
And lacks the truth, then where is the truth?

Commentary:

"Now don't be nervous," the Master said. "Sit down and don't jump around. Don't cry right in front of me like that. Really, you are undisciplined disciples. Listen to my verse. It discusses the true and the false and the principles of motion and stillness. If you can understand it and bear it in mind, you won't deviate from the Sudden Teaching."

"Turn the light around," said the Master. "Shine it inside at your own self-nature, and you can know the truth. To find your true mind is simply to separate yourself from all the false forms and images of this world. If there is no truth within your own mind, where will you find the truth? The truth is not apart from the self-nature; apart from the self-nature there is no truth."

Sutra:

Sentient beings understand motion.
Insentient beings do not move.
If you cultivate the work of non-movement,
Like insentient beings, you will not move.
If you seek the true non-movement,
In movement, there is non-movement.
Non-movement is non-movement, but
Things without sentience lack the Buddha-seed.
Fully able to discriminate among marks,
But unmoving in the primary meaning:
The very act of viewing in this way,
Itself is the function of true suchness.

Commentary:

Do not seek non-movement apart from movement, for it is just within movement that stillness can be found. All sentient beings move, but if you can be still while remaining sentient, that is true non-movement. If, as a sentient being, you are able to clearly distinguish the marks of all dharmas, not with your consciousness but with wisdom, you can give proof to the attainment of the substantive principle of your self-nature and achieve the ultimate state. That is true, proper non-movement.

Sutra:

I tell you, students of the Way,
Apply your minds with effort and take care,
At the gate of the Great Vehicle
Do not grasp the wisdom of birth and death.

If there is response at these words,
Then let us discuss the Buddha's meaning together.
If there is no response,
Join your hands together and make others glad.
The basis of this school is non-contention.
Contention is not the meaning of the Way.
For in grasping at the Dharma doors of contradiction and contention,
The self-nature enters birth and death.

Commentary:

You are face to face with the Great Vehicle Buddhadharma; do not continue to grasp at your understanding which binds you up in birth and death, at the kind of wisdom that is still attached to marks. If you can't understand what I am trying to tell you, then put your hands together to please living beings. My school of Sudden Enlightenment is based on the cultivation of the patience of unproduced Dharmas. There should be no debating. When you argue with others you lose the meaning of the Way.

Debating, the thoughts of victory and defeat
Stand in contradiction to the Way.
Giving rise to the four-mark mind,
How can samadhi be obtained?

If you insist on arguing, your self-nature won't escape the revolving wheel. Giving rise to the marks of a self, others, living beings, and a life, you will certainly continue to undergo birth and death.

Sutra:

When the followers heard this verse, they understood its meaning and bowed down before the Master. They made up their minds to practice in accord with the Dharma and not to argue, knowing that the Great Master would not remain long in the world.

The Senior Seated Fa Hai bowed again and asked, "After the High Master enters extinction, who will inherit the robe and Dharma?"

Commentary:

Fa Hai never forgets himself. No doubt he wanted the robe and bowl for himself.

Sutra:

The Master said, "Since the time I lectured on the Dharma in the Ta Fan Temple, transcriptions of my lectures have been circulated. They are to be called *The Dharma Jewel Platform Sutra*. Protect and transmit them in order to take humankind across. If you speak according to them, you will be speaking the Orthodox Dharma. I will explain the Dharma to you, but I will not transmit the robe, because your roots of faith are pure and ripe. You certainly have no doubts and are worthy of the great Work. According to the meaning of the transmission verse of the First Patriarch Bodhidharma, the robe should not be transmitted. His verse said,

Originally I came to this land,
Transmitting Dharma, saving living beings.

One flower opens; five petals and
The fruit comes to bear of itself."

Commentary:

The students didn't have tape-recorders as we do, so they wrote down their notes with brush and ink and compared them among themselves.

"You should take good care of these lectures," the Master said. "They are Dharma jewels. Print and distribute them and so take living beings across. I know that you all believe in me, and so I don't need to transmit the robe. Besides, the Great Master Bodhidharma said that beginning with the Sixth Patriarch the robe should not be transmitted. He said, 'I originally came to China in order to transmit the right Dharma and take across all these confused living beings. From me, this one flower, in the future five petals will open–the Second, Third, Fourth, Fifth and Sixth Patriarchs. And the fruit will come to bear of itself; that is, there will be no need to transmit the robe. Transmitting the Dharma will suffice.'

This is why the Fifth Patriarch told the Sixth Patriarch, "As the robe is a source of contention, do not transmit it. Should you continue to transmit it, your life will hang by a thread."

"The fruit comes to bear of itself." You should know that the fruit which ripens in this line is just all of you who have taken refuge with me. The first character of your Dharma-names is "Kuo" and it means "fruit" or "result." So don't forget to ripen.

All of you should ripen right away. Most importantly don't be lazy! Bodhidharma gave you all predictions long ago. The Sixth Patriarch himself said, "The Bodhi fruit accomplishes itself." They both knew that, in the future, there would be all of you disciples in America with the first name "Kuo," fruit. The fruit they spoke of is just all of you. That fruit is you; you are that fruit. The two are one.

Sutra:

The Master added, "All of you Good Knowing Advisors should purify your minds and listen to my explanation of the Dharma. If you wish to realize all knowledge, you must understand the Samadhi of One Mark and the Samadhi of One Conduct.

"If you do not dwell in marks anywhere and do not give rise to hate or love, do not grasp or reject, and do not calculate advantage or disadvantage, production and destruction while in the midst of marks, but instead remain tranquil, calm, and yielding, then you will have achieved the Samadhi of One Mark.

"In all places, whether walking, standing, sitting, or lying down, to maintain a straight and uniform mind, to attain the unmoving Bodhimanda and the true realization of the Pure Land. That is called the Samadhi of One Conduct."

Commentary:

"Wash your minds clean," said the Master, "and get rid of greed, hate, and delusion. If you wish to realize all knowledge, you need to understand the Samadhi of One Mark, which consists in not dwelling in marks, and the Samadhi of One Conduct, which consists in not dwelling in conduct.

The Samadhi of One Mark: whether you are in a good place or a bad place, whether moving or still, do not dwell in marks. While in the midst of marks, do not give rise to dislike or to fondness.

Neither love nor hate
Should move the mind;
The mind should not
Grasp or reject.

If you have a thought of love, you will grasp at the object of your desire. The twelve conditioned causes say, "love conditions grasping, grasping conditions existence..."

To reject means to cast away. If you hate something then you reject it. Love and hate cause grasping and rejecting. Do not calculate advantage and disadvantage. If you think, "What's in it for me?" you are just being greedy, self-seeking, and impure. Do you understand? You should not have such thoughts.

You should remain tranquil, with nothing at all to do, and calm, like water without waves. "No waves" means no afflictions, no love, no hate, no grasping, no rejecting, no advantage, no disadvantage, no success and no failure. You should be yielding, like empty space. Take a look: everything comes from empty space and yet empty space does nothing at all. It does not set itself up as boss and say, "Go be born! Go die!" Everything is born and dies within it, undergoing transformations in a most natural way without the slightest difficulty. Yield and be flexible. If you are flexible then whatever happens just happens. That's the way it is. There is no greed, hatred, or delusion; there is nothing at all. With few wants, one is content, being without longing or self-seeking.

It is no use to think, "Wait until my book gets published. I will be a famous scholar."

You may want to do something strange to make the world take notice of you; but you should not have such ideas. You should decrease your desires, no matter what they are, and always be content.

Knowing enough, you're always happy.
Able to be patient, you're at peace.

If you can be tranquil, calm, and yielding, and leave marks while in the midst of them, if you can transcend the dust while in the dust, just that is the Samadhi of One Mark.

The Samadhi of One Conduct: no matter where you are, in a good place, a bad place, a wholesome place, an unwholesome place, a right place, a wrong place–walking, standing, sitting or lying down–maintain a direct mind. The direct mind is the Bodhimandala. Students of the Buddhadharma should not be devious. Be direct in your thoughts, words, and deeds. Speak your mind; don't think east and speak west. The straight mind is the Bodhimandala. If the cause is not straight, the result will be crooked. Your mind should be uniform and of one purity. You who cultivate the Way: toward others, toward yourself, toward everything, be straightforward. Don't try to trick people out of their money, no matter how poor you are. If you borrow a little money and return it right away, you have not lost the virtue of a gentleman, but if you borrow and don't return it, your position is very low.

Be an unmoving Bodhimandala with a straightforward mind, for that is the realization of the Pure Land and is called the Samadhi of One Conduct.

Sutra:

"One who perfects the two samadhis is like earth in which seeds are planted; buried in the ground, they are nourished and grow, ripening and bearing fruit. The One Mark and One Conduct are just like that.

"I now speak the Dharma which is like the falling of the timely rain, moistening the great earth. Your

Buddha-nature is like the seeds which, receiving moisture, will sprout and grow. Those who receive my teaching will surely obtain Bodhi and those who practice my conduct will certainly certify to the wonderful fruit. Listen to my verse:

The mind-ground contains every seed;
Under the universal rain they all sprout
Flower and feeling–Sudden Enlightenment:
The Bodhi-fruit accomplishes itself."

After speaking the verse the Master said, "Dharma is not dual nor is the mind, and the Way is pure and without marks. All of you take care not to contemplate stillness or empty the mind. The mind is basically pure and does not grasp or reject anything. Each of you work hard, and go well, in harmony with circumstances."

At that time, his followers made obeisance and withdrew.

Commentary:

The timely rain falls just when it is needed. If it falls too soon, it may drown the crops, and if it comes too late, they may wither and die. The Sixth Patriarch's Dharma is like the timely rain which moistens all of the great earth. Your own inherent Buddha-nature is like seeds which receive the moisture and flourish ripening into Bodhi-fruits. The Bodhi-sprouts become Bodhi-fruits.

The Master went on, "You who understand my doctrine are certain to obtain Bodhi. If you cultivate according to this method, you will surely obtain the wonderful Bodhi-fruit. Now that I have spoken so much Dharma for you, you are probably all flustered, so pay attention while I speak this verse. Purify your minds!

> *Your self-nature contains every seed;*
> *At the timely rain they all sprout.*
> *When sentient beings suddenly enlighten,*
> *The Flower opens, the fruit is ripened.*
> *And the Bodhi-fruit accomplishes itself.*

The wonderful fruit of Bodhi ripens of itself. Bodhidharma said, "The fruit comes to bear of itself," and the Sixth Patriarch said, "The Bodhi fruit accomplishes itself." They were speaking of all of you who have the Dharma name "Kuo" (fruit). You should ripen throughout the world. All places should reap this fruit. What fruit? The Bodhi-fruit. The Sixth Patriarch was afraid that you might not have understood and so he spoke it very clearly. "The Bodhi fruit accomplishes itself." You should all ripen on your own. I cannot help you. If you don't ripen you are just cheating yourselves. So ripen!

Isn't this strange? Your Dharma names all begin with the word "fruit," and our School's transmission verse says also:

> *Contemplating, cultivating the*
> *ever blissful fruit;*
> *Personally transmitting the*
> *unconditioned teaching.*

In the future all of you will personally transmit the unconditioned teaching.

The Master went on, "My Sudden Enlightenment Dharma door is not two, it is one. What is the one? It is just the Sudden Teaching. The mind is not two either; therefore it should return to the one. The Way we cultivate is pure and without marks.

"Although it is without marks, don't make the mistake of contemplating stillness because that is just another attachment. Do not loiter in dull emptiness either, because the mind of living beings is naturally and fundamentally pure. The original substance of the mind is pure and immaculate, without grasping or rejecting.

"Work hard, all of you. Go forward and don't be lazy. Go where circumstances take you and build Bodhimandalas. Be good, cultivate good conduct and work hard."

Sutra:

On the eighth day of the seventh month, the Master suddenly said to his disciples, "I wish to return to Hsin Chou. Quickly ready a boat and oars."

The great assembly entreated him earnestly to stay, but the Master said, "All Buddhas appear in the world and then are seen to enter Nirvana. This body of mine must return somewhere."

The assembly said, "Master, you are leaving, but sooner or later you will return."

The Master said, "Falling leaves return to the root. There was no day on which I came."

They further asked, "Who has received the transmission of the Right Dharma-eye Treasury?"

The Master said, "The one who has the Way obtains it; the one without a mind penetrates it."

Commentary:

"Patriarch," said the assembly, "you are leaving now, but we can't believe that you will enter Nirvana. Sooner or later you will come back, won't you?"

The Master said, “Just as leaves fall and return to the root of the trees, I must go. Besides, there was no day on which I came.”

The Chinese text reads, “When I came I had no mouth,” but this is a misprint for the word “day.” However, you can also explain it as, “When I came I had no mouth.” On the day when the Patriarch came into this world, he had no mouth; that is, he had no words. He did not speak Dharma when he came and he did not speak Dharma when he left; coming and going he did not speak Dharma. The Dharma does not increase or decrease and although he spoke Dharma for so many years, he never spoke Dharma at all.

There are no fixed Dharmas. You can explain it any way you wish, as long as you are in accord with principle. But if you don’t explain it correctly, you can explain your listeners right into the hells, and that is taking the unfixed Dharma too far.

The Patriarch’s disciples, unable to bear the thought of their Master’s imminent departure, tried to delay him with questions until the Master, in exasperation, probably decided that they were just too much trouble. “I’m getting out of here,” he probably thought.

The “Right Dharma-eye Treasury” refers to the robe and bowl. So many disciples, and yet not one of them knew who had received the Dharma transmission. If they hadn’t been greedy for it themselves, they wouldn’t have asked this question. Why else would they be “standing by the river and gazing out into the sea?” If you weren’t longing for the sea, why would you be standing there? Everyone thought the robe and bowl was extremely important, but the Sixth Patriarch was not a business man. If he had been, at $65.00 a transmission, he could have made a lot of money.

“Who got the transmission? The one who has the Way obtains it; the one without a mind penetrates it. Whoever has no self-seeking mind understands my Dharma, because he has obtained the Samadhis of the One Mark and the One Conduct."

The Sixth Patriarch's Dharma is to be found in these verses and these principles, and if you cultivate according to them you will obtain his Dharma.

Sutra:

They further asked, "In the future, there won't be any difficulties, will there?

The Master said, "Five or six years after my extinction, a man will come to take my head. Listen to my verse:

Offerings to the parents with bowed head.
There must be food in the mouth.
When the difficulty of 'Man' is met,
The officials will be Yang and Liu.

Commentary:

Remembering the demonic difficulties which had beset the Master during his lifetime–assassination attempts, arson, thievery, and spying–the Master's disciples wondered what would happen when he was gone.

I know that the Sutra does not record all of the hardships the Master underwent. There were at least six attempts made to steal the robe and bowl and the thieves were armed and prepared to kill the Master, if necessary. So his disciples asked hopefully, "There won't be any difficulties like that in the future, will there? No one will want to kill us, will they? Will they try to kill us instead of you?"

While he was alive, they tried to take his life. After his death, they tried to steal his head. In those days it wasn't easy to be Patriarch. It's not so difficult today, however, so don't retreat.

The Sixth Patriarch's verse was a prophecy. No one understood it at the time, but later it came true. Five or six years after the Master's death, a Korean monk named Chin Ta Pei hired Chan Ching Man of Hung Chou to steal the Patriarch's head and bring it back to Korea so that he could make offerings to it.

Chan Ching Man was poor and hungry and so he took the money because "there must be food in the mouth." The Korean monk was no doubt very rich.

At the time of the "difficulty" of Chan Chin "Man," the Magistrate was named Liu T'ien and the Governor was named Yang K'an.

The flesh-body of the Patriarch was housed in the pagoda. Having heard the Master's prediction, his disciples had bound his neck with sheets of iron for protection. Chan Ching Man chopped at it with his knife, but he wasn't able to remove the Master's head. He made a lot of noise, and when the Bhikshus came running to catch him they saw a man wearing white mourning clothes run from the pagoda. The Bhikshus reported the incident to the police and within five days the thief was arrested and brought to Nan Hua Temple to be tried.

"Why did you try to steal the Sixth Patriarch's head?" they asked.

"A Korean monk paid me to do it," he said, "and I was hungry, so I took his money."

The Magistrate turned to the Master's disciple Ling T'ao and said, "What do we do now?"

Ling T'ao said, "According to the law, he deserves to die, but in the Buddha's teaching there are no friends or enemies. Besides, the Master predicted this would happen. Let him go."

"The Buddha's gate is indeed wide," said the Magistrate, and he set the criminal free.

Sutra:

The Master also said, "Seventy years after my departure, two Bodhisattvas, one who has left home and one who is a layman will simultaneously come from the east to propagate and transform. They will establish my School, build and restore monasteries, and glorify the Dharma for its heirs."

Commentary:

The Bodhisattva who had left home was Patriarch Ma Tsu Tao I. He built many monasteries in China. It is said, "Ma Tsu built the temples and Pai Chang wrote the rules." Pai Chang was Ma Tsu's Dharma successor.

The Bodhisattva who had not left home was P'ang Yün, the enlightened layman. His entire family was enlightened, wife, daughter, and son, and they all went to Nirvana. Layman P'ang had been incredibly wealthy, but he built a big boat one day, put all of his money in it, sailed out to sea, and dumped it overboard.

Some say that the two Bodhisattvas are Dhyana Master Huang Po and layman P'ei Hsiu. You may explain it any way you like, as long as you pick two people: a monk and a layman.

Layman P'ang gave all his money as a gift to use for remodeling the Dragon Palace at the bottom of the sea. He returned to his home and took up a lowly occupation, and in the midst of their bitter poverty, the P'ang family cultivated the Way.

One day, Mr. P'ang sighed,

It's hard, it's hard
It's really just as hard as putting seeds
On all the leaves
Of trees in the yard.

"What do you know, old man?" said Mrs. P'ang. "It's not hard at all. In fact,

It's easy, it's easy
It's easy, because I find
On the tip of every blade of grass
The Patriarch's mind."

She thought it was easy and he thought it was hard. Then their little daughter came and disagreed with both of them:

It's not easy,
It's not hard;
I eat when I'm hungry and
I sleep when I'm tired!

"There's nothing to it!" she said.

Although Mr. P'ang was married, he and his wife were like good friends and did not carry on like ordinary men and women. As a consequence, they became enlightened. Lay people should all imitate their inconceivable purity.

Sutra:

The assembly made obeisance again and asked, "Will you please let us know for how many generations the teaching has been transmitted since the first Buddhas and Patriarchs appeared in the world?"

The Master said, "The Buddhas of antiquity who have responded to appear in the world are numberless and uncountable."

Commentary:

"Their number is incalculable," said the Master. "Besides, I never learned to read or write and I'm not very good at arithmetic. So let's not count them."

Sutra:

"But now I will begin with the last seven Buddhas. In the Past 'Adorned Eon' there were Vipashyin Buddha, Shikhin Buddha, and Vishvabhu Buddha. In the present 'Worthy Eon' there have been Krakucchanda Buddha, Kanakamuni Buddha, Kashyapa Buddha, and Shakyamuni Buddha."

Commentary:

In the Adorned Eon (Alamkarakalpa) a thousand Buddhas appeared in the world. The 998th Buddha of that kalpa was Vipashyin Buddha. His name means "Victorious Contemplation," "Every Kind of Contemplation," "Victorious View," or "Every Kind of View." If you just remember "Vipashyin Buddha" that will do for general purposes.

"Shikhin Buddha." Shikhin is translated as "fire." "Vishvabhu Buddha" was the last Buddha of the Adorned Eon.

We are now living in the Worthy Eon (Bhadrakalpa), so-called because many worthy sages will appear during it.

Of the thousand Buddhas of this eon, Krakucchanda Buddha was the first. His name means "Worthy of Offerings," because he should receive the offerings of humans and gods. His name also means "Adornment."

The second Buddha was Kanakamuni, the third, Kashyapa, and the fourth, Shakyamuni. These are the most recent Buddhas.

Sutra:

"From Shakyamuni Buddha, the transmission went to Arya Mahakashyapa, Arya Ananda, Arya Sanakavasa, Arya Upagupta, Arya Dhrtaka, Arya Miccaka, Arya Vasumitra, Arya Buddhanandi, Arya Buddhamitra, Arya Parshva..."

Commentary:

Shakyamuni Buddha, in the midst of the millions of humans and gods who were circumambulating him, picked up a flower and Mahakashyapa, the First Patriarch, had to smile. No one knew what was happening when Shakyamuni Buddha said, "I have the Right Dharma-eye Treasury, the wonderful mind of Nirvana, the real mark, which is unmarked. This is the mind-to-mind transmission, transmitted outside the teaching. I have already given it to Mahakashyapa in mind-to-mind transmission."

The Third Patriarch, the Venerable Sanakavasa, was born wearing clothes, and as he grew, his clothes grew along with him. After he left home under Arya Ananda, his clothes changed into a great Samghati robe. Just before he died, he said, "This robe will not decay until Shakyamuni Buddha's Dharma is completely extinguished."

The Tenth Patriarch, Arya Parshva, lived in his mother's womb for more than sixty years. He was born with white hair and a white beard, just like Lao Tzu in China.

Lao Tzu lived in his mother's womb for eighty-one years and was born with white hair and a long white beard. They named him "Lao Tzu" which means "Old Child," but he was actually a reincarnation of Mahakashyapa. He was reborn in China because Shakyamuni Buddha had noticed that the Chinese had good karmic roots. Most of them did not believe in the Buddha, however, so Mahakashyapa was sent to China to found the religion of Taoism, which is the same as the Brahman religion of India and which cultivates purity of conduct.

Arya Parshva, the Tenth Patriarch, was born with a liking for cultivation. When he met the Ninth Patriarch, Buddhamitra, he left home and the Dharma door of the Buddha's mind-seal was transmitted to him.

Sutra:

> **"...Arya Punyayashas, Mahasattva Ashvaghosha, Arya Kapimala, Mahasattva Nagarjuna, Arya Kanadeva, Arya Rahulata, Arya Sanghanandi, Arya Gayashata..."**

Commentary:

When the Eleventh Patriarch, Punyayashas, met Parshva he asked him, "How can I realize Buddhahood?"

Parshva said, "You wish to realize Buddhahood? It is just your present non-realization."

Punyayashas said, "You say that my present non-realization is the Buddha, but how can I know that?"

Parshva replied, "How can you know that your present non-realization is not the Buddha?"

With that question and that answer, Punyayashas became enlightened and received the Dharma transmission. Later on, he met the Great Master Ashvaghosha, the Eleventh Patriarch. Mahasattva Ashvaghosha was extremely intelligent. Punyayashas knew that Ashvaghosha's conditions were ripe–he was ready to become the twelfth Patriarch. When Punyayashas went to teach him, Ashvaghosha asked, "How can I know the Buddha?'"

Punyayashas said, "You wish to know the Buddha? He is just your not knowing."

Ashvaghosha said, "Not knowing the Buddha, how can I know that my not knowing is the Buddha?"

Punyayashas said, "If you do not know the Buddha, how can you know that your not knowing is not the Buddha?"

Ashvaghosha said, "Ah! So this is the meaning of sawing! You say this and I say that, and we hack at the principle like sawing through a piece of wood."

Punyayashas replied, "Ah! So that is the meaning of wood! But what is the meaning of sawing?"

Ashvaghosha said, "It's just what you are! And what is the meaning of wood?"

Punyayashas said, "You have just been sawed open by me; you have just been liberated by me."

Ashvaghosha was instantaneously enlightened. He left home, received the transmission, and became the Twelfth Patriarch. He was called Ashvaghosha, "horse cry," because when he spoke the Dharma all the horses cried out. He was a Mahasattva, that is, a "great being," a great Bodhisattva.

Nagarjuna Bodhisattva, the Fourteenth Patriarch, is the one who went to the Dragon Palace and brought back the *Avatamsaka Sutra*. He was very, very wise.

Sanghanandi, the Seventeenth Patriarch, asked Gayashata, the Eighteenth Patriarch, "How old are you?"

The child replied, "I'm one hundred years old."

"But you're so young," said the Patriarch, "how can you be a hundred years old?"

"If I were a hundred years old and did not understand the Buddhadharma, I would not be as good as a one-day-old baby who did."

Hearing such an intelligent answer, the Seventeenth Patriarch let the child leave the home life under him and later transmitted the Dharma to him.

Sutra:

"...Arya Kumarata, Arya Jayata, Arya Vasubandhu, Arya Manorhita, Arya Haklena, Arya Aryasimha, Arya Basiasita, Arya Punyamitra, Arya Prajnatara, Arya Bodhidharma, Great Master Hui K'o, Great Master Seng Ts'an, Great Master Tao Hsin, Great Master Hung Jen, and I, Hui Neng, am the Thirty-Third Patriarch. Thus the transmission has been handed down from patriarch to patriarch. In the future transmit it accordingly from generation to generation. Do not allow it to become extinct."

The assembly heard and faithfully accepted what the Master had said, bowed, and withdrew.

Commentary:

Aryasimha, the Twenty-Fourth Patriarch, was a native of Central India. In his practice of the Buddhadharma, he traveled to Kashmir. The King of Kashmir did not believe in the Buddha, but instead followed two non-Buddhist leaders who were intent on destroying Buddhism. As Bhikshus were not allowed within the country, the King demanded of Aryasimha, "Have you ended birth and death?"

Aryasimha wanted to convert the King. "I have ended it," he answered.

"The Buddha's teaching says that practicing the Bodhisattva way, you must give up your head, your eyes, your brains, and your blood. You must give up whatever someone happens to need. Now, I need your head. Give it to me! Since you have ended birth and death, you must give me your head. Can you do it?"

"I don't even have birth or death," said Aryasimha. "What does it matter if I lose my head? It's yours. Take it."

The King sliced off Aryasimha's head but instead of blood, a milky white fluid ran out of his neck. The King's arm fell to the ground. No one cut it off; it fell off by itself because he had murdered an Arhat. The King then put the two leaders of the non-Buddhist religion to death, but there was nothing special about their executions. They bled just like everyone else. The King prohibited their non-Buddhist religion and spread the Buddhadharma widely.

Sutra:

On the third day of the eighth month of the year Kuei Ch'ou, the second year of the Hsien T'ien reign (A.A. 713), after a meal in Kuo En Temple, the Master

said, "Each of you take your seat, for I am going to say goodbye."

Fa Hai said, "What teaching dharma will the High Master leave behind so that confused people can be led to see the Buddha-nature?"

The Master said, "All of you please listen carefully. If those of future generations recognize living beings, they will have perceived the Buddha-nature. If they do not recognize living beings, they may seek the Buddha throughout many eons, but he will be difficult to meet.

"I will now teach you how to recognize the living beings within your mind and how to see the Buddha-nature there. If you wish to see the Buddha, simply recognize living beings, for it is living beings who are confused about the Buddha and not the Buddha who is confused about living beings.

"When enlightened to the self-nature, the living being is a Buddha. If confused about the self-nature, the Buddha is a living being. When the self-nature is impartial, the living being is the Buddha. When the self-nature is biased, the Buddha is a living being.

"If your thoughts are devious and malicious, the Buddha dwells within the living being, but by means of one impartial thought, the living being becomes a Buddha. Our minds have their own Buddha and that Buddha is the true Buddha. If the mind does not have its own Buddha, where can the true Buddha be sought? Your own minds are the Buddha; have no further doubts. Nothing can be established outside the mind, for the original mind produces the ten thousand dharmas. Therefore the Sutras say, 'The mind produced, all

dharmas are produced; the mind extinguished, all dharmas are extinguished.'"

Commentary:

The Great Master instructed his disciples to take their seats. In Buddhism, everything has a fixed order. Those who take precepts first stand or sit in front of those who take them later. If you have held precepts for even one day longer, you sit in front.

Once again Fa Hai, number one, heard that the Sixth Patriarch was going, and so he acted as spokesman. He was the oldest, so naturally he was higher than everyone else. "What Dharma will you leave with us, High Master, so that we can teach the deluded ones of future generations to understand the mind and see the nature?"

The Master said, "If you want to find the Buddha, you must look among living beings. If you recognize living beings, you recognize the Buddha-nature." Why does Never-Slighting Bodhisattva bow before everyone he meets? Because he knows that everyone is a Buddha, he will accomplish Buddhahood himself. If he saw everyone as a demon, he would become a demon.

See the Buddha within your own mind; don't seek him outside. If you wish to see the Buddha you must first respect living beings and recognize them all as the Buddha; then you've understood the mind and seen your nature. Confused living beings do not recognize the Buddha, but the Buddha recognizes living beings.

If you are biased and continually pick at other people's faults, even if you are a Buddha, you turn into a living being. Living beings and the Buddha are a thought apart.

Buddha is mind; mind is Buddha. Right thoughts are the Buddha; deviant thoughts are the demon. Pure thoughts are the

Buddha; defiled thoughts are the demon. Take a look at your thoughts. If you can keep your mind clean, that is the real Buddha. Without a clear, pure, genuine Buddha-mind, where can you go to find the Buddha? You'll never find him. The Buddha is made in your mind; do not seek him outside.

Nothing is separate from the self-nature. Nothing is separate from your own mind. The ten thousand dharmas are all produced from your mind, not from outside.

The Buddha spoke all dharmas
For the minds of living beings.
If there were no minds,
What use would dharmas be?

Sutra:

"Now, to say goodbye, I will leave you a verse called the 'Self-Nature's True Buddha Verse.' People of the future who understand its meaning will see their original mind and realize the Buddha Way. The verse runs:

The true-suchness self-nature
is the true Buddha.
Deviant views, the three poisons,
are the demon king.

Commentary:

The most important part of the *Platform Sutra* is this last verse. It explains everything extremely well. The Sixth Patriarch left it not just for the people of his day, but for us, now, to cultivate according to its principles. He saw that you and I would be here listening. We all have a share, and we should cultivate according to this verse because we are all people of future generations, not animals. The animals of future generations will have to be reborn as people before they can have a share. The Sixth Patriarch spoke this verse for people, not animals. Animals who wish to become Buddhas must first be reborn as human beings.

We should not lose this opportunity.

"The true-suchness self-nature is the true Buddha." The self-nature is your mind. Your true-suchness self-nature is also called the real mark, the Tathagata Store, the Buddha-nature, and your own nature. True suchness is just your own nature which is the true Buddha.

"Deviant views, the three poisons, are the demon king." If you know the true Buddha, you should also know the demon king. The demon king is just your deviant views: greed, hate, and delusion, the three poisons. Greed for riches, greed for sex, greed for anything at all is nothing but poison.

If, after you leave home, you are still greedy and self-seeking, that too is poison. If you scheme to get more disciples, that is poison.

So, you see, we have been here for a long time and not many have taken refuge and become disciples. Those who take refuge must do it on their own. No one advises them. If I told you to take refuge with me, you might wonder if I had the right to be your teacher and Good Knowing Advisor. I don't know myself whether I am a Good Knowing Advisor, and so I do not go about it in this way.

Sutra:

> ***At times of deviant confusion***
> ***the demon king is in the house;***

But when you have proper views
the Buddha is in the hall.
Deviant views, the three poisons
produced within the nature,
Are just the demon king
come to dwell in the house.
Proper views casting out
three poisons of the mind
Transform the demon into Buddha–
true, not false.

Commentary:

"Deviant confusion" is ignorance. Ignorance creates love and desire, and that is the demon king dwelling in your house.

If you have proper views and not the wrong ones of greed, hate, and delusion, then your mind is pure and the Buddha is in the hall.

The Buddha and the demon are both manifested from your own nature. When you hold deviant views, the three poisons arise, and the demon comes to dwell in your house. What is your house? Your body.

Proper views spontaneously expel the three poisons, and the demon immediately changes into Buddha. This principle is absolutely true; it cannot possibly be false. You need only hold proper views, and that is the Buddha. Improper views are the demon.

Sutra:

Dharma-body, Reward-body,
and Transformation-body:

Fundamentally the three bodies
are one body.
Seeing that for yourself
within your own nature
Is the Bodhi-cause
for realizing Buddhahood.
The pure nature is originally produced
from the Transformation-body.
The pure nature is ever-present within
the Transformation-body,
One's nature leads the Transformation-body
down the right road.
And in the future the full perfection
is truly without end.

Commentary:

Although spoken of as three, the clear, pure Dharma-body, the perfect, full Reward-body, and the hundred thousand myriads of Transformation bodies are fundamentally one. The three bodies are simply transformations of your one body. This is called "Three in one, one in three."

Your seeing for yourself the true Buddha within your self-nature is a cause for your future realization of Buddhahood. It is a seed of Buddhahood. Having planted the Bodhi-seed, you will certainly reap the Bodhi-fruit and become a Buddha.

The clear, pure self-nature originally arises from the Transformation-body. Your pure self-nature, your pure Dharma-body, is within your Transformation body.

In the future, your Bodhi self-nature will be perfected, and the perfect, full Reward-body will be truly inexhaustible.

Sutra:

> ***The root cause of purity***
> ***is the lust nature,***
> ***For once rid of lust,***
> ***the substance of the nature is pure.***
> ***Each of you, within your natures;***
> ***abandon the five desires.***
> ***In an instant, see your nature–***
> ***it is true.***

Commentary:

Everyone has sexual desire, but you do not need to be afraid of it. In *The Shurangama Sutra* we read about Ucchusma, the "Fire-Head Vajra" whose sexual desire was unbearably intense when he first began to cultivate. But he was able to discipline and temper the fire of lust, transforming it into the fire of wisdom and transforming himself into the "Fire-Head Vajra."

"The root cause of purity is the lust nature." Proper thoughts are the cause of purity in the nature, and deviant thoughts the cause of impurity. Therefore cut off the nature of sexual desire, which means transform it. This certainly is not telling you to castrate yourself. That's not the answer. Just change your thoughts and make them pure in nature. You don't have to cut off sexual desire. Don't cut it off, transform it instead. Transform lust into purity, which is simply proper knowledge and proper views. The lust within the nature is simply deviant knowledge and deviant views.

"Once rid of lust, the substance of the nature is pure." To get rid of lust means to transform it. You don't have to throw it away, all you have to do is transform it. You don't have to throw it away, all you have to do is change your thoughts and direct them to the pure nature. That is the clear, pure, substance of the self-nature, the Dharma-body.

The five desires are for wealth, sex, fame, food, and sleep. They may also be explained as forms, sounds, smells, tastes, tangible objects, and objects of the mind. In general, stay far away from them; do not have deviant thoughts within your self-nature. Cultivate proper knowledge and proper views, and abandon the five desires. Once you leave the five desires, you can see the nature in an instant and obtain your own true-suchness wonderful nature.

Sutra:

If in this life you encounter
the door of the Sudden Teaching
You will be suddenly enlightened to your self-nature,
and see the Honored of the World.
If you wish to cultivate
and aspire to Buddhahood,
You won't know where the truth
is to be sought
Unless you can see the truth
within your own mind,
This truth which is the cause
of realizing Buddhahood.
Not to see your self-nature
but to seek the Buddha outside:
If you think that way, you are

deluded indeed.
I now leave behind
the Dharma-door of the Sudden Teaching
To liberate worldly people
who must cultivate themselves.
I announce to you
and to future students of the Way:
If you do not hold these views
you will only waste your time.

Commentary:

Having encountered the Sudden Teaching of the Dhyana School, you may become instantly enlightened and understand your original mind and see your original nature. At that moment you will personally meet the World Honored Ones, the Buddhas of the ten directions; you can see them all.

Unless you apply effort in the self-nature instead of looking outside, you will never find the genuine Buddha. Understand your mind and see your nature: that is the way to realize Buddhahood.

If you do not turn the light around and seek within yourself, but run outside instead to look for the Buddha, you are being stupid, stupid, extremely stupid.

You must cultivate the Dharma of Sudden Enlightenment on your own. Do not fail to cultivate. If you do not hold the notions expressed in this verse, you are wasting your time. You'll never obtain the smallest advantage.

Sutra:

Having spoken the verse the Master continued, "All of you should take care. After my extinction, do not act with worldly emotion. If you weep in sorrow, receive condolences, or wear mourning clothes, you are not my disciples, for that is contrary to the proper Dharma. Simply recognize your own original mind and see your own original nature which is neither moving nor still, neither produced nor extinguished, neither coming nor going, neither right nor wrong, neither dwelling nor departing."

Commentary:

The Master said, "Unlike common, vulgar, worldly folk, do not make an emotional display of your feelings. Don't behave like that. Don't weep tears like rain to irrigate the fields. My disciples have to obey me! If you do such things, not only are you not my disciples, but you are also contradicting the Buddhadharma.

"Do not strike up false thinking. Don't fail to put it down. Don't fail to break through it. You must see through it, smash it, and put it all down. Then you can be free."

"If we are not supposed to mourn, then what should we do?" the disciples wondered.

"Recognize your original mind. What is it like? It doesn't move and it isn't still. It doesn't come or go. It's not right or wrong, good or bad, black or white, long or short. It doesn't stay and it doesn't leave. It's neither here nor there. Work to see the self-nature; understand your mind. Then you will not have wasted your time."

Sutra:

"Because I am afraid that your confused minds will misunderstand my intention, I will instruct you again so that you may see your nature. After my extinction, continue to cultivate accordingly, as if I were still present. Should you disregard my teaching, then even if I were to remain in the world, you would obtain no benefit."

He further spoke this verse:

Firm, firm: Do not cultivate the good.
High, high: Do not do evil.
Still, still: Cut off sight and sound.
Vast, vast: The mind unattached.

Commentary:

"Firm, firm" means not moving: "thus, thus unmoving," clear, clear, and constantly bright. "Do not cultivate the good," does not mean that you should not cultivate good. It just means that you should not be attached when you cultivate the good. Don't be like that greedy-minded ghost Emperor Wu of Liang who thought, "Look at all my merit!"

"High, high," means happy and cheerful, independent and content from morning to night. Do not do evil does not mean that you can think, "I am not attached to doing evil, so it's no problem." Attached or not attached, you should not do evil. What is evil? Killing, stealing, and sexual misconduct.

Of the ten-thousand evils
Licentiousness is the worst.
Do not walk down
This road of death.

Do not walk this road. Do not do evil.

"Still, still: Cut off sight and sound." This state is peaceful, comfortable, and happy. Still, still, quiet, quiet, you cut off sight and sound by not producing deviant thoughts at the gates of the six sense organs. It is all right to have proper thoughts, but cut off the deviant ones. Cut off deviant sights and sounds. For example, if people are speaking improperly, don't listen.

"Vast, vast: The mind unattached." This mind's capacity extends throughout the universe and fills up heaven and earth. It is high, great, broad, vast, limitless, and unbounded, and it is not attached anywhere.

Sutra:

After speaking this verse, the Master sat upright until the third watch, when suddenly he said to his disciples, "I am going!" In an instant he changed, and a rare fragrance filled the room. A white rainbow linked with the earth, and the trees in the wood turned white. The birds and the beasts cried out in sorrow.

Commentary:

The Master sat meditating with his disciples until the middle of the night, at twelve o'clock, when he said, "The time has come to go. See you all again!" His energy was cut off and he no longer moved. He had entered Nirvana. "He changed" means that he moved to a new house. Who moved? The flesh-body Bodhisattva!

The forest turned white because the white rainbow light shone on it. You could also say that the trees knew the Master was dead and so they expressed their grief by wearing the white clothes of mourning.

All the animals on the mountain cried uncontrollably. Grass and trees seem to be without feelings, but they put on mourning clothes; birds and beasts ordinarily don't understand very much, but they showed forth a spiritual nature and wept.

Sutra:

In the eleventh month, a dispute arose among the officials, disciples, Sangha, and laity of the three countries of Kuang Chou, Shao Chou, and Hsin Chou as to who should receive the true body.

As they could not agree, they lit incense and prayed saying, "The Master will be returned to the place indicated by the incense smoke."

The smoke went directly to Ts'ao Hsi and so, on the thirteenth day of the eleventh month, the reliquary and the transmitted robe and bowl were returned there. In the following year, on the twenty-fifth day of the seventh month, the body was removed from the reliquary and Disciple Fang Pien anointed it with incense paste. Remembering the prophecy that his head would be taken, the disciples wrapped sheets of iron and lacquered cloth around his neck for protection and then placed his body in the pagoda. Just then a white light appeared within the pagoda, shot up into the sky, and did not fade for three days. The Magistrate of Shao Chou reported this to the Emperor and received an imperial order to erect a stone tablet commemorating the Master's conduct in the Way.

The Master's springs and autumns were seventy-six. The robe was transmitted to him when he was twenty-four and when he was thirty-nine his hair was cut. For thirty-seven years he spoke Dharma to benefit living

beings. Forty-three men inherited his Dharma, and an uncountable number awoke to the Way and overstepped the common lot. The robe of belief transmitted from Bodhidharma, the Mo Na robe and precious bowl conferred by Emperor Chung Tsung, as well as the lifelike image sculpted by Fang Pien and other articles of the Way, were entrusted to the attendant in charge of the stupa and were permanently retained at the Pao Lin Bodhimandala for the Bodhimanda's protection.

***The Platfom Sutra* has been transmitted to set forth the principles of our school, to glorify the Triple Jewel, and to benefit all living beings.**

Commentary:

Those from Kuang Chou wanted to take the body to Fa Hsing Temple. "The Sixth Patriarch had his head shaved here. He should return here now to receive offerings."

The Hsin Chou people all said, "The Great Master is a native of Hsin Chou. He should return there!" and those of Shao Chou insisted that since the Patriarch had expounded his teaching there he should not be returned to that place.

While the Patriarch was alive, they had never quarreled over him, for he had been most independent. But now the Master had completed the stillness and everyone felt as if they personally had the right to remove his body and make offerings to it.

"Wasn't the Sixth Patriarch originally from Hsin Chou? And didn't the Master himself say, 'Falling leaves return to the root?'"

"But the Sixth Patriarch himself built Nan Hua Temple," said those of Shao Chou. "He really should return there."

"The Patriarch left home in Kuang Chou. He let his hair fall there and his Dharma should all fall back to us!"

The text says that "they could not agree," and that indicates that the situation was extremely grave; it was a crisis. Everyone was trying to take the body away by force. They argued and argued until one intelligent person said, "Stop! While he was alive, we obeyed the Master's instructions. Now that he has died, we should still listen to him. Let's ask the Master to decide!"

"But he's already dead," they said. "How can he tell us where he wants to go?"

"The Master has great spiritual powers," he said, "And he knows all of our thoughts. It must displease him to see us here fighting over the right to make offerings to his body. Let's light some incense, and in whatever direction the smoke drifts, that is where the Master wants to go. Then no one can argue about it."

The smoke went straight to Nan Hua Temple and there was nothing that the people from Kuang Chou and Hsin Chou could say.

The lectures are now complete and the Sutra has been explained. You have undergone much suffering, but I don't know whether you realized it was suffering or not. If you felt it was suffering, you are just a common person, but if you did not feel that it was suffering, then you are just a rock or a piece of wood. Well, was it suffering?

As to my explanation, I don't know whether I explained well or badly, and I also don't know if you listened well or badly. Good and bad–get rid of them both! Explaining is just explaining and listening is just listening.

We have met because of a karmic affinity. We have heard the story of the Sixth Patriarch's life and of his cultivation of the Way. You should not look for good or bad points, but look instead to see whether you believe. Advance down the right road and retreat from the wrong.

You should cultivate according to the Dharma. Memorize the last verse of this Sutra and recite it often, for if you reflect on its meaning you will certainly realize Buddhahood. And don't discriminate as to whether I explained the Sutra well or not. Just look to see whether or not you cultivate. If you cultivate, what is bad is good, but if you do not cultivate, what is good is bad.

Now I am going to ask you a question. The Sixth Patriarch was an illiterate, and illiterates cannot have much knowledge. How could someone who couldn't even read speak a Sutra? What does this mean?

[Student: "I think the Sutra shows that you don't need a lot of scholarly learning in order to become enlightened. The Sudden Teaching is just the mind, realizing the mind, and we should *do* it.]

Who else has a view? This is a democracy. Speak up!

[Student: "In the Sixth Patriarch's Dharma explanation, where could a word arise?"]

[Student: "The principles contained in the Sutra are so clear and out in front, that, every time I try to say something about them, I get tied up in dualism and feel hopelessly overwhelmed."]

Does anyone else have an opinion?

[Student: "Master, when the Sixth Patriarch was about to enter Nirvana, he said, 'See you later.' Where is he now?"]

He comes right from where you are speaking!

Now, why was it that the Master never learned to read? During the time of the Sixth Patriarch, schools were not available to all, and to attend, you had to have money. The Sixth Patriarch's family was extremely poor, because his father was an honest official who never took bribes. As a boy, even getting food to eat was a problem for the Master, so of course he couldn't go to school. It was a question of environment, then. He never learned to read because his family was poor and because schools were not available.

But there is yet another reason. Why did the Sixth Patriarch choose to appear in a poor family? He did it to show us that even illiterates can realize Buddhahood and become Patriarchs. Thus he raised the hopes of those who could not read.

Seeing the Sixth Patriarch, everyone thought, "He never went to school but he cultivated and obtained the fruit of the Way. We can do it too!" It is not the case that if you can't read, you can't cultivate. If you think, "Only educated people can cultivate," you are holding a prejudice. The Sixth Patriarch appeared to cause us all to lay down such prejudices. As I see it, these are three reasons why the Sixth Patriarch never learned to read. There's one more thing you should recognize clearly about the Sixth Patriarch. He was not lazy. He always practiced the Buddhadharma. He became enlightened and after his enlightenment he spoke the *Platform Sutra*. Being able to read is just worldly knowledge. The Sixth Patriarch understood his mind, saw his nature, and opened up to his inherent wisdom. Because this Sutra was spoken from the bright light of this wisdom, its value is incomparable. It is the same as Sutras spoken by the Buddha, so do not take him lightly just because he couldn't read.

The Sutra is now complete, and, after teaching it, I make that statement to all of you.

General Index

J

K

L

M

N

O

P

V

W

People & Places Index

Buddhist Text Translation Society Publication

Buddhist Text Translation Society
International Translation Institute

http://www.bttsonline.org

1777 Murchison Drive,
Burlingame, California 94010-4504 USA
Phone: 650-692-5912 Fax: 650-692-5056

When Buddhism first came to China from India, one of the most important tasks required for its establishment was the translation of the Buddhist scriptures from Sanskrit into Chinese. This work involved a great many people, such as the renowned monk National Master Kumarajiva (fifth century), who led an assembly of over 800 people to work on the translation of the Tripitaka (Buddhist canon) for over a decade. Because of the work of individuals such as these, nearly the entire Buddhist Tripitaka of over a thousand texts exists to the present day in Chinese.

Now the banner of the Buddha's Teachings is being firmly planted in Western soil, and the same translation work is being done from Chinese into English. Since 1970, the Buddhist Text Translation Society (BTTS) has been making a paramount contribution toward this goal. Aware that the Buddhist Tripitaka is a work of such magnitude that its translation could never be entrusted to a single person, the BTTS, emulating the translation assemblies of ancient times, does not publish a work until it has passed through four committees for primary translation, revision, editing, and certification. The leaders of these committees are Bhikshus (monks) and Bhikshunis (nuns) who have devoted their lives to the study and practice of the Buddha's teachings. For this reason, all of the works of the BTTS put an emphasis on what the principles of the Buddha's teachings mean in terms of actual practice and not simply hypothetical conjecture.

The translations of canonical works by the Buddhist Text Translation Society are accompanied by extensive commentaries by the Venerable Tripitaka Master Hsuan Hua.

BTTS Publications

Buddhist Sutras. Amitabha Sutra, Dharma Flower (Lotus) Sutra, Flower Adornment (Avatamsaka) Sutra, Heart Sutra & Verses without a Stand, Shurangama Sutra, Sixth Patriarch Sutra, Sutra in Forty-two Sections, Sutra of the Past Vows of Earth Store Bodhisattva, Vajra Prajna Paramita (Diamond) Sutra.

Commentarial Literature. Buddha Root Farm, City of 10000 Buddhas Recitation Handbook, Filiality: The Human Source, Herein Lies the Treasure-trove, Listen to Yourself Think Everything Over, Shastra on the Door to Understanding the Hundred Dharmas, Song of Enlightenment, The Ten Dharma Realms Are Not beyond a Single Thought, Venerable Master Hua's Talks on Dharma, Venerable Master Hua's Talks on Dharma during the 1993 Trip to Taiwan, Water Mirror Reflecting Heaven.

Biographical. In Memory of the Venerable Master Hsuan Hua, Pictorial Biography of the Venerable Master Hsü Yün, Records of High Sanghans, Records of the Life of the Venerable Master Hsüan Hua, Three Steps One Bow, World Peace Gathering, News from True Cultivators, Open Your Eyes Take a Look at the World, With One Heart Bowing to the City of 10000 Buddhas.

Children's Books. Cherishing Life, Human Roots: Buddhist Stories for Young Readers.

Musics, Novels and Brochures. Songs for Awakening, Awakening, The Three Cart Patriarch, City of 10000 Buddhas Color Brochure, Celebrisi's Journey, Heng Ch'au's Journal.

The Buddhist Monthly–Vajra Bodhi Sea is a monthly journal of orthodox Buddhism which has been published by the Dharma Realm Buddhist Association, formerly known as the Sino-American Buddhist Association, since 1970. Each issue contains the most recent translations of the Buddhist canon by the Buddhist Text Translation Society. Also included in each issue are a biography of a great Patriarch of Buddhism from the ancient past, sketches of the lives of contemporary monastics and lay-followers around the world, articles on practice, and other material. The journal is bilingual, Chinese and English

Please visit our web-site at **www.bttsonline.org** for the latest publications and for ordering information.

The Dharma Realm Buddhist Association

Mission

The Dharma Realm Buddhist Association (formerly the Sino-American Buddhist Association) was founded by the Venerable Master Hsuan Hua in the United States of America in 1959. Taking the Dharma Realm as its scope, the Association aims to disseminate the genuine teachings of the Buddha throughout the world. The Association is dedicated to translating the Buddhist canon, propagating the Orthodox Dharma, promoting ethical education, and bringing benefit and happiness to all beings. Its hope is that individuals, families, the society, the nation, and the entire world will, under the transforming influence of the Buddhadharma, gradually reach the state of ultimate truth and goodness.

The Founder

The Venerable Master, whose names were An Tse and To Lun, received the Dharma name Hsuan Hua and the transmission of Dharma from Venerable Master Hsu Yun in the lineage of the Wei Yang Sect. He was born in Manchuria, China, at the beginning of the century. At nineteen, he entered the monastic order and dwelt in a hut by his mother's grave to practice filial piety. He meditated, studied the teachings, ate only one meal a day, and slept sitting up. In 1948 he went to Hong Kong, where he established the Buddhist Lecture Hall and other Way-places. In 1962 he brought the Proper Dharma to the West, lecturing on several dozen Mahayana Sutras in the United States. Over the years, the Master established more than twenty monasteries of Proper Dharma under the auspices of the Dharma Realm Buddhist Association and the City of Ten Thousand Buddhas. He also founded centers for the translation of the Buddhist canon and for education to spread the influence of the Dharma in the East and West. The Master manifested the stillness in the United States in 1995. Through his lifelong, selfless dedication to teaching living beings with wisdom and compassion, he influenced countless people to change their faults and to walk upon the pure, bright path to enlightenment.

Dharma Propagation, Buddhist Text Translation, and Education

The Venerable Master Hua's three great vows after leaving the home-life were (1) to propagate the Dharma, (2) to translate the Buddhist Canon, and (3) to promote education. In order to make these vows a reality, the Venerable Master based himself on the Three Principles and the Six Guidelines. Courageously facing every hardship, he founded monasteries, schools, and centers in the West, drawing in living beings and teaching them on a vast scale. Over the years, he founded the following institutions:

The City of Ten Thousand Buddhas and Its Branches

In propagating the Proper Dharma, the Venerable Master not only trained people but also founded Way-places where the Dharma wheel could turn and living beings could be saved. He wanted to provide cultivators with pure places to practice in accord with the Buddha's regulations. Over the years, he founded many Way-places of Proper Dharma. In the United States and Canada, these include the City of Ten Thousand Buddhas; Gold Mountain Monastery; Gold Sage Monastery; Gold Wheel Monastery; Gold Summit Monastery; Gold Buddha Monastery; Avatamsaka Monastery; Long Beach Monastery; the City of the Dharma Realm; Berkeley Buddhist Monastery; Avatamsaka Hermitage; and Blessings, Prosperity, and Longevity Monastery. In Taiwan, there are the Dharma Realm Buddhist Books Distribution Association, Dharma Realm Monastery, and Amitabha Monastery. In Malaysia, there are Tze Yun Tung Monastery, Deng Bi An Monastery, and Lotus Vihara. In Hong Kong, there are the Buddhist Lecture Hall and Cixing Monastery.

Purchased in 1974, the City of Ten Thousand Buddhas is the hub of the Dharma Realm Buddhist Association. The City is located in Talmage, Mendocino County, California, 110 miles north of San Francisco. Eighty of the 488 acres of land are in active use. The remaining acreage consists of meadows, orchards, and woods. With over seventy large buildings containing over 2,000 rooms, blessed with serenity and fresh, clean air, it is the first large Buddhist monastic community in the United States. It is also an international center for the Proper Dharma.

Although the Venerable Master Hua was the Ninth Patriarch in the Weiyang Sect of the Chan School, the monasteries he founded emphasize all of the five main practices of Mahayana Buddhism (Chan meditation, Pure Land, esoteric, Vinaya (moral discipline), and doctrinal studies). This accords with the Buddha's words: "The Dharma is level and equal, with no high or low." At the City of Ten Thousand Buddhas, the rules of purity are rigorously observed. Residents of the City strive to regulate their own conduct and to cultivate with vigor. Taking refuge in the Proper Dharma, they lead pure and selfless lives, and attain peace in body and mind. The Sutras are expounded and the Dharma wheel is turned daily. Residents dedicate themselves wholeheartedly to making Buddhism flourish. Monks and nuns in all the monasteries take one meal a day, always wear their precept sash, and follow the Three Principles:

Freezing, we do not scheme.
Starving, we do not beg.
Dying of poverty, we ask for nothing.
According with conditions, we do not change.
Not changing, we accord with conditions.
We adhere firmly to our three great principles.
We renounce our lives to do the Buddha's work.
We take the responsibility to mold our own destinies.
We rectify our lives to fulfill the Sanghan's role.
Encountering specific matters,
  we understand the principles.
Understanding the principles,
  we apply them in specific matters.
We carry on the single pulse of
  the Patriarchs' mind-transmission.

The monasteries also follow the Six Guidelines: not contending, not being greedy, not seeking, not being selfish, not pursuing personal advantage, and not lying.

International Translation Institute

The Venerable Master vowed to translate the Buddhist Canon (Tripitaka) into Western languages so that it would be widely accessible throughout the world. In 1973, he founded the International Translation Institute on Washington Street in San Francisco for the purpose of translating Buddhist scriptures into English and other languages. In 1977, the Institute was merged into Dharma Realm Buddhist University as the Institute for the Translation of Buddhist Texts. In 1991, the Venerable Master purchased a large building in

Burlingame (south of San Francisco) and established the International Translation Institute there for the purpose of translating and publishing Buddhist texts. To date, in addition to publishing over one hundred volumes of Buddhist texts in Chinese, the Association has published more than one hundred volumes of English, French, Spanish, Vietnamese, and Japanese translations of Buddhist texts, as well as bilingual (Chinese and English) editions. Audio and video tapes also continue to be produced. The monthly journal Vajra Bodhi Sea, which has been in circulation for nearly thirty years, has been published in bilingual (Chinese and English) format in recent years.

In the past, the difficult and vast mission of translating the Buddhist canon in China was sponsored and supported by the emperors and kings themselves. In our time, the Venerable Master encouraged his disciples to cooperatively shoulder this heavy responsibility, producing books and audio tapes and using the medium of language to turn the wheel of Proper Dharma and do the great work of the Buddha. All those who aspire to devote themselves to this work of sages should uphold the Eight Guidelines of the International Translation Institute:

1. One must free oneself from the motives of personal fame and profit.
2. One must cultivate a respectful and sincere attitude free from arrogance and conceit.
3. One must refrain from aggrandizing one's work and denigrating that of others.
4. One must not establish oneself as the standard of correctness and suppress the work of others with one's fault-finding.
5. One must take the Buddha-mind as one's own mind.
6. One must use the wisdom of Dharma-Selecting Vision to determine true principles.
7. One must request Virtuous Elders of the ten directions to certify one's translations.
8. One must endeavor to propagate the teachings by printing Sutras, Shastra texts, and Vinaya texts when the translations are certified as being correct.

These are the Venerable Master's vows, and participants in the work of translation should strive to realize them.

Instilling Goodness Elementary School, Developing Virtue Secondary School, Dharma Realm Buddhist University

"Education is the best national defense." The Venerable Master Hua saw clearly that in order to save the world, it is essential to promote good education. If we want to save the world, we have to bring about a complete change in people's minds and guide them to cast out unwholesomeness and to pursue goodness. To this end the Master founded Instilling Goodness Elementary School in 1974, and Developing Virtue Secondary School and Dharma Realm Buddhist University in 1976.

In an education embodying the spirit of Buddhism, the elementary school teaches students to be filial to parents, the secondary school teaches students to be good citizens, and the university teaches such virtues as humaneness and righteousness. Instilling Goodness Elementary School and Developing Virtue Secondary School combine the best of contemporary and traditional methods and of Western and Eastern cultures. They emphasize moral virtue and spiritual development, and aim to guide students to become good and capable citizens who will benefit humankind. The schools offer a bilingual (Chinese/English) program where boys and girls study separately. In addition to standard academic courses, the curriculum includes ethics, meditation, Buddhist studies, and so on, giving students a foundation in virtue and guiding them to understand themselves and explore the truths of the universe. Branches of the schools (Sunday schools) have been established at branch monasteries with the aim of propagating filial piety and ethical education.

Dharma Realm Buddhist University, whose curriculum focuses on the Proper Dharma, does not merely transmit academic knowledge. It emphasizes a foundation in virtue, which expands into the study of how to help all living beings discover their inherent nature. Thus, Dharma Realm Buddhist University advocates a spirit of shared inquiry and free exchange of ideas, encouraging students to study various canonical texts and use different experiences and learning styles to tap their inherent wisdom and fathom the meanings of those texts. Students are encouraged to practice the principles they have understood and apply the Buddhadharma in their lives, thereby nurturing their wisdom and virtue. The University aims to produce outstanding individuals of high moral character who will be able to bring benefit to all sentient beings.

Sangha and Laity Training Programs

In the Dharma-ending Age, in both Eastern and Western societies there are very few monasteries that actually practice the Buddha's regulations and strictly uphold the precepts. Teachers with genuine wisdom and understanding, capable of guiding those who aspire to pursue careers in Buddhism, are very rare. The Venerable Master founded the Sangha and Laity Training Programs in 1982 with the goals of raising the caliber of the Sangha, perpetuating the Proper Dharma, providing professional training for Buddhists around the world on both practical and theoretical levels, and transmitting the wisdom of the Buddha.

The Sangha Training Program gives monastics a solid foundation in Buddhist studies and practice, training them in the practical affairs of Buddhism and Sangha management. After graduation, students will be able to assume various responsibilities related to Buddhism in monasteries, institutions, and other settings. The program emphasizes a thorough knowledge of Buddhism, understanding of the scriptures, earnest cultivation, strict observance of precepts, and the development of a virtuous character, so that students will be able to propagate the Proper Dharma and perpetuate the Buddha's wisdom. The Laity Training Program offers courses to help laypeople develop correct views, study and practice the teachings, and understand monastic regulations and ceremonies, so that they will be able to contribute their abilities in Buddhist organizations.

Let Us Go Forward Together

In this Dharma-ending Age when the world is becoming increasingly dangerous and evil, the Dharma Realm Buddhist Association, in consonance with its guiding principles, opens the doors of its monasteries and centers to those of all religions and nationalities. Anyone who is devoted to humaneness, righteousness, virtue, and the pursuit of truth, and who wishes to understand him or herself and help humankind, is welcome to come study and practice with us. May we together bring benefit and happiness to all living beings.

Dharma Realm Buddhist Association Branches

Home Page: **http:\\www.drba.org**
Main Branch:
The City of Ten Thousand Buddhas
P.O. Box 217, 2001 Talmage Road, Talmage, CA 95481-0217 USA
Tel: (707) 462-0939 Fax: (707) 462-0949

The City of the Dharma Realm
1029 West Capitol Avenue, West Sacramento, CA 95691 USA
Tel: (916) 374-8268

The International Translation Institute
1777 Murchison Drive, Burlingame, CA 94010-4504 USA
Tel: (650) 692-5912 Fax: (650) 692-5056

Institute for World Religions (Berkeley Buddhist Monastery)
2304 McKinley Avenue, Berkeley, CA 94703 USA
Tel: (510) 848-3440 Fax: (510) 548-4551

Gold Mountain Monastery
800 Sacramento Street, San Francisco, CA 94108 USA
Tel: (415) 421-6117 Fax: (415) 788-6001

Gold Sage Monastery
11455 Clayton Road, San Jose, CA 95127 USA
Tel: (408) 923-7243 Fax: (408) 923-1064

Gold Summit Monastery
233-1st Avenue, West Seattle, WA 98119 USA
Tel: (206) 284-6690 Fax: (206) 284-6918

Gold Wheel Monastery
235 North Avenue 58, Los Angeles, CA 90042 USA
Tel: (213) 258-6668

Blessings, Prosperity, & Longevity Monastery
4140 Long Beach Boulevard, Long Beach, CA 90807 USA
Tel: (562) 595-4966

Long Beach Moaastery
3361 East Ocean Boulevard, Long Beach, CA 90803 USA
Tel: (562) 438-8902

Avatamsaka Hermitage
11721 Beall Mountain Road, Potomac, MD 20854-1128 USA
Tel: (301) 299-3693

Avatamsaka Monastery
1009-4th Avenue, S.W. Calgary, AB T2P OK8 Canada
Tel: (403) 269-2960

Gold Buddha Monastery
248 E. 11th Avenue, Vancouver, B.C. V5T 2C3 Canada
Tel: (604) 709-0248 Fax: (604) 684-3754

Dharma Realm Buddhist Books Distribution Society
11th Floor, 85 Chung-hsiao E. Road, Sec. 6, Taipei, R.O.C.
Tel: (02) 2786-3022, 2786-2474
Fax: (02) 2786-2674

Dharma Realm Sagely Monastery
20, Tong-hsi Shan-chuang, Hsing-lung Village, Liu-kuei
Kaohsiung County, Taiwan, R.O.C.
Tel: (07) 689-3717 Fax: (07) 689-3870

Amitabha Monastery
7, Su-chien-hui, Chih-nan Village, Shou-feng,
Hualien Country, Taiwan, R.O.C.
Tel: (07) 865-1956 Fax: (07) 865-3426

Tze Yun Tung Temple
Batu 5½, Jalan Sungai Besi,
Salak Selatan 57100 Kuala Lumpur, Malaysia
Tel: (03) 7982-6560 Fax: (03) 7980-1272

Kun Yam Thong Temple
161, Jalan Ampang, 50450 Kuala Lumpur, Malaysia
Tel: (03) 2164-8055 Fax: (03) 2163-7118

Lotus Vihara
136, Jalan Sekolah, 45600 Batang Berjuntai,
Selangor Darul Ehsan, Malaysia
Tel: (03) 3271-9439

Buddhist Lecture Hall
31 Wong Nei Chong Road, Top Floor Happy Valley,
Hong Kong, China
Tel/Fax: 2572-7644

Verse of Transference

May the merit and virtue accrued from this work,
Adorn the Buddha's Pure Lands,
Repaying four kinds of kindness above,
And aiding those suffering in the paths below.

May those who see and hear of this,
All bring forth the resolve for Bodhi,
And when this retribution body is over,
Be born together in ultimate bliss.

Dharma Protector Wei T'o Bodhisattva